A HAUNTED ATLAS OF WESTERN NEW YORK

a Spooky Guide to the Strange and Unusual

Amanda R. Woomer

(Haunted Atlas of Western New York)

ISBN 978-0-578-59948-9

Printed in USA by Spook-Eats Publishing

FOR JED.

ALWAYS.

CONTENTS

NIAGARA COUNTY

ERIE COUNTY

INTRODUCTION

Humans are fickle creatures.

We love our technology—smartphones, social media, streaming television services, GPS—and without it, we'd be lost. We're addicted to being connected. For many of us, the scariest thing we can imagine is misplacing our phone. 21st Century comforts have robbed us of the terrors of the night that our ancestors knew all too well. Perhaps that's why so many people are fascinated by the paranormal.

In this fast-paced world, there shouldn't be any room left for things that go bump in the night. Yet, people are always eager to hear stories of cursed roads, haunted houses, and creatures lurking in the woods. It connects us to where we came from—the monsters that once hid in our closets—and reminds us that sometimes, we should be afraid of the dark. If nothing else, it makes our mundane lives a bit more exciting.

For some, merely hearing these stories is enough to feed their hunger for all things strange. For others, they seek to experience the unexplained for themselves.

If you venture down haunted roads at night, hunting urban legends…

If you wander through cemeteries and find yourself asking questions to no one in particular…

If you lace up your hiking boots and run along an overgrown trail, searching for shadows among the trees…

If you scan the landscape as you're driving for any sign of Bigfoot…

If you're desperate to believe in the bizarre to add a bit of spice to your life…This book is for you.

We're moving away from the ghost stories around the campfire and seeking the unknown for ourselves. We're getting our hands dirty and standing face to face with some of the most haunted, mysterious, and unusual places west of the Genesee River.

Travel with me, as we visit over 100 haunted locations scattered around Western New York. From schools and churches to abandoned orphanages and insane asylums, with a few hiking trails and cryptids thrown in just for fun, explore all the haunts that Western New York has to offer.

These spooky locations have everything you'd expect from a good ghost story. Some are a bit mundane with claims of just cold spots and unexplained noises. However, some come with the package deal: full-body apparitions, ghosts caught on camera, physical contact, and so much more. I've decided to include every haunted place I could find right here in Western New York to cater to whatever kind of paranormal enthusiast you might be. So don't be afraid to hop in your car, break the binding of this book, take notes in the margins, and have your own haunted adventure.

Eat at Spook-Eats recommended bars and restaurants. Walk through history in one of our many cemeteries. Become one with nature in a state park. Learn something new at a haunted museum. Get to know our beloved community's dark and grisly side.

History belongs to everyone. Haunted history belongs to the weirdos.

Things are about to get strange around here, so hold on tight and follow me. That is if you're not scared.

-a.r.w.

ABOUT SPOOK-EATS

Spook-Eats is a travel website where we visit haunted restaurants, bars, and hotels, trying the food, telling the ghost stories, and searching for spirits of all kinds.

To learn more about Spook-Eats, you can find us on Facebook, Instagram, and Twitter, as well as our website www.spookeats.com.

Throughout the Haunted Atlas of Western New York, keep an eye out for our Spook-Eats stamp of approval. These are haunted bars, restaurants, and hotels in the Western New York region. Each of them is open to the general public so you might get a chance to experience ghostly activity. And to think, all it will cost is the price of a pint of beer, an appetizer, or a room.

For history buffs, keep an eye out for our NRHP stamp. These are National Registered Historic Places.

AN IMPORTANT NOTE

Spook-Eats and the author of this book do not support or endorse trespassing to any haunted locations. Before visiting any haunted site, you must obtain the proper permits/permission and be respectful of private property, schools, posted signs, and cemeteries. Even if cemeteries are closed to new burials, please be courteous and treat the sacred ground as if it is precious—because it is. All coordinates are approximate and may require a bit of investigating if they're off the beaten path.

Happy haunting!

A HAUNTED ATLAS OF WESTERN NEW YORK

a Spooky Guide to the Strange and Unusual

Amanda R. Woomer

BUFFALO PROPER

BUFFALO PROPER

Buffalo is the second-largest city in New York State and is home to over 250,000 people. The Buffalo area was inhabited before the 17th Century by the local Iroquois. Eventually, French settlers arrived, and after the American Revolution, the newly founded state of New York began its westward expansion. During the War of 1812, all but four buildings in Buffalo were burned. The city rebuilt itself during the 19th and 20th Centuries through immigration and the construction of the Erie Canal.

1. Allendale Theatre
2. Buffalo Central Terminal
3. Buffalo Museum of Science
4. Buffalo Naval Park
5. Buffalo Public School 61
6. Buffum Street Cemetery
7. Canisius College
8. Coatsworth Mansion
9. Episcopal Church of the Ascension
10. Flint Hill
11. German Roman Catholic Orphan Asylum
12. Gypsy Parlor
13. Iron Island Museum
14. Koessler Admin Building
15. The Mansion on Delaware
16. Maytham Mansion
17. Medaille College
18. North Street
19. St. Mary's School for the Deaf
20. Shea's Performing Arts Center
21. Statler City Hotel
22. Swannie House
23. Town Ballroom

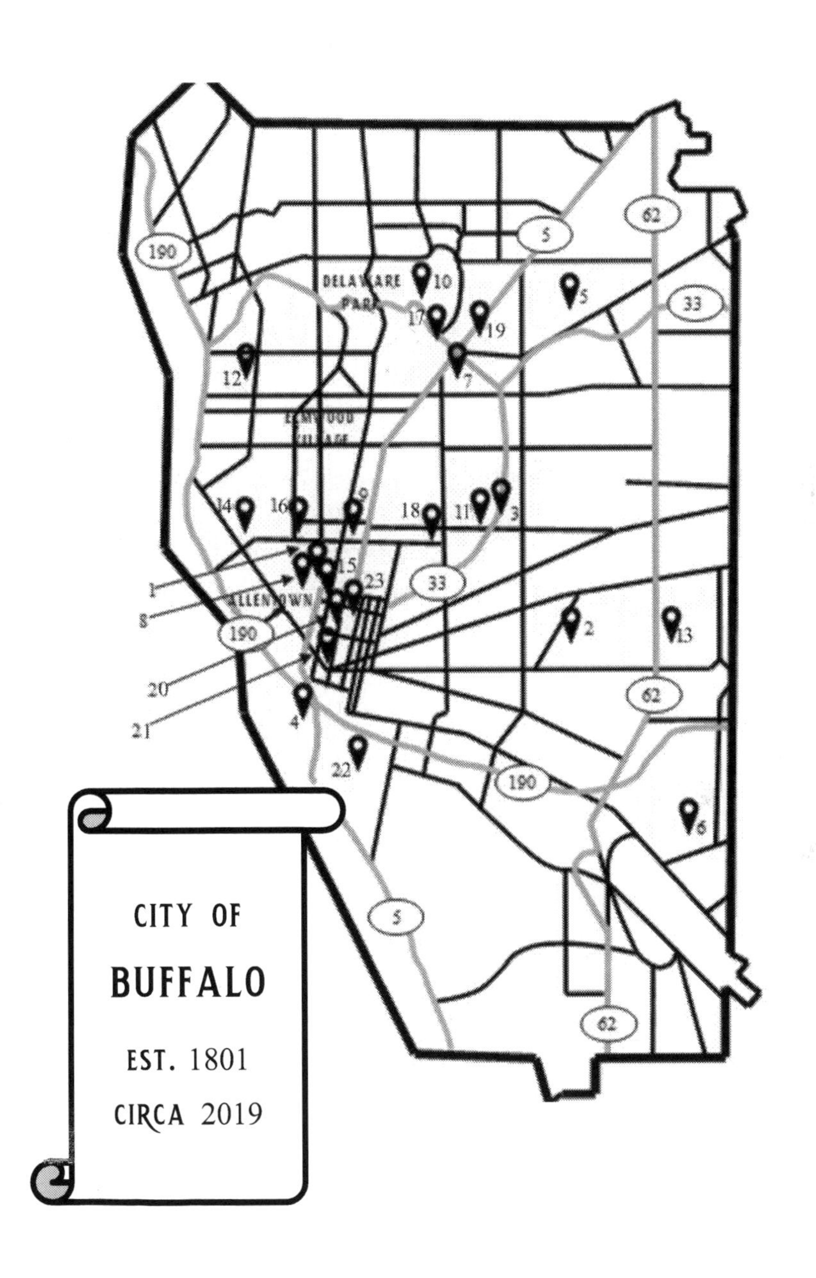
CITY OF
BUFFALO
EST. 1801
CIRCA 2019
DELAWARE PARK
ELMWOOD VILLAGE
ALLENTOWN
190
5
62
33
1
2
3
4
5
6
7
8
9
10
11
12
13
14
15
16
17
18
19
20
21
22
23

ALLENDALE THEATRE

203 Allen Street, Buffalo, New York, 14201
42.899570°, -78.877560°
www.theatreofyouth.org

The Allendale Theatre may not be the oldest theatre in Western New York. After all, it was only built in 1913. But that doesn't mean it hasn't made an impact on the local theatre scene, and maybe the spooky scene too.

The Allendale Theatre was built by Levin Michaels in the Neo-Classical Revival style and was originally home to silent films and photoplays. It did have a span of growing pains and acted as a XXX movie theatre for a few years before it was saved from demolition in 1986 by the Allentown Association. Today, the Allendale Theatre is home to TOY (Theatre of Youth) which performs family-friendly shows and workshops to over 30,000 local children each year.

Ghost stories and theatres seem to go hand in hand wherever you might travel. Many paranormal researchers believe that ghosts gather energy from electrical sources such as extension cords, power strips, lights, and computers. These are all things that many theatres use to put on performances nowadays, making these locations a veritable buffet for the spirit world. The Allendale Theatre only celebrated its centennial a few years ago, but, thanks to the technology it uses daily, it has just as much paranormal activity as Buffalo's oldest theatres.

Many stories come from members of the tech crew who report extra performers and even a phantom audience during closed rehearsals. The classic claim of movement in the corner of your eye has been documented by performers and audience members alike. Voices are heard in the otherwise empty theatre. Crew members say that activity seems to come alive around midnight where unexplained noises echo through the theatre and props go missing.

FUN FACT: Home of TOY, it is the only professional theatre company in Western New York dedicated to families and young audiences. Perfect for bringing the kids!

The Allendale Theatre is located in the heart of the Allentown historic district. Because it is home to TOY, school groups are always welcome. For those of us who left elementary school far behind us, the Allendale Theatre and the Theatre of Youth is open to the general public for performances throughout the year.

EXPERIENCE:
Theatre

OPEN TO THE PUBLIC:
Yes

HANDICAP ACCESSIBLE:
Yes

Important Info:
Box Office Hours of Operation:
Tuesday-Friday:
12:00-4:00pm
Contact:
(716) 884-4400

Admission:
Tickets range from $15-28 depending on seat selection.

BUFFALO CENTRAL TERMINAL

495 Paderewski Drive, Buffalo, New York, 14212
42.889718°, -78.830683°
www.buffalocentralterminal.org

One of Buffalo's most impressive and beautiful structures has not had the easiest life in the Queen City. Built in 1929, the beautiful Art Deco train station opened just months before the Great Depression and offered shops, a restaurant, and soda fountain. Sadly, it didn't last too long as Buffalo's premier train station. Over the last century, it has had a rough time (reaching such a low point as to be sold for only $1). The train station closed its doors in 1979. But luckily in 2003, it was selected to be restored by the Preservation League of New York State, and since then, it has seen new life.

Like so many other historic buildings throughout Western New York, people have rallied around it in the hopes of restoring it. Annually, the Buffalo Central Terminal hosts over 40 fundraising events. Today, it is even home to such festivities as Buffalo's own Dyngus Day celebrations as well as Oktoberfest and their annual Central Terminal Car Show.

As seen on *Ghost Hunters* season 4, episode 17.

It was recently announced that the Central Terminal's former waiting room and restaurant would be restored to its former glory in a $5 million project. This newest remodel will offer people even more opportunities to experience one of Buffalo's unique and beautiful buildings, filled with history and ghost stories.

Buffalo Central Terminal was featured on SyFy's *Ghost Hunters*, including their live Halloween special. According to claims, the train station is home to several shadow figures. Occasionally, the Terminal is open to the public for ghost tours and hunts. Keep an eye on their website for special events and tickets.

FUN FACT: It is the 10th tallest building in Buffalo.

EXPERIENCE:

Landmark/Ghost Tour

OPEN TO THE PUBLIC:

Yes

HANDICAP ACCESSIBLE:

Partial. No elevator on tours.

BUFFALO MUSEUM OF SCIENCE

1020 Humboldt Parkway, Buffalo, New York, 14211
42.906074°, -78.843384°
www.sciencebuff.org

If you grew up in Buffalo, then you visited the Buffalo Museum of Science on more than one occasion when the Ancient Egypt exhibit came to town. The museum has gone through quite a transformation over the years. They've severely downsized their dinosaur exhibit and put away the giant Sequoia and Lucy the beloved Australopithecus afarensis. The museum is redefining itself and bringing in world-famous exhibitions such as Body Worlds and Mummies of the World (both of which I highly recommend). But there are some things about the museum that will never change. That includes their haunting.

The museum isn't advertising the fact that some strange things are happening after hours. But volunteers at the Buffalo Museum of Science know that there is something paranormal happening in the building that has been part of Buffalo for almost 100 years now.

Most employees agree that there is something on the third floor. There have been unexplained noises, voices calling out people's names, shadows, and orbs of light seen with the naked eye. The third floor is now home to the hands-on learning section of the museum, with a recently updated exhibit on earth science, weather, and geology. But don't be afraid to take the kids to this part of the museum—most of the activity here happens after hours. According to a former employee, the museum seems to come alive at night when it's empty.

TIP: The Kellogg Observatory is finally open once more! 30-minute visits are available on Wednesdays for $15-25. Reservations are required and can be made the day of.

The activity in the building which opened in 1929 spiked when a collection of shrunken heads arrived. During this time a "dark cloud" seemed to come to the museum, and a bizarre wave of misfortune followed the staff members who handled those heads.

The museum is home to artifacts from around the world. Some of these items supposedly include protection spells and curses, therefore, it is impossible to pinpoint a single haunted object or haunting, for that matter.

EXPERIENCE:
Museum

OPEN TO THE PUBLIC:
Yes

HANDICAP ACCESSIBLE:
Yes. Kellogg Observatory is not.

Important Info:
Hours of Operation:
Monday-Tuesday:
10:00am-4:00pm
Wednesday:
10:00am-9:00pm
Thursday-Sunday:
10:00am-4:00pm
Contact:
(716) 896-5200

Admission:
Adults: $13
Children under 17: $10
Senior, student, and veteran discounts available.

*There may be additional charges for touring exhibits

BUFFALO NAVAL PARK

Military Park 1 Naval Park Cove, Buffalo, New York, 14202
42.877640°, -78.879709°
www.buffalonavalpark.org

The Buffalo Naval Park always makes an appearance on various lists around Halloween time, highlighting the most haunted locations throughout Western New York. And for some pretty compelling reasons.

The Naval Park is made up of three different ships—the destroyer *USS The Sullivans*, the guided-missile cruiser *USS Little Rock*, and the World War II submarine *USS Croaker*. Oh, and every single one of them is supposedly haunted.

FUN FACT: All branches of the armed forces are represented in the exhibits.

The Naval Park, itself, opened to the public in 1979. But each of the ships has their own history, leading to some curious phenomenon experienced by volunteers and employees, guests, and even boy scout troops.

The *USS The Sullivans* was launched in 1943 and is named after the five Sullivan brothers: George, Francis, Joseph, Madison, and Albert. The five brothers refused to be separated during their service in World War II, and sadly, all five of them perished in 1942. The *USS The Sullivans* served in both World War II and the Korean War until it was decommissioned in 1965. It found a home in the Buffalo Naval Park in 1977, and since then paranormal activity has run amuck.

As seen on *Ghost Hunters* season 9, episode 18.

Guests to the *USS The Sullivans* report having electrical issues such as cameras not working correctly, batteries dying, and even memory cards wiping out photos. Lights turn off without reason while some people also report seeing unexplained balls of light. The sound of bangs and voices echo through the empty ship, and some say they notice a mist following them. There is a portrait of the Sullivan brothers on board the vessel. According to claims, it is impossible to take a clear photo of the painting. The most disturbing reports tell of an apparition seen in the bowels of the ship—a floating torso with a badly burned face.

> **FUN FACT:** This is the largest inland park of its kind in the country.

The *USS Little Rock* was commissioned too late to see any combat in World War II. Instead, she spent a fair amount of time in the Caribbean and the Mediterranean. She came to the Buffalo Naval Park at the same time as the *USS The Sullivans* and is a favorite haunt for history buffs and ghosts alike.

There have been reports of ghostly activity on the *USS Little Rock* ranging from faucets turning on and off and the sound of footsteps and voices to even the sight of shadowy figures. The *USS Little Rock* is also said to be home to a sad, lonely sailor who enjoys following women around the ship in the hopes of getting some attention from them.

The newest addition to the Buffalo Naval Park family is the World War II submarine *USS Croaker*, arriving in Buffalo in 1988. Serving in the Pacific during World War II, she was finally decommissioned in 1968 and eventually was opened to the public as a museum at the Naval Park.

Perhaps the most frightening ship at the museum, the *USS Croaker* is said to be home to an angry spirit named John. He is known to pull on peoples' hair, breathe on the back of their necks, and even manages to block entire passageways, forcing guests to leave.

The Buffalo Naval Park is open to the public as a museum and runs seven days a week from April to November. Overnight encampments are available for Boy Scouts and Girl Scouts, school groups, etc. and allow campers to spend a night on the *USS Little Rock*. The price for the overnight stay is $55 per person, regardless of age, and covers the cost of dinner, breakfast, the overnight stay, and a tour of the entire park.

TIP: Last ticket is sold one hour prior to close.

EXPERIENCE:
Museum/Landmark

OPEN TO THE PUBLIC:
Yes

HANDICAP ACCESSIBLE:
Partial

Important Info:
Summer Hours:
Daily
10:00am-5:00pm
Winter Hours:
Daily
10:00am-4:00pm

For overnight stays, contact leslie@buffalonavalpark.org

Admission:
Adults (13-64): $15
Seniors (65+): $12
Veterans: $10
Active duty: Free
Children (5-12): $9

BUFFALO PUBLIC SCHOOL #61

Buffalo Public School #61 is also known as the Arthur O. Eve School of Distinction. It is one of 45 elementary schools in the city of Buffalo, offering equal and high-quality education for each of its students. The Buffalo public school system was founded in 1838, and today there are over 70 facilities including pre-k, elementary, high school, and adult education.

According to legend, a young boy died while on the second floor of the school in the 1970s. They say his ghost has haunted the halls of his alma mater ever since. The haunting is a relatively quiet one, which in the case of PS #61 (a school for pre-K-4th graders) is a blessing. There are no signs of an evil haunt—hardly any signs of a haunt for that matter. The school isn't plagued with unexplained shouts and screams, no apparitions, and nothing that has been caught on camera. But if the ghost stories are to be believed, there is one occurrence each year that reminds the staff of the school's tragic past.

In the room located directly below where the boy perished (said to be an English Language Arts classroom), the ceiling tiles fall, spelling out the word HELP. It's hard to prove whether or not this extraordinary claim is real (you know: pics or it didn't happen). Nevertheless, it makes for a great ghost story and helps keep the legend of Buffalo Public School #61 alive.

EXPERIENCE:

School

OPEN TO THE PUBLIC:

No

BUFFUM STREET CEMETERY

Seneca Indian Park, Buffalo, New York, 14210
42.854722°, -78.801944°

There isn't much left of the Buffum Street Cemetery on the corner of Buffum Street and Fields Avenue. What was once an ancient Native American burial mound as well as a cemetery for Christian Seneca, is now Buffalo's Seneca Indian Park. Sadly, only a boulder acting as a monument marks the sacred grounds today. The park was dedicated in 1912, but the graves have been disturbed multiple times over the years as the community surrounding the cemetery continues to develop.

The Buffum Street Cemetery was once the final resting place of the Seneca Chief, Red Jacket, and Mary Jemison, the White Woman of the Genesee. Mary Jemison was moved from Buffum Street to the Seneca Council House in what is now Letchworth State Park in 1874. In 1884, Red Jacket was removed from the Seneca cemetery and brought to Buffalo's largest cemetery where a statue of the leader of the Wolf Clan still stands.

Each time the sacred burial ground is disturbed (as recent as 2009 thanks to a local sewer company), it seems as if reports of paranormal activity spikes. An apparition of a Native American boy has been spotted around the park, and dogs and children avoid the park entirely. It seems the houses surrounding

Buffum Street Cemetery have experienced overflow activity from the park. Many families report objects moving in their homes, lights turning on and off, unexplained sounds, and even shadow people.

In recent years, Buffum Street Cemetery has been the center of a new controversy with the Maritime Charter School hoping to build a high school and gymnasium on the land.

> **FUN FACT:** Mary Jemison was captured during the French and Indian War and chose to remain a Seneca instead of returning to British Colonial rule.

The future of the burial ground and the charter school are still unknown. But if we've learned anything from the movie *Poltergeist*, it's that you probably don't want to build anything on sacred land.

EXPERIENCE:

Burial Ground/Park

OPEN TO THE PUBLIC:

Yes

HANDICAP ACCESSIBLE:

Partial. Steps to boulder.

CANISIUS COLLEGE

2001 Main Street, Buffalo, New York, 14208
42.925263°, -78.850856°
www.canisius.edu

Canisius College is, quite easily, the most haunted college in all of Buffalo.

Founded in 1870 by the Jesuits, Canisius was the first Catholic college in Buffalo. Starting with only one building on Washington Street, Canisius now has 37 buildings resting on 72 acres of land. The college was an all-male school until 1965. Since the ladies have joined in, the school has grown to over 3,000 students.

> **FUN FACT:** Canisius is one of 28 Jesuit Catholic colleges in the country.

Both current students and alumni have an impressive collection of ghost stories. These tales don't revolve around a single building. The entire campus, including residence halls and even the chapel, seems to be haunted.

There are at least three residence halls with paranormal claims. Frisch Five has been the site of at least three hangings on the fifth floor, including one in the bathroom where doors slam shut and voices are heard. On the fourth floor of Lyons Hall, nuns are seen wandering in the dark. And in Dugan Residence Hall, the fourth-floor women's bathroom is home to some ghostly activity including lights turning on and off on their own.

The chapel is a hot spot when it comes to paranormal activity. Students claim to hear loud banging and voices coming from the confessionals. Some even report seeing an old man wandering around (it is believed that he is a former priest).

And, of course, we can't forget the campus's theatre: Marie Maday Theatre. There are stories of a spirit named Marie, who is said to haunt the costume room. Students involved in productions are supposed to say goodbye to her before leaving for the night. Otherwise, things might not go so well in the next production.

The number of ghost stories is astounding when it comes to Canisius College. It seems as if students are unfazed by the activity on their campus with how willing they are to talk about their own experiences. If you ever meet a Canisius alum, don't be afraid to ask them about the stories surrounding their alma mater… they might surprise you.

EXPERIENCE:
School

OPEN TO THE PUBLIC:
Partial

COATSWORTH MANSION

49 Cottage Street, Buffalo, New York, 14201
42.897510°, -78.879650°

If you can afford to spend over $1000 a month, you could live in one of Buffalo's most haunted houses! The beautiful four-story home at 49 Cottage Street has been restored and transformed into luxury apartments. In the style of Second Empire Fantasy Architecture (that's just fun to say), this towering home is sometimes called "The Jewel of Allentown."

There's a bit of discrepancy over just when the Coatsworth Mansion was built, with dates ranging anywhere from 1865 to 1879. Built by Thomas Coatsworth for his wife, Electra, he made his fortune after the Civil War and built one of the first grain elevators in Buffalo. The Coatsworth family remained there, taking meticulous care of the home until they moved to Lincoln Woods Lane at the turn of the 20th Century. Over the years, the mansion was also home to the Brothers of Mercy and the local Carmelite nuns. It fell into a state of disrepair until developer Noel Sutton got his hands on it and transformed it into what it is today.

Recently, there have been tales of ghostly activity coming from the mansion. And it doesn't matter if you're inside the house or outside.

Residents experience cold spots and unexplained noises, though, for one of Buffalo's most historic homes, drafts and creaks aren't that peculiar. Full-body apparitions, on the other hand, well that's something of which to take notice.

> **FUN FACT:** Theodore Roosevelt supposedly stopped by the house while visiting Buffalo.

The most frequently seen apparition around the house is the spirit of a nun, no doubt leftover from the house's days as a home for the Carmelite sisters.

Despite the haunting, 49 Cottage Street has no problem filling its apartments. The stunning house has been saved from demolition and has found new life in the heart of Downtown Buffalo. You'll have a hard time getting access to see the interior of the restored mansion unless you know someone on the inside. But if the legends are real, you just have to walk by and look up at the windows. With any luck, you'll see a nun staring back at you.

EXPERIENCE:

Private Residence

OPEN TO THE PUBLIC:

No

EPISCOPAL CHURCH OF THE ASCENSION

16 Linwood Avenue, Buffalo, New York, 14209
42.902610°, -78.871210°

Completed in 1873, the Episcopal Church of the Ascension called Linwood Avenue its home until 2015, when the parish moved to the Church of the Good Shephard. Since then, the church has been left in a state of limbo—it's set to transform into senior housing, but after years of setbacks, it remains empty.

Even when Ascension was bustling with a congregation, there were claims of paranormal activity. Of course, many of the reports revolved around unexplained sounds as well as electrical issues. Could it have just been that the building was well over a century old? It could be. But many people think there's more to this haunting than just a building settling.

Many visitors and members of the congregation have shared stories of seeing a full-body apparition of a man throughout the entire building. He's been spotted so many times, that he's recognized as a former priest.

But the late father isn't the only spirit lurking in the old church (and no, we're not talking about the Holy Spirit, either).

According to legend, Ascension was once home to an abusive priest, and his actions left a dark mark on the church. Many feel as if there is a "bad vibe" in the sanctuary. This bad juju was so strong that at one point in time, the church was blessed in the hopes of ridding itself of the negativity.

The Church of the Ascension still sits empty at the time of publication, so access to the haunted chapel isn't likely anytime soon.

EXPERIENCE:

Church

OPEN TO THE PUBLIC:

No

FLINT HILL

84 Parkside Avenue, Buffalo, New York, 14214
42.936161°, -78.858039°

Flint Hill is a fascinating piece of Buffalo history that has been forgotten over time. It's an unassuming bit of land in the city, nestled between Scajaquada Creek and Jewett Parkway. It may not look like much now. But it is, in fact, a burial mound that we have built on top of over the centuries.

> **FUN FACT:** There were over 30 battles in the Niagara Frontier during the War of 1812.

The land once belonged to Judge Erastus Granger (a close friend and ally to Red Jacket and the Seneca Nation at the time), and it became the winter campground for the American troops during the War of 1812. Unfortunately, these troops were led by the less than adequate General Alex Smyth. Smyth decided to abandon his men once the harsh Western New York winter arrived, ordering the soldiers to stay put until spring.

What resulted was the death of over 300 men, all victims to poor planning and (a complete lack of) leadership.

Illness swept through the men as winter arrived, and those who didn't succumb to sickness would meet their end as they froze and starved to death. It was nearly impossible to bury the dead (up to 10 men dying each day) in the frozen limestone ground, so many of the graves were only a foot deep. Eventually, the bodies were moved to the nearby meadow. They're still there to this day, but a meadow no longer marks their final resting place, but rather, the Delaware Park Golf Course.

Right near the fourth hole along the course, there is a boulder that was placed in 1896 to mark the location where 300 soldiers from the War of 1812 still lie.

Today, there are reports of shadowy figures wandering around the golf course. But even those who may not believe in the spirits of the dead still notice something a bit "off" when it comes to the fourth hole of the golf course. Many golfers report feeling as if the ground around that particular hole moves on its own, making it nearly impossible to make the shot. Some think that the golfers are just bitter… but there's no denying that they seem to always miss at Delaware Park's fourth hole.

TIP: Visit on a Monday morning before the golf course opens.

EXPERIENCE:
Burial Ground/Park

OPEN TO THE PUBLIC:
Yes

HANDICAP ACCESSIBLE:
Yes

GERMAN ROMAN CATHOLIC ORPHAN ASYLUM

564 Dodge Street, Buffalo, New York, 14208
42.905825°, -78.846537°

One of Buffalo's lesser-known haunts has a pretty intimidating name attached to it. Throw in the fact that the building was abandoned for years, and you can be sure that some ghost stories are floating around the German Catholic Orphan Asylum.

The orphanage was an extension of St. Mary's Church, built between 1874 and 1875. Over the next 80 years, the nuns of the establishment cared for over 15,000 children, seeing its busiest time during the Great Depression when parents couldn't care for their children. After a fire that devastated the main building in 1956, the orphanage closed its doors to the kids but remained open into the 1990s as a preparatory seminary.

The complex was left abandoned, but that didn't stop urbexers and paranormal investigators from exploring the grounds. According to claims, the orphanage is home to strange noises, including children laughing as well as the sound of running water when the service was turned off for years. The most interesting claim to fame is the colorful orbs that appear in photographs taken inside the orphanage.

In 2010, the buildings were saved from the wrecking ball. The two three-storied brick buildings of the former orphanage as well as the chapel have been restored and transformed into low-income apartments steps away from the Buffalo Museum of Science.

In the past, the orphanage wasn't accessible to the public (unless you wanted to be that person who gets caught breaking into an asbestos-laden building). And it looks like unless you know a resident, you're still not getting access. But it's impressive to see just how beautiful the historic buildings have been restored. It's even more impressive to keep a piece of Buffalo's history alive, especially for the kids who called the German Catholic Orphan Asylum their home. For some, it was the only happy home they ever knew.

EXPERIENCE:

Private Residence

OPEN TO THE PUBLIC:

No

GYPSY PARLOR

376 Grant Street, Buffalo, New York, 14213
42.924162°, -78.890148°
www.thegypsyparlor.com

Even though the Gypsy Parlor only opened in 2013, the building dates back to 1890 and is now the home to one of the hottest bars in the West Side of Buffalo.

> **TIP:** You can rent the billiards room for a few private rounds of pool.

When you enter the Gypsy Parlor, it is like walking back in time with old photos on the wall, dim lighting, Victorian furniture, and even a billiards room off to the side. Gabrielle Mattina has created a watering hole that offers unique dishes inspired by cuisines from all over the world. Stop in and try the Gypsy Parlor's famous stuffed bread, pastelillos, or Gypsy Juice.

And the people crowding around the bar are just as eclectic as the food and drink served here. There's trivia night on Mondays, and the famous Tutu Tuesday with $2 drinks and pastelillos (but only if you wear a tutu). There's also Bohemian Belly Dance Nights on Wednesdays, karaoke on Thursdays, dance parties on Saturdays, and even tango dancing on Sundays. And you can almost always find a fortune teller or tarot card reader setting up their table near the dining room.

When asking if a place is haunted, the best answer you can get is, "You have to see the basement!" Before the Gypsy Parlor opened, Todd Mattina restored much of the place, possibly riling up any energy that was lingering in the basement and beyond. Others think that the tarot readings encourage the haunting. Either way, it just adds to the charm of this unique watering hole.

As you sit at the bar drinking your Gypsy Juice or Witch's Brew, ask the bartenders if they have any good ghost stories. Most of the employees are incredible storytellers, and they'll have a few tales about unexplained noises throughout the building that is sure to send a shiver down your spine... it's that, or the hard liquor you're enjoying a little too much.

TIP: No tutu? No problem! They offer a colorful collection for you to choose from.

EXPERIENCE:
Restaurant/Bar

OPEN TO THE PUBLIC:
Yes

HANDICAP ACCESSIBLE:
No

Important Info:
Hours of Operation:
Monday-Thursday:
5:00pm-4:00am
Friday:
2:30pm-4:00am
Saturday:
5:00pm-4:00am
Sunday:
11:00am-4:00am
Contact:
(716) 551-0001

IRON ISLAND MUSEUM

998 East Lovejoy Street, Buffalo, New York, 14206
42.890037°, -78.811407°
www.ironislandmuseum.com

Formerly a church built in 1883, Iron Island Museum is considered to be one of the most haunted places in Western New York. The church closed its doors in the 1940s and, remained empty until 1956 when it became a funeral home. During its years as a funeral home, it waked many residents, including the current owners' brother and son, Jimmy. It was donated in 2000 to the Iron Island Preservation Society of Lovejoy. Since Linda and her mother, Marge, have taken over, it has become a beacon for paranormal investigators in the region.

The museum is separated into various sections, each one boasting its own exhibits and hauntings. There's the railroad room and the military room, filled with artifacts from wars fought throughout the 20th Century. The Chapel has a small room off to the side that has a single ladder leading up to the attic. If anyone is brave enough to climb it, you'll find the beautiful original stained glass windows still hanging up there, and possibly a ghost.

> **FUN FACT:** It's called "Iron Island" because the neighborhood is surrounded by train tracks.

It is believed that the museum is haunted by the ghost of Edgar Zernicke, whose cremated remains went unclaimed for years. Iron Island is also haunted by the spirits of two six-year-old boys whose funerals were held there in the 1960s (aside from Jimmy). People have reported hearing their names called by children, both audibly with their own ears as well as in EVPs. The coat rack is thought to be a vortex, stirring up psychic energy, and the attic is home to a grumpy spirit known by many investigators as the night watchman.

> As seen on *Ghost Hunters* season 4, episode 14, *Ghost Lab* season 2, episode 8, and *My Ghost Story* season 2, episode 2.

The best time of year to visit one of Buffalo's prime haunts is in October leading up to Halloween (no surprise there). Iron Island opens its doors to the public, hosting events such as a haunted happy hour and a haunted food truck rodeo. It's just one of the many fun ways Marge and Linda have managed to keep Iron Island Museum going stronger than ever.

The museum is open to the public with both guided and self-guided tours. You can also rent the space on weekends for private ghost hunts for $35 per person for groups of five or more. You'll have access to the entire building from the basement to the chapel, and even the museum exhibits. These special hunts go from 7:00pm-2:00am, and they have a functioning kitchen and dining area (with heat!) that offers a great base camp for investigations. For those who

> **~~FUN~~ FACT:** Dozens of ashes went unclaimed in the basement. One was even found knocked over.

might require sustenance (aka coffee), they do allow you to bring food and drinks for the evening. Alcohol is not permitted.

Iron Island Museum lives up to its reputation as being haunted by restless spirits: some are playful and curious, while others are a bit more intimidating and grumpy. Linda and Marge are open to the idea of the haunting and encourage those interested in the afterlife to visit with an open mind… Iron Island is sure to make a believer out of you.

EXPERIENCE:
Museum/Ghost Hunt

OPEN TO THE PUBLIC:
Yes

HANDICAP ACCESSIBLE:
Yes

Important Info:
Museum Hours of Operation:
Thursday:
6:00-8:30pm
Friday-Saturday:
10:00am-12:30pm

Overnight investigations available Saturday-Sunday. Email ljhgold@aol.com for more info.

Admission:

Self-guided tours: $2

Guided ghost tours: $5 (reservations recommended)

Private overnight ghost hunt: $35 per person (minimum of five participants).

KOESSLER ADMIN BUILDING

320 Porter Avenue, Buffalo, New York, 14201
42.902498°, -78.891031°
www.dyc.edu

Even though it's a co-ed college today, D'Youville was established as an all-girls school when it first opened in 1908. Founded by the Grey Nuns who also founded Holy Angels Academy, the college is named after their patron saint Marie-Marguerette D'Youville. It was the first college to offer baccalaureate degrees to women in Western New York, and it also introduced the first four-year undergrad nursing program in 1942. By the time the 1970s rolled around, men were allowed to enroll, and since then, it has grown to more than 3,000 students with over 50 majors available.

FUN FACT: The Grey Nuns were founded in Montreal in 1737.

The Koessler Administration Building opened in 1874 and initially acted as the home of Holy Angels Academy until the young ladies of D'Youville came along. Legend has it that the four-story, red brick building was once an orphanage, but there are no records that prove this is true. It was, however, the very first place where the students of D'Youville attended classes over 100 years ago. Even though it is the oldest building on campus, it is still the core building of D'Youville today.

Many believe that the paranormal activity in the old building stems from a fire that erupted on the upper floors in the late 1870s. At the time, students at the boarding school of Holy Angels and nuns lived on the third and fourth floors. Local legend claims that there was one nun that refused to leave her home, proclaiming that Mother D'Youville would save her beloved school (technically she wasn't wrong). Luckily, she was removed by firemen, but many believe her spirit has returned to haunt the Koessler building.

But the activity at D'Youville doesn't stop with ghostly nuns. Security guards report seeing strange lights throughout the upper floors of the building. Doors will unlock on their own and footsteps can be heard echoing down empty halls. There are also stories of a young girl running through the fourth floor, possibly a former student of Holy Angels.

FUN FACT: The statue of Sister D'Youville includes a kitten, a child (symbolizing her work with orphans), and a replica of her key to the Grey Nun's motherhouse.

Students of D'Youville who visit the Koessler Administration Building at night report a sense of fear and dread when they arrive on the third and fourth floors. It could be ghosts… or the fact that they're breaking into a building in the middle of the night. Tough call to make.

EXPERIENCE:

School

OPEN TO THE PUBLIC:

Partial

THE MANSION ON DELAWARE AVENUE

414 Delaware Avenue, Buffalo, New York, 14202
42.895650°, -78.875610°
www.mansionondelaware.com

One of the hottest wedding venues in Buffalo was built in 1870 in the Second Empire Style. Strangely enough, the Mansion went through three owners in its first year of existence. Charles Sternberg died before the house was completed. John Condit Smith died shortly after purchasing the home. Finally, Samuel Curtis Trubee came along and managed to own it for years. Trubee turned the family home into a hotel during the Pan-American Exposition in 1901, charging $3 a night (that would be almost $90 by today's standards). By the time the Great Depression hit Buffalo, it is rumored that the Mansion had converted into a bordello, and not surprisingly, the building was abandoned from the late 1970s until 2001.

Today, the Mansion is a popular venue for Buffalo couples and their weddings, and it is also the only butler service hotel in the Buffalo area. Celebrities stay here when they're performing in town, and I hear the service

FUN FACT: The Mansion is the only AAA Four Diamond Hotel in Buffalo.

is so excellent that some guests refuse to leave. Legend has it that the spirit of a little girl haunts the upper floor. Guests and staff alike have reported hearing her laughter as well as the sound of furniture moving by unseen hands.

The Mansion on Delaware Avenue offers luxury service with rooms starting at $199 a night. If you're not looking to drop a pretty penny on an overnight stay, the Mansion does host events such as weddings, birthday parties, charity balls, and fundraisers. During the summer months, they hold their Cocktails on the Lawn event where the grounds of the mansion are open to the public. Of course, you still have to purchase a ticket for $20 to attend, but then you have a chance to experience the food, drink, and haunted history of Millionaire's Row.

TIP: Request a room in the back or up higher to avoid ambient street noise.

EXPERIENCE:
Hotel/Event Venue

Contact:
(716) 886-3300

OPEN TO THE PUBLIC:
Yes

HANDICAP ACCESSIBLE:
Yes

MAYTHAM MANSIONS

26 Richmond Avenue, Buffalo, New York, 14222
42.902861°, -78.881611°

The Maytham Mansions are two Queen Anne style houses along Symphony Circle near Kleinhans Music Hall. Both buildings are breathtaking 19th Century mansions, but it is the one located at 26 Richmond Avenue that is said to be the home of a haunting.

> **FUN FACT:** Before the street was paved, locals would race their horses along Richmond Avenue with Symphony Circle acting as the finish line.

Constructed in 1892, the mansion was built for one of the Maytham brothers (the other brother living in the house next door at 71 Symphony Circle). The Maythams were best known for their family tugboat business, Maytham Towing and Wrecking. Today, their family home is infamous in the Allentown Historic District for being haunted.

Built on what was once Black Rock Burying Ground, the historic home was initially a private residence for wealthy families. Through the years, it became a home for women known as El Nathan, before becoming the administration building for Buffalo's Philharmonic Orchestra until 2013. No matter who inhabits the impressive home, though, one thing remains the same: its ghost stories.

Visitors to the Maytham Mansion claim that desks have been rearranged, a black mist is in the basement, and there are cold spots throughout the house. A full-body apparition of a little girl is seen on the stairs, and an older woman is spotted near the front door. No one knows who these spirits are, but everyone who has seen them has agreed that they don't feel malevolent.

EXPERIENCE:

Private Building

OPEN TO THE PUBLIC:

No

MEDAILLE COLLEGE

18 Agassiz Circle, Buffalo, New York, 14214
42.928608°, -78.855954°
www.medaille.edu

Even though Medaille College was established in 1937, it dates back to 1875 and the Sisters of St. Joseph. Originally named Mount St. Joseph Teachers College, the college began as a school to train teachers and offered baccalaureate degrees in education to women. In 1968, the school became co-educational and experienced a facelift, including a name change. Eventually, the school was named after the founder of the Sisters of St. Joseph, Father Jean Pierre Médaille, and Medaille College as we know it was born.

According to stories surrounding the newer college, a young boy hanged himself on the fourth floor of the main campus building and his restless spirit has haunted the premises ever since. The story goes further thanks to a student simply known as Hannah. After using an Ouija board at a party, she began to have vivid dreams of the boy who had hanged himself. According to the boy's spirit, he killed himself after experiencing abuse from one of the nuns. There are also reports of ghostly students sitting at the desks of empty classrooms.

EXPERIENCE:

School

OPEN TO THE PUBLIC:

Partial

NORTH STREET

North Street, Buffalo, New York, 14201
42.902240°, -78.875120°

Much of Downtown Buffalo has gone through some growing pains since it was first settled in 1789. Few roads have gone through a metamorphosis quite like North Street along the perimeter of Allentown.

What is now a road that passes through some of the most famous streets in all of Buffalo, once connected two cemeteries: the Delaware-North and the Black Rock burying grounds.

Black Rock burying ground is the older of the two cemeteries once found along North Street, with many dead already buried there at the beginning of the 19th Century. Eventually, the land turned out to be too low and not safe or suitable for burial. Many families dug up their dead and brought them to their new home at Lot 88 on North Street. A part of this new cemetery was also a potter's field where those who died in the local poorhouse were interred. Eventually, most of the bodies were moved, though many believe that some bodies remain.

FUN FACT: A potter's field dates back to biblical times. The first one was purchased with the 30 pieces of silver given to Judas and used as a burial ground for strangers, criminals, and the poor.

Delaware-North burial ground was established in the 1830s and was a small lot for families to bury their dead (only five acres of usable land). However, much like Black Rock, the ground was found to be unsuitable for burial—natural springs flooded the area. By the 1870s, most of the bodies were transferred to another cemetery as well. Today, the old burial ground is now the location for the Lenox Hotel. However, there are no reports that the

Lenox Hotel is haunted by those who once rested beneath the ground. But there are still plenty of ghost stories that are part of the North Street culture.

Several houses that now stand where Black Rock cemetery once stood are believed to be haunted. None of the claims sound malicious, but one owner believes that the spirit of a female is jealous of the living. People living and visiting these homes report objects moving on their own, the bathroom door locking on more than one occasion, and lights flashing off and on. Many also report seeing the apparition of a woman and a child.

It's hard to pinpoint a single spot on North Street that could be considered the most haunted. If you're up for a walk, grab some Tim Hortons and wander from Symphony Circle (and the nearby Maytham Mansions) and make your way towards Jefferson Avenue. You'll see pieces of Buffalo's history such as the Theodore Roosevelt Inaugural Site to your right down Delaware Avenue. And if you're lucky, you might experience a slice of Buffalo's forgotten past along North Street.

EXPERIENCE:

Burial Ground/Haunted Road

OPEN TO THE PUBLIC:

Yes

HANDICAP ACCESSIBLE:

Yes

ST. MARY'S SCHOOL FOR THE DEAF

St. Mary's School for the Deaf has been serving the deaf community in Western New York for over 160 years. It was established in 1853 as LeCouteulx St. Mary's Benevolent Society for the Deaf and Dumb, and only a year later a home was built for the school in Buffalo. Within five years, the school was in session with a handful of boys and girls. In 1898, the current school opened on Main Street with over 150 pupils, and since then, the school has grown into a vital part of the city of Buffalo and the surrounding counties of Western New York.

Of course, St. Mary's isn't home to just award-winning education for children and young adults—it is also home to several ghost stories.

One story stems from the death of a small boy who tragically drowned in the swimming pool, which is now the school gymnasium.

The most famous claim surrounding St. Mary's might connect the school to the beloved nuns that founded it over a century ago. According to legend, students have seen nuns wandering along the third floor. They have also seen the bell of the school move without any explanation. But there's no sense of negativity or fear when it comes to the ghost stories. Many believe that it is merely the sisters watching over their school.

EXPERIENCE:

School

OPEN TO THE PUBLIC:

No

SHEA'S PERFORMING ARTS CENTER

650 Main Street, Buffalo, New York, 14202
42.891890°, -78.872676°
www.sheas.org

It should come as no surprise that Buffalo's biggest theatre has its own ghost story (like all good theatres should).

Shea's was built by Michael Shea in 1926 in the Neo-Spanish Baroque style and is one of four Louis Comfort Tiffany designed theatres in the country. In its early days, it was home to silent films and today hosts nationally touring companies performing Broadway-style shows.

Like most buildings in the Buffalo area, it was abandoned and fell into a state of disrepair in the 1960s. And again, like most buildings in the Buffalo area, it was saved from demolition, and in 1995 the Interior Restoration Program began. Over the last 20 years, volunteers have worked diligently to restore Shea's to its original grandeur and glory, and throughout the renovations, some ghostly activity has been stirred up.

Spirits may roam the theatre's catwalk, backstage area, and foyer. But the most famous ghost in Shea's is its original owner, Michael Shea. Even though he passed away in 1934, Shea's spirit refuses to leave his beloved theatre. Performers, staff, and patrons have seen him, generally reveling in the glory of his creation.

The usual telltale signs of a haunt are here: doors slamming shut and lights turning on and off. But there is also the even more extraordinary claim of full-body apparitions. Michael Shea has appeared throughout the theatre over the years and even speaks to volunteers, asking them, "Isn't this place magnificent?"

Yes, Mr. Shea, it is.

Shea's Performing Arts Center offers historical tours from 10:00am-1:00pm on select days during the week. Reservations are recommended.

If you're looking to grab a bite to eat before a performance, head to Shea's Bistro & Bar. They serve cocktails and meals, specially themed around the show you're about to see. Try their matzo ball soup before *Fiddler on the Roof*, sip on a Red Lion cocktail for *The Lion King*, or nibble on some hush puppies before *The Book of Mormon*. The menu is always changing, offering visitors a unique experience with each show that comes to town.

EXPERIENCE:

Theatre/Restaurant/Bar/ Event Venue

OPEN TO THE PUBLIC:

Yes

HANDICAP ACCESSIBLE:

Partial. No elevator to upper floors.

Important Info:
Box Office Hours of Operation:
Sunday:
Closed
Monday-Friday:
10:00am-5:00pm
Saturday:
10:00am-2:00pm
Doors open one hour prior to each performance.
Contact:
(716) 847-1410

STATLER CITY HOTEL

SPOOK APPROVED EATS

107 Delaware Avenue, Buffalo, New York, 14202
42.887330°, -78.877000°
www.statlercity.com

> As seen on *Paranormal Lockdown* season 2, episode 7.

In the heyday of the Queen City's glamorous years, the Statler City was one of the most luxurious places to be seen. Built in 1921, it hosted first-class guests such as Al Capone, Richard Nixon, and even Dean Martin. Sadly, it closed in the 1980s and was left abandoned for 15 years. It wasn't until renovations began that the ghostly activity started to be noticed.

Paranormal claims vary from ghostly voices and full-body apparitions to people being touched by unseen hands. In the Terrace Room, a legless apparition has been seen as well as shadows and unexplainable glowing. The old pool area is supposedly home to a darker entity which is known to grab people aggressively and scream.

Currently, the Statler is not a functioning hotel. However, there are several ways that you can experience a vital part of Buffalo's history. The historic hotel acts as a luxury banquet hall and wedding venue, and it also offers tours and even private ghost hunts of the upper floors. For a more laid back approach to the Statler, the Lobby Bar is open Wednesday-Sunday starting at 4:00pm and offers a variety of food and drink specials.

For more information on ghost tours at

the Statler, visit www.statlerghosttours.com or email conor@statlercity.com for group rates.

EXPERIENCE:

Restaurant/Bar/
Event Venue/Ghost Hunt

OPEN TO THE PUBLIC:

Yes

HANDICAP ACCESSIBLE:

Partial. No elevator to upper floors.

Important Info:
Lobby Bar Hours of Operation:
Sunday-Tuesday: Closed
Wednesday-Thursday: 4:00-10:00pm
Friday-Saturday: 4:00pm-2:00am
Contact:
(716) 853-3300

SWANNIE HOUSE

170 Ohio Street, Buffalo, New York, 14203
42.872220°, -78.871800°

The Swannie House is the second oldest bar in Buffalo, second only to Ulrich's which opened 18 years prior. Established in 1886, the Swannie House found its home on the corner of Ohio and Michigan Streets in 1892, and it has been a tavern ever since.

The Swanerski Family originally owned the pub, but due to the tension between the Irish and Polish communities in the First Ward, they eventually changed their name to Swannie. For over a century, the Swannie House has been a favorite watering hole of the locals as well as a hot spot for lunch breaks for nearby factory workers. With 100 years of revelers coming and going, it should be no surprise that some of their residual energy still lingers in this place.

There are no EVPs, no objects that move, and no voices that call out to employees when they're all alone. The Swannie House does, however, have its own ghost.

Bob Nowak was a young man who worked at the Swannie House before the current owner, Tim Wiles, bought it in 1983. He enjoyed drinking and smoking and was liked by everyone who came to the tavern. However, one night on his

> **TIP:** The Swannie House is cash only.

way home from the Swannie House, Bob died tragically in a car accident on the corner of Roanoke and Seneca. When Wiles bought the place from Bob's mother, she gave him a photo of her son to hang on the bar's walls. Ever since "Swannie House" Bob's photo has been behind the bar, the Swannie House has experienced nothing but success.

Of course, Swannie House Bob's presence wasn't always felt on the premises, and when he finally made himself known, he caused quite a stir. One of the employees saw Bob wandering through the basement and was convinced someone had broken into the bar. Every time Bob is seen, he is wearing black slacks, a white shirt, and a skinny black tie. And whether or not employees see him, Tim Wiles is convinced he's there.

> **TIP:** Look for "Swannie House" Bob's photo behind the bar on the left-hand side beside the door.

"I'm not the bar owner… I'm the gatekeeper," Wiles says as he sits in his usual corner by the front window.

Wiles truly believes that someone is looking out for him and the Swannie House and is helping to keep it going even into the 21st Century.

Today, the Swannie House still acts as a tavern with a menu of quintessential Buffalo comfort food including beef on weck, deep-fried stuffed banana peppers, hearty chili, and killer wings. Oh, and it was also named the best fish fry in all of Buffalo! As if you needed more of a reason to visit.

EXPERIENCE:
Restaurant/Bar

OPEN TO THE PUBLIC:
Yes

HANDICAP ACCESSIBLE:
No

Important Info:
Hours of Operation:
Daily:
11:00-4:00am

TOWN BALLROOM

681 Main Street, Buffalo, New York, 14203
42.892387°, -78.871615°
www.townballroom.com

A staple in the entertainment industry throughout the 20th Century, the Town Ballroom has been known by many names, including Sphere Entertainment, UB's Pfeiffer Theatre, Studio Arena, and the Town Casino. Many of music's most celebrated acts passed through its doors, including Nat King Cole, Frank Sinatra, and Les Paul. Today, it continues to be a cornerstone of Buffalo's music scene, hosting a slew of acts each month. Good luck beating headliners link King Cole and Sinatra, though.

Supposedly, the Town Ballroom was home to a speakeasy in the basement during the dreaded years of Prohibition and even welcomed the infamous Al Capone. He hosted wild parties and gambling circles which seem to continue today, causing confusion and fear among staff members. People report hearing the sound of laughter and music echoing up from the basement in an otherwise empty building. Security alarms are triggered, and there has even been a young blonde woman spotted in a Victorian dress.

You can check out the Town Ballroom for yourself at one of their many concerts and events held throughout the year. They have some pretty impressive acts with ticket prices that won't break your piggy bank! However, no one under 12 is admitted, and an adult must accompany patrons under 16 years. Be sure to check events to see what the age restriction might be.

EXPERIENCE:

Event Venue

OPEN TO THE PUBLIC:

Yes

HANDICAP ACCESSIBLE:

Yes. Call ahead to reserve a spot: (716) 852-3900

Important Info:
Box Office Hours of Operation:
Monday-Friday: 12:00-5:00pm
Saturday-Sunday: Closed
When attending an event, you must bring ID to enter.

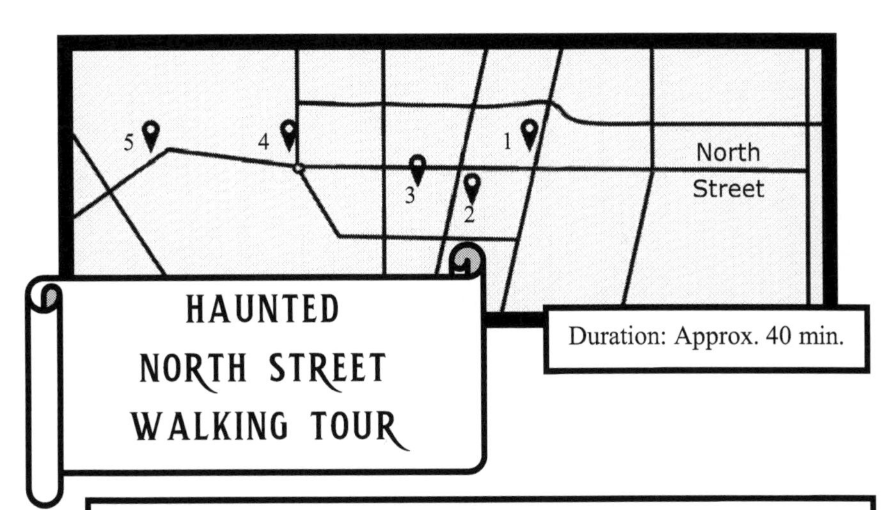

HAUNTED NORTH STREET WALKING TOUR

North Street is filled with both hauntings and history, and this little walking tour will show you both. Head west on Jefferson Avenue (if you don't feel obligated to walk the length of North Street or would like to cut off about 15 minutes of this walk, begin on Main Street, still heading west). Just past Main Street, you'll hit Linwood Avenue on your right where the empty **Episcopal Church of the Ascension (1)** still awaits its fate. Continue to Delaware Avenue and look to your left to see the **Theodore Roosevelt Inaugural Site (2)**. It's there Teddy Roosevelt was sworn in as president after William McKinley was assassinated. Consider stopping in for a guided tour. Backtrack to North Street and continue west. On your left will be the **Lenox Hotel (3)**, built on one of Buffalo's oldest cemeteries. There are no reports of a haunting, but it is the longest-running hotel in Buffalo and their restaurant has gourmet mac 'n cheese, so consider stopping in. As you exit the hotel, turn left and continue to Symphony Circle near Kleinhans Music Hall where you'll see the **Maytham Mansions (4)** to your right at 26 Richmond Avenue. Follow North Street as it turns into Porter Avenue where you'll end your tour at the statue of **Sister Marguerette D'Youville and the Koessler Admin Building (5)**. To reward yourself, I recommend celebrating at Community Beer Works, located just down the street at 520 7th Street for the perfect taste of Buffalo beer. Cheers!

GENESEE COUNTY

GENESEE COUNTY

The Seneca word Gen-nis'-hee-yo means "the Beautiful Valley." The history of the region dates back to the Ice Age (10,000-12,000 years ago). With evidence of Paleo-Indian artifacts such as tools, ceramics, and leather, it is one of the most important archaeological sites in the country. The county, itself, was officially established in 1803, making it one of the oldest counties in the area.

GENESEE
COUNTY
98
1
BASOM
63
BYRON
BERGEN
5
INDIAN
FALLS
33
2
90
90
4
6
PEMBROKE
BATAVIA
5
33
CORFU
3
98
63
DARIEN
CENTER
EAST
BETHANY
19
20
EST. 1803

BERGEN HOUSE

6571 West Sweden Road, Bergen, New York, 14416
43.0968862°, -77.9753675°

The Bergen House was built in 1858 and has an impressive collection of history and haunts. It's located next to the Bergen-Byron Swamp which is over 10,000 years old, and some believe witches visited the swamp to hold ceremonies and rituals in days gone by.

Whether witches worked on the land or not, there is something strange happening on the Bergen House's property.

From orphans and runaway slaves to Bigfoot and a young woman committing suicide in the barn, there are stories all throughout the property, not just inside the house. The apparition of a woman is seen walking up the long driveway leading up to the house. There have also been figures seen standing in the barn and looking out the windows of the house (some of them have even been caught on camera). People have been spotted in the trees surrounding the house, leading many to believe that the spirits of lynched runaway slaves still wander the grounds. Inside the house, there are disembodied voices and growls as well as shadow people and the spirit of a grumpy older man and several children on the upper floor of the house (sometimes known to play with living children).

FUN FACT: Aside from ghosts, there are also claims of Bigfoot and fairies on the property.

Stories abound of objects moving and orbs as large as your fist flying through the air. People have been scratched in the séance room, and there are even reports of levitation. According to Cathy, the current owner (who also happened to grow up in the house), there are very different types of spirits haunting the Bergen House. She describes the activity as the day-shift and the night-shift. During the day, the ghosts seem curious and playful while after the sun sets, things get a bit darker (both literally and figuratively).

The three-bedroom house offers tours and ghost hunts throughout the year. Private hunts begin at $300 for the first eight participants ($25 extra for each additional person after that). Hunts run from 7:00pm-3:00am from April to November. Luckily, they do allow you to bring your own food and drink for your investigation (no alcohol please!). However, it is on a carry-in, carry-out basis, so be sure to not leave anything behind as this is a family's home.

> **TIP:** The owners have moved into the house to protect it from vandals and trespassers, so it's best to call ahead to ask if you can stop by:
> (585) 297-0191

As a precaution, they do supply sage and holy water for you upon departure if you're concerned about anyone (or anything) following you home.

EXPERIENCE:

Ghost Hunt/Ghost Tour

OPEN TO THE PUBLIC:

Yes

HANDICAP ACCESSIBLE:

No

BIG FALLS

Gilmore Road, Corfu, New York, 14036
43.026096°, -78.399805°

Now don't expect the sweeping views of Devil's Hole or the picturesque hiking trails like Eternal Flame Falls. There is no hiking trail for Indian Falls (in fact, there isn't even parking). But that doesn't stop those curious about Big Falls' ghost story from checking out the waterfall of Tonawanda Creek for themselves.

> **FUN FACT:** The falls are where Tonawanda Creek flows over the Onondaga Escarpment.

The area that is now home to Indian Falls was once Seneca land. Because the Seneca of this region were allied with the British, they were forced to give up the territory to the newly formed United States after the Revolutionary War. It is the birthplace of Ely Parker, the first Native American to be Commissioner of Indian Affairs under President Ulysses S. Grant. And it's also home to two pairs of entities.

The first ghostly duo comes from the 1950s—a pair of brothers who drowned. The second pair comes from the end of the 20th Century. It is believed a husband fell into the falls and drowned, and the wife, unable to live without her husband, jumped in after him. Both couples have been spotted by locals as well as orbs and even unexplained red lights.

While this may not be the most enjoyable hike, you can see the "Big Falls" from the west side of the New York State Route 77 bridge over Tonawanda Creek. Or better yet, grab a bite to eat at the Log Cabin restaurant to view the falls with a beer and some of their famous BBQ.

EXPERIENCE:

Natural Wonder

OPEN TO THE PUBLIC:

Yes

HANDICAP ACCESSIBLE:

Yes

Important Info:
The (not haunted) Log Cabin Restaurant is located at:
1227 Gilmore Rd.
Corfu, NY 14036

Hours of Operation:
Sunday:
12:00pm-12:00am
Monday-Thursday:
11:00am-12:00am
Friday-Saturday:
11:00am-2:00am

DARIEN LAKE

9993 Alleghany Road, Darien Center, New York, 14040
42.9245989°, -78.3895383°
www.sixflags.com/darienlake

Not many people think of an amusement park as someplace that might be haunted. But Western New York's ever-popular Darien Lake is home to roller coasters and rides, a water park, a campground, and some ghostly activity, too.

By 1983, *The Viper* was constructed, and Darien Lake as we know it has been entertaining Western New York families ever since. They offer attractions like *The Predator* (New York's largest wooden roller coaster), *Ride of Steel* (New York's tallest roller coaster), and the ever-terrifying *Skycoaster* where people actually pay to be hoisted 180 feet in the air before swinging over the entire park.

But among the bright lights, laser show, and junk food, Darien Lake has experienced its fair share of tragedy since opening.

In July 1987, three campers were struck by lightning, killing them while they slept in their tents. In 2009, the body of a Pennsylvania man was found in one of the park's lakes. And in 2011, an Iraq War veteran fell from the *Ride of Steel.* It seems as if death and tragedy have always been a part of Darien Lake's otherwise colorful history.

Because of the large crowds and ambient noise, it is almost impossible to experience any of Darien Lake's paranormal activity during a visit. But security and staff have plenty of stories to share after the customers go home and the rides shut down at night.

Security guards have answered false alarms throughout the park. Lights from the rides will turn back on after being successfully shut down. Shadow figures have been seen in the park after hours, forcing staff to run around trying to find them long after they've vanished. There are also stories of a phantom swimmer who likes to enjoy the water park after hours.

Darien Lake is open from May through October, with day passes starting at $44.99 if you purchase them in advance (day-of passes cost an additional $15). There's no guarantee that you'll experience anything paranormal while visiting the amusement park. But Darien Lake is probably the most fun you'll have visiting a haunted location. You're likely to have so much fun that you'll forget about the park's tragic past and ghostly activity.

TIP: Be sure to bring an additional $20 with you as parking is not included with your ticket.

EXPERIENCE:
Amusement Park

OPEN TO THE PUBLIC:
Yes

HANDICAP ACCESSIBLE:
Yes

Important Info:
Hours of Operation:
Daily (from Father's Day-August):
10:30am-9:30pm
For other times, check the calendar on their website for up to date hours.

Admission:
(At the Gate)

Adults: $59.99
Children under 48": $39.99
Children 2 and under: Free

OLD WEST MAIN STREET CEMETERY

West Main Street, Batavia, New York, 14020
42.9992179°, -78.1906862°

Batavia's first graveyard was established in 1806 just after the town was settled. However, there isn't much left of the old cemetery today. After less than 20 years, the land the cemetery was on was deemed unfit for burial. Located on the banks of Tonawanda Creek, the waters regularly flooded the area, disturbing the dead. In 1823, many of the bodies were removed from the old West Main Street Cemetery and brought to Batavia Cemetery which is still accepting burials today.

Sadly, not everyone left the site of the former cemetery along Tonawanda Creek. Locals report seeing the spirit of a woman in a long gray dress wandering along the north bank. Many believe that she was buried in an unmarked grave, and because of that, her remains were left behind.

The creek as a whole runs for 90 miles, so the likelihood of seeing the gray lady along the north bank is pretty slim. But it does take you past some other haunted locations through Western New York, so it might be worth it to try.

FUN FACT: The Batavia Cemetery is home to William Morgan's grave, an anti-Masonic activist. His body, however, disappeared in 1824.

If you can't manage to find the site of Batavia's original cemetery, you can always head towards East Main Street and visit the historic Batavia Cemetery on Harvester Avenue. It may not be haunted, but it is listed on the National Register of Historic Places and is the final resting place to over 8,000 individuals.

EXPERIENCE:

Burial Ground

OPEN TO THE PUBLIC:

Yes. But only if you can find it.

SANDHILL ROAD

Sandhill Road, Basom, New York, 14013
43.0573132°, -78.4404556°

Just about a mile onto the Tonawanda Reservation might be the most terrifying haunted road in Western New York. Not so much for the stories surrounding it (that honor goes to Pigman Road), but rather, for what bizarre things people have reported seeing over the years.

Sandhill Road runs along Tonawanda Creek (another hot spot for paranormal activity). Travelers who make their way along this street claim to see changelings.

> **TIP:** Sandhill Road is also known as Hopkins Road.

For Europeans, changelings are a fairy child left behind in place of a human child taken to the land of the fairies. It might be upsetting to think that something can sneak into your house and steal your kid only to leave a sickly replacement behind in its stead. But that is child's play. The changelings of Native American lore are a bit more disturbing, especially if one crosses your path in the middle of the night on an empty road. People report seeing humans with animal features such as a fox tail or deer antlers. According to legend, these changelings are shamans and witches who are caught in mid-transformation.

There have also been reports of little people. Of course, the most famous little people come from Ireland (leprechauns). But there are stories of little people from cultures all over the world such as Greece, the Philippines, Hawaii, New Zealand, and Indonesia. The Native American legend says that

> **FUN FACT:** Shapeshifting is found in some of the world's oldest epic poems like *The Iliad* and *The Epic of Gilgamesh*.

little people tend to inhabit areas near large bodies of water, such as the Great Lakes. The stories go a bit further and say that little people tend to live inside sandy hills (what's the name of this road, again?).

As if changelings and little people weren't enough, shapeshifters have also been spotted nearby. For a three-mile stretch of road, Sandhill sure does pack a paranormal punch.

EXPERIENCE:

Haunted Road

OPEN TO THE PUBLIC:

Yes

HANDICAP ACCESSIBLE:

Yes

SEYMOUR PLACE

201 East Main Street, Batavia, New York, 14020
42.9975412°, -78.181652°
www.goart.org

Built in 1831 by Hezekiah Eldredge (officially the coolest name ever) as the Bank of Genesee, it didn't receive the name Seymour Place until 2010. In 1886 the mansion was sold to the Batavia Club (a community men's club), and it stayed in their possession until 2002 when it was donated to the Genesee-Orleans Regional Arts Council. Today, it is home to GO ART! and offers art exhibits, lectures, and workshops, as well as social events. But even though it's now an art gallery, I have a feeling none of the spirits helped with those paintings (to see that, you'll have to head to Lily Dale).

Patrons and students share their haunted experiences throughout Seymour Place. People report smelling cigar smoke and seeing imprints of someone sitting in chairs next to them when no one is around. EVPs have been captured, and white shadow people have been seen up on the second floor. A psychic medium has reported sensing the spirit of a young girl in a room just to the left of the bar, though the child has never made herself known to anyone else. There is also a full-body apparition of a man in the bar. He is tall and dressed in clothes from the 1960s (finally, not another stuffy Victorian phantom!). Sometimes he is alone. Other times he is surrounded by ghostly men, no doubt former members of the Batavia Club.

> **TIP:** You can book Tavern 2.o.1. for a private event.

If you're looking to catch Seymour Place's groovy ghost, be sure to swing by Tavern 2.o.1. for a liquid refreshment. The bar is open on Thursdays during Seymour Place's events and gallery hours. Prices start at $2 for a soda and run up to $27 for a bottle of pinot noir. They offer wine, beer, mead, nonalcoholic beverages, and mixed cocktails, including the John Daly and The Redhead.

Seymour Place offers a 15 minute guided tour of their beloved building for $5 and is available during their office hours. Private ghost hunts are also available upon request, costing investigators $300 for the night, running from 7:00pm-2:00am.

EXPERIENCE:
Event Venue/Bar/Ghost Hunt

OPEN TO THE PUBLIC:
Yes

HANDICAP ACCESSIBLE:
Partial. First floor only.

Important Info:
Hours of Operation:
Thursday-Friday:
11:00am-7:00pm
Saturday:
11:00am-4:00pm
and by appointment
Contact:
(585) 343-9313

ALLEGANY COUNTY

ALLEGANY COUNTY

Not to be confused with the town of Allegany over in Cattaraugus County, Allegany was home to the Seneca until Europeans permanently settled it after the American Revolution. The name supposedly dates back to a Lenape legend of a tribe called Allegewi. Today, Allegany is home to several famous universities as well as theatre companies, museums (including one dedicated to cheese), and libraries. It was also the birthplace of Charles "Pa" Ingalls, father of Laura Ingalls Wilder, author of *Little House on the Prairie.*

1. Alfred State
2. Alfred University
3. Allegany County Poorhouse
4. Angelica Inn
5. The Pink House
6. Spring Valley Road

ALLEGANY
COUNTY
305
17
4
3
ANGELICA
6
BLACK
CREEK
ALFRED
1
2
86
WELLSVILLE
5
417
19
EST. 1806

ALFRED STATE

10 Upper College Drive, Alfred, New York, 14802
42.254550°, -77.799159°
www.alfredstate.edu

Alfred State University opened its doors in 1908 and today offers more than 70 majors to 3,500 students. There are currently (lucky number) 13 residence halls on campus with MacKenzie North, South, East, and West acting as a suite option for students.

According to a story told by the *Rochester Times-Union* in 1987, the architect of the MacKenzie Complex committed suicide by jumping from the south corridor of the complex. The reason? The school changed the design of the building from a swastika to what it is today (which still very much resembles a swastika). There is no evidence currently available on this supposed suicide from over 40 years ago. However, many students living in the MacKenzie Complex have experienced enough ghostly activity to convince us that there may be some truth to this morbid tale.

Stories tell of ghostly apparitions appearing throughout the housing complex, especially the southern corridor. There are reported cold spots in various rooms as well as lights mysteriously turning off and on. As if this wasn't enough to make people cautious, some students decided to play with an Ouija board in one of the suites, successfully stirring up the activity.

EXPERIENCE:

School

OPEN TO THE PUBLIC:

Partial

ALFRED UNIVERSITY

1 Saxon Drive, Alfred, New York, 14802
42.253879°, -77.788161°
www.alfred.edu

Most universities in Western New York have their haunted hall, dormitory, or library. But that's all it usually is—a single building. Alfred University is one of the exceptions. There is not one, not two, but three buildings that are said to be home to not only paranormal activity but full-body apparitions, too.

Alfred University was founded in 1836 as a small college. However, over the years it has expanded and now educates over 2,000 students in 40 majors and 50 minors.

> **FUN FACT:** Alfred University was one of the first coeducational schools in America.

One of the more modern buildings, built in the 20th Century, is the Herrick Memorial Library. Founded in 1881, the current library was constructed only in 1956. It is home to 100,000 journals, 130,000 physical texts, 800,000 e-books, and one ghost. No one knows who he is or where he came from. Still, students and staff at Herrick Library report seeing the manifestation of a little boy running through the rows of books on the second floor.

One of the more impressive buildings on campus (let's be honest: *the* most impressive building on campus) is the Allen Steinheim Museum. Also known as Steinheim Castle, the building does, in fact, look like a castle. Today, it is home to the CDC (career development center). Construction on the Steinheim began in 1875 by Professor Ida Kenyon who started to build the structure from locally sourced stones and trees. More than 8,000 kinds of rock from within three miles of the school and 800 kinds of wood can be seen in the Steinheim along with the school's state of the art career center. People who visit the beautiful structure report witnessing the apparition of a woman. Many believe that it might be Professor Kenyon, returning to the castle she built for herself all those years ago.

Castles and libraries may be impressive haunts, but the most famous haunted location at Alfred University is known as The Brick.

> **TIP:** Reach out to the Paranormal Investigators of Alfred University student group. They have plenty of tales to tell!

The Brick was built in 1858 and was initially used to house female students on campus. Originally called Boarding Hall and Ladies Hall, the students' nickname finally stuck, and in 1933, the residence hall was renamed The Brick. With just under 100 students living there, The Brick is one of the prime housing locations at Alfred, and people are just dying to get in (see what I did there?). Ghost stories abound, but that doesn't stop students from battling to be able to live in the dorm. Students report the sound of loud bangs as well as objects moving on their own. The Brick is also home to a soldier that has been seen silently walking the halls. Legend says the dorm building was an infirmary during the Civil War. However, the university has stated that it was an infirmary during World War II, not the American Civil War. Either way, a full-body apparition joins the already impressive paranormal claims at The Brick. It makes you wonder why on earth anyone would want to spend a night there.

EXPERIENCE:
School

OPEN TO THE PUBLIC:
Partial

ALLEGANY COUNTY POORHOUSE

Karr Valley Road, Angelica, New York 14709
42.298141°, -77.978940°

> **~~FUN~~ FACT:** Instead of going to a poorhouse, some paupers chose to sell themselves into indentured servitude.

As you begin to research the history of any region, the dark part of humanity begins to show its ugly head, and Western New York is no different. The Buffalo Psych Center (page 31) is thought to have been ahead of its time in offering a peaceful home for some of Western New York's undesirables. The Allegany County Poorhouse, on the other hand, was not nearly as successful in providing a clean, safe, and welcoming environment for its patients.

In 1824, a law was passed saying that each county in New York State needed its own poorhouse. These establishments were seen as an economical way to provide relief for families that couldn't provide for themselves. Of course, unless you're like Ebenezer Scrooge, you know the poorhouses did nothing to provide quality living conditions. Nevertheless, the Allegany County Poorhouse was opened in 1831, and it had a troubled time over the next 130 years.

There were 17 rooms for 70 inmates, and Dr. John Norton described the poorhouse in 1864 as having "very bad conditions, with no ventilation, old, rotten, and filthy…" Mattresses were made of straw with vermin living inside, the old and sick didn't have proper nourishment, and those deemed insane were tethered to their beds.

In 1923, a fire erupted in the home, killing seven women who were all bed-ridden and one firefighter. Along with the human casualties, the fire also destroyed all of the records of the establishment, making it almost impossible to know the Allegany County Poorhouse's complete history. After the devastating fire, it was rebuilt as a home for the elderly and remained open until the 1960s. Sadly, since then, the Allegany County Poorhouse has fallen into a massive state of disrepair, vegetation taking over the buildings, and it has become all but forgotten by the county and the state.

FUN FACT: "Sleep tight, don't let the bed bugs bite," comes from old beds held up by ropes (the tighter they were, the more comfortable your bed would be), and many mattresses were stuffed with straw, making it a home for bugs.

Abandoned buildings are homing beacons for urban explorers and paranormal investigators. Photos of the abandoned buildings at the Allegany County Poorhouse are both incredible and heartbreaking, and so are the stories of the empty structure.

The number one claim that visitors to the poorhouse share is the overwhelming sense that someone has just walked out of the room. That's a bit unnerving when you think that the place has been empty for the last 60 years.

Objects throughout the home such as rocking chairs and tricycles move on their own.

Places such as asylums, hospitals, and poorhouses have an energy about them that is unlike anything else in this world, and you're sure to feel it at the Allegany County Poorhouse.

EXPERIENCE:

Landmark

OPEN TO THE PUBLIC:

No

ANGELICA INN

66 West Main Street, Angelica, New York, 14709
42.307137°, -78.019375°

After the Revolutionary War, the region surrounding Angelica experienced a boost in both population and wealth. The land that now makes up much of Western New York was purchased by Robert Morris, Founding Father, a significant financier of the American Revolution, and signer of the Declaration of Independence (now that's quite the resume). Eventually, parts of this land were given to Captain Philip Church, who, in 1802, founded a town and decided to name it after his mother, Angelica Schuyler Church. You know: sister to Elizabeth Schuyler and sister-in-law to Alexander Hamilton? Cue Lin-Manuel Miranda!

The gorgeous Victorian mansion was built in 1886 by Clara and Frank Smith. But it wasn't until the 1980s that it finally became a bed and breakfast. The Angelica Inn lasted for several decades, offering a unique hotel experience until it closed its doors for good in 2011. Since then, the antique furniture has been auctioned off, and the house sold in 2016 for $79,900 with still no sign of it reopening to the public.

It's easy to get an eerie feeling about the inn. The once elegant single-family home is now an empty shell. Stories tell that there is even a mausoleum in the back.

Paranormal activity has been reported throughout the grand mansion and even the smaller second house on site.

The ballroom that sits on the third floor is home to what one guest referred to as a silvery shimmering presence. Lights have been known to flicker, and music boxes play by themselves. When the inn was a functioning B&B, an unseen entity would knock on the front door in the middle of the night, and the sound of banging on the steps would echo through the entire building.

TIP: Just four doors from the inn is the Angelica Sweet Shop, home to the famous Angelica salt rising bread. For the perfect Angelica experience, try it toasted with butter!

Sadly, it's not likely that anyone will be checking in to the historic bed and breakfast any time soon. In 2012, all of the furniture (including the 1864 Square Steinway grand piano, original to the house) was auctioned off. Since then, the Queen Anne mansion with her stained-glass windows, crystal chandeliers, and wide front porch has sat on Main Street. She's still empty and quiet, waiting for someone to put her out of her misery. Here's hoping it's not the wrecking ball.

EXPERIENCE:

Hotel

OPEN TO THE PUBLIC:

No

THE PINK HOUSE

193 West State Street, Wellsville, New York, 14895
42.116939°, -77.950552°

As the name might suggest, the Pink House is a pink Victorian mansion nestled on the corner of West State Street and Brooklyn Avenue. It may look like the home of a fairy tale princess or a six-year-old's dream home, but, in fact, it was once the site of several tragic and mysterious deaths.

According to the legend of the Pink House, a young woman named Frances Farnum was engaged to E.B. Hall, the man who built the Pink House. But as fate would have it, she was still in love with her childhood sweetheart, Hanford Lennox Gordon. Frances's father didn't approve of her affections towards Gordon since he was nowhere near as wealthy as Hall. He forged a pair of letters and sent them to Frances and Gordon, successfully ending their relationship (there's quality parenting for you). The next time Frances saw Gordon, he ignored her. Unable to handle the pain of her broken heart, Frances drowned herself in the fountain of the Pink House.

There is technically no hard evidence of Frances's suicide. Still, many believe that Hanford Lennox Gordon's 1857 poem, *Pauline*, tells the story of the young woman's death. But it would seem Frances's suicide was only the beginning of the legend that still haunts the Pink House to this day.

As the story progresses, E.B. Hall went on to marry Frances's sister, Antoinette, and the couple moved into the Pink House with their two-year-old daughter shortly after. Betrayed by her sister and fiancé, the ghost of Frances led the little girl through the Pink House to the fountain where the child was found drowned the next day.

> **TIP:** Security is tight around the house, so it's best to get permission before your visit, or simply enjoy it from the sidewalk.

Interestingly, there has not been any recent ghostly activity, and the current owners of the mansion (descendants of the Hall family) try to downplay the dark history of the house. Whether the ghost of a scorned lover killed her niece out of vengeance or not, there is no denying the child died tragically in the fountain. It would seem that is enough to tarnish the reputation of the beautiful pink mansion in Wellsville.

EXPERIENCE:

Private Residence

OPEN TO THE PUBLIC:

No

SPRING VALLEY ROAD

Spring Valley Road, Black Creek, New York, 14714
42.266521°, -78.209845°

No matter where you go in the country (and Western New York for that matter), there are always legends surrounding Bigfoot sightings. Why should Allegany County be any different? A hot spot for Bigfoot and paranormal activity can be traced to Spring Valley Road, a four-mile stretch that takes you through innocent-looking farmland.

> **FUN FACT:** The first documented Bigfoot sighting was in Sacketts Harbor, NY in 1818.

The Bigfoot scare in Black Creek only lasted for about three years from 1973-1976, but the stories have managed to put Spring Valley Road on the paranormal map. The locals in the area began having strange encounters with a cryptid that many believe was a Bigfoot.

Within three years, cabins were damaged, and livestock were mutilated. Dogs would chase after nothing, barking viciously, and people would report the sound of footsteps outside of their tents and cabins. Along with each sighting came a horrible smell (similar to reports of Florida's Skunk Ape), only adding to the fear people experienced along Spring Valley Road. At first, witnesses were mostly campers and high schoolers. Eventually, those traveling along Spring Valley Road began to see thc humanoids (yes, that's plural) in the surrounding woods and even in their headlights.

Each experience with the creature is unique, but the descriptions tend to be the same: large and white, and it moves at a terrifying speed.

No one knows for sure what these white creatures are. Some think it may be a ghost while others are convinced it has to be extraterrestrial. Most, however, tend to agree that it's most likely an albino Bigfoot.

Since the mayhem of the 1970s, sightings have died down. However, there have still been several Bigfoot sightings in the area, particularly in the 1990s.

One of these sightings took place in Wellsville, less than 30 miles from Spring Valley Road (and home of the Pink House). The eyewitness reports walking near River Road, along the Genesee River when she and her cousin saw a figure that stood almost seven feet tall… and it was white. This white Bigfoot doesn't seem to be specific to Allegany County. There are reports in other parts of the country (particularly Pennsylvania) that also tell of a white Bigfoot.

The white Bigfoot that people see on Spring Valley Road may not be unique to Western New York. But you have to admit that the stories surrounding the small road near Route 305 are impressive, and have lasted for decades. The next time you drive along Spring Valley Road, it might be smart to have your high beams on just in case a Bigfoot crosses your path. Oh, and a camera too—because you'd be the first to capture any physical evidence that the albino Bigfoot of Black Creek actually exists.

EXPERIENCE:

Cryptid Sighting/Haunted Road

OPEN TO THE PUBLIC:

Yes

HANDICAP ACCESSIBLE:

Yes

CATTARAUGUS COUNTY

CATTARAUGUS COUNTY

Once the traditional home of the extinct Wenrohronon Indians, Cattaraugus County is now famous for Allegany State Park, Holiday Valley Ski Resort, and Griffis Sculpture Park. At one time, the land went claimed by Pennsylvania, New York, and Massachusetts, until it was founded as a New York county in 1808. The name Cattaraugus comes from the Seneca word for "bad smelling banks." Despite its tragic name, the land has since proven to be one of the most naturally beautiful counties in all of Western New York.

1. Allegany State Park
2. Ashford Hollow Witch
3. Dudley Hotel
4. East Otto Cemetery
5. Gurnsey Hollow Cemetery
6. Hencoop Schoolhouse and Cemetery
7. Henrietta Road
8. Hinsdale House
9. J.N. Adam Hospital
10. Randy's Up the River Bar & Grill
11. St. Bonaventure
12. Salamanca Historical Society Museum
13. Wildwood Sanitarium
14. Wing Hollow
15. Zoar Valley

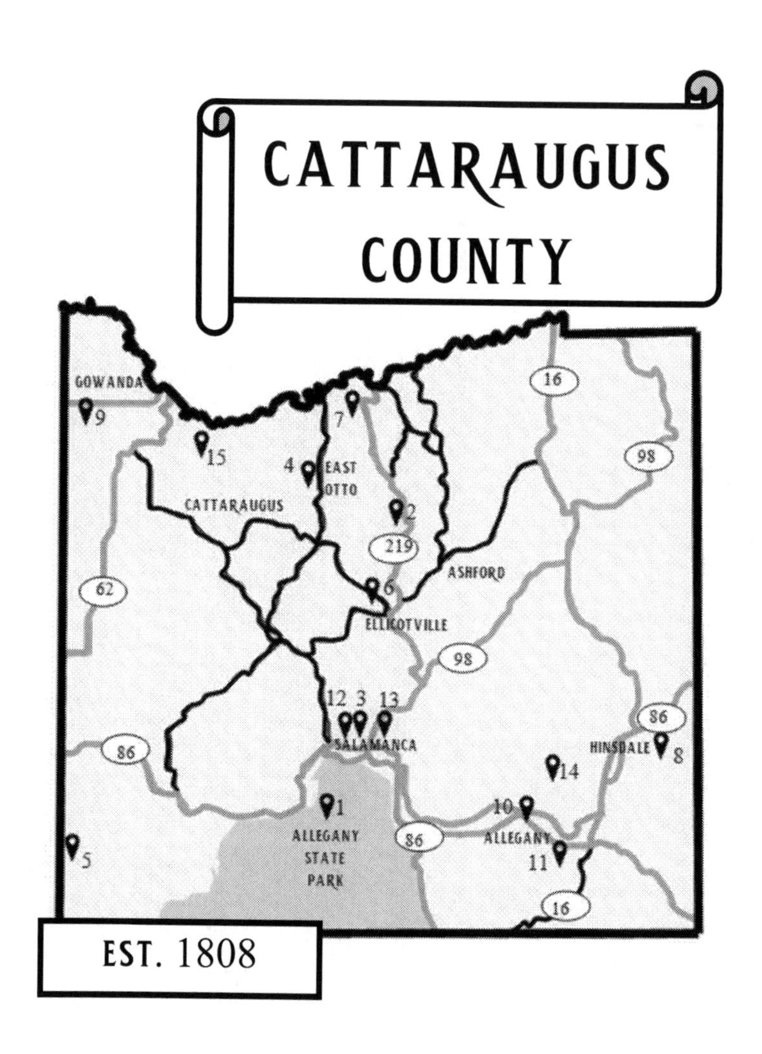
CATTARAUGUS
COUNTY
GOWANDA
9
15
4
EAST
OTTO
7
CATTARAUGUS
2
219
16
98
62
6
ASHFORD
ELLICOTVILLE
98
12 3 13
SALAMANCA
86
86
HINSDALE
8
14
1
ALLEGANY
STATE
PARK
10
86
ALLEGANY
11
5
16
EST. 1808

ALLEGANY STATE PARK

2373 ASP Route 1, Salamanca, New York, 14779
42.124161°, -78.708291°

It was once the home of the Iroquois with their tales of the Great Snake of the Allegany. But it wasn't until 1921 when the "wilderness playground of Western New York" was officially dedicated.

> **FUN FACT:** With over 60,000 square acres, Allegany is one of the largest state parks in the country.

Over the last century, the legends of Allegany have been forgotten by guests hiking, fishing, and camping in the Red House and Quaker Run areas. But in recent years, more and more people have come forward with their own spooky tales revolving around the hiking trails and cabins that you can rent yourself.

Near Cabin No. 2 at Stony Cabin Trail in the Quaker Run section of the park, multiple people have reported seeing a little girl playing all by herself. When they approach her to ask where her parents are, she vanishes.

The ever-popular Thunder Rocks are home to a woman in an 1800s white dress and bonnet, seen most often by hunters and hikers.

One of the most famous apparitions is the "flannel man." Since the 1980s, he's been spotted multiple times and is always described in the same way: a

tall, thin man with a beard, jeans, and (of course) a flannel shirt. Most often, he is seen in the field across from the Quaker rental office. He's also been spotted on the road leading to Quaker Lake, as well as ASP3 near Science Lake, and Quaker Run Creek near Group Camp No. 5. No one knows who the flannel man is, but it doesn't seem like he's going anywhere any time soon.

But perhaps the strangest place in the park is the Witch's Walk, also known as Ga'hai to the Seneca. For those brave enough to venture to the Witch's Walk, it is located along the Alleghany River between Bay State and Route 280 as you head into the Quaker Run section of the state park. The reports range from the mundane to the bizarre: people feeling uneasy to spotting creatures that look half-human, half-animal (changelings). Mysterious orbs of light can be seen on the mountaintop, and many have reported hearing the sound of drums that grow louder the higher up the hill you venture. According to legend, it was once home to witches and is even the supposed site of Confederate treasure.

TIP: If you're camping, Quaker Run is more rugged and remote while Red House has more to do with a beach, store, and restaurant.

To experience the supernatural of Allegany State Park, you can visit for a meal, a hike, and even a camping trip! The state park is open all year round and offers both natural beauty and a chance to experience the ancient and supernatural as well.

EXPERIENCE:
Park

OPEN TO THE PUBLIC:
Yes

HANDICAP ACCESSIBLE:
Partial

Important Info:
You can reserve a cottage, cabin, and camp site, through Reserve America:

www.reserveamerica.com/explore/allegany-state-park/NY/31/overview

ASHFORD HOLLOW WITCH

Rohr Hill Road, Ashford, New York, 14171
42.379084°, -78.677826°

History is filled with outcasts, and, unfortunately, many times, those outcasts are accused of being witches. The most infamous case of witch hysteria in America was found in Salem, Massachusetts in 1692. Luckily, for Sophia Disch, Ashford Hollow wasn't gripped with any traumatic trials or executions. Instead, gossip and folklore led to the birth of the Ashford Hollow Witch.

Sophia Disch was born in 1833 to Lewis and Salome Disch. When she was 29 years old, her mother died, leaving her and her father alone on the family farm. Sophia would spend the next 16 years caring for her elderly father and running the household. Because of this, Sophia never married and, subsequently, never had children.

In the 19th Century, when a woman chose not to marry, it raised some questions in the community, and that is precisely what happened to Sophia Disch. The people in the community began questioning the woman and her life choices, and by the time her father died when she was 45 years old, she was an outcast.

> **FUN FACT:** The first witch-hunt in America dates to 1645, but punishments for witchcraft date back to Hammurabi's Code (c. 18th Century BCE).

For the rest of her life, Sophia was reclusive, living on her family's farm and keeping to herself. Her secrecy and privacy added to the witchcraft rumors, and by the time Sophia died, she was all alone.

According to claims, Sophia died in 1909 from a heart attack or aneurysm while chopping wood. When she was found, she was wearing 13 petticoats to keep herself warm. Some think she had lost her mind while others still clung to the witch claims.

Today, Sophia is buried along with her parents under a single headstone on the edge of the former Rohr Hill Cemetery. If the legend is true, the Disch family is buried far from any other graves because they had an unknown disease that could be spread even in death. Unfortunately, in 1890, a fire swept through Ashford Hollow destroying all the town's records, so there is no hard evidence of disease in the Disch family... or witchcraft for that matter.

TIP: The tombstone is located between Griffis Sculpture Park and 8850 Rohr Hill Road. Coming from Sculpture Park, it will be on your left.

EXPERIENCE:

Grave

OPEN TO THE PUBLIC:

Partial—be aware of posted signs.

HANDICAP ACCESSIBLE:

No

DUDLEY HOTEL

132 Main Street, Salamanca, New York, 14779
42.159341°, -78.714588°

Nestled right along Salamanca's Main Street (and directly across from another haunted location you'll read about in 21 pages), lies what remains of the once bustling and historic Dudley Hotel.

Built in 1868, the Dudley Hotel was present during Salamanca's prosperous railroad years and was built right nearby the Salamanca station on the Erie Railroad. Because of its prime location, the Dudley has hosted an impressive lineup of guests over the years, including Franklin Delano Roosevelt, and in more recent years, Hillary Rodham Clinton.

> **FUN FACT:** In 1832, the railroad was chartered to connect NYC to Buffalo. Eventually, it reached as far west as Chicago.

The hotel was nearly destroyed by a fire in 1880 but was rebuilt and opened its doors once more for the people of Salamanca and Cattaraugus County until they closed for good in 2014. Potential buyers have visited the historic hotel over the years, but none seem willing to invest in it, and so it continues to sit vacant on Main Street. And like so many other haunted buildings in Western New York, many believe that the quiet, abandoned halls are the perfect breeding ground for a haunting.

Several spirits are said to haunt the Dudley Hotel—both before it closed its door and now that it sits empty.

The ghost of Mr. Charles Dudley, the original owner of the hotel, has been seen wandering through the hotel halls and the first floor. Many think he is checking in to see how his hotel is faring. Another apparition is simply known as "George." There is also the spirit of a former employee who is said to haunt the basement.

As if anyone could be surprised, the ominous basement is said to be the hub of the activity, particularly, the laundry room. One former housekeeper had such a fright while down there that she fled from the building and never returned.

Other nameless apparitions have been known to haunt the kitchen. This has led many investigators to believe that the haunting is the cause of former employees and not guests as none of the guest rooms have been reported to be haunted.

Sadly, there is no "checking in" at the Dudley Hotel… at least for now. There have been several public ghost hunts at the Dudley since they closed their doors in 2014. Aside from that, however, we'll have to wait impatiently until someone brave enough purchases the Dudley Hotel and breathes new life into her once more.

EXPERIENCE:

Hotel

OPEN TO THE PUBLIC:

No

EAST OTTO CEMETERY

7940 Mill Street, East Otto, New York, 14729
42.390200°, -78.758700°

> **TIP:** East Otto Cemetery is sometimes confused with North Otto Cemetery. Make sure you have the address entered correctly and not just "East Otto Cemetery" in search engines.

The town of East Otto was founded in 1854, and it's believed some of the earliest settlers used this cemetery. It's an innocent looking burial ground with no towering monuments or celebrity graves among the tombstones. However, East Otto Cemetery has managed to make quite a name for itself in the paranormal community for being one of the… noisier… cemeteries in Western New York.

Two headless women haunt the otherwise silent graves. They only appear to visitors at night, and there have been multiple reports from locals of the sound of women screaming. How headless women might scream is another question entirely...

What are these two women screaming about? Well, supposedly there is also the apparition of a man who marches through the cemetery, wielding an ax. We can only assume he's the one responsible for the headless women, and maybe he's cursed to spend eternity with his victims. We'll never know for sure until the two ladies stop screaming and start

talking.

The cemetery is open to the general public from dawn until dusk. Even though it is situated on a quiet country road, it is still wise to follow the rules of the burial ground. Please respect both the living who are trying to sleep nearby and the dead who just won't shut up.

EXPERIENCE:

Cemetery

OPEN TO THE PUBLIC:

Yes

HANDICAP ACCESSIBLE:

Yes

GURNSEY HOLLOW CEMETERY

11907 Gurnsey Hollow Road, Frewsburg, New York, 14738
42.029582°, -79.003516°

Gurnsey Hollow Cemetery is considered by many to be one of the most haunted cemeteries in Western New York. Perhaps not as (in)famous as Goodleburg, Gurnsey Hollow's history is just as tragic and its reputation is just as unnerving.

The cemetery, itself, dates back to the early 1800s and hasn't been used in decades unless you count the local teens who use it as a late-night rendezvous point. Fire pits, trash, and graffiti dot the once hallowed ground. But the initial signs of disrespect are complemented by the continued tales and urban legends surrounding the old cemetery.

There is a cross on one side of the cemetery, and according to local folklore, all visitors must kiss the cross before leaving the cemetery. If you don't, a whole lot of bad juju will follow you home (aka you'll die).

Urban legends aside, Gurnsey Hollow Cemetery was the sight of a tragedy that has left a scar on the land. In the early days of the town of Frewsburg, there was a mentally ill child (some historians claim it was a boy, others say it

TIP: The address places it in Frewsburg which is in Chautauqua County. However, it is located in Cattaraugus County.

was a girl). Sadly, this child was the victim of the townsfolk's fears and hatred. Eventually, a gang from the village chased the child into the cemetery where they were stoned to death and buried.

This child isn't the only one that calls Gurnsey Hollow their final resting place. A fair amount of graves belong to children from a smallpox epidemic years ago. With the death of so many children, it would be expected that we would have some playful spirits in the hollow.

TIP: A large stone blocks the entrance, so you will have to get out of your car and walk to the cemetery.

People report hearing loud giggles and the sound of children talking. Others claim to have their hair tugged, and there is even a ghostly apparition of a small boy who likes to follow curious visitors to the gate. Glowing tombstones, balls of light, and the sight of children playing in the surrounding woods have all been reported. The young child who was stoned to death is believed to terrorize any late-night visitors for fear another child will meet the same fate. Guests have also reported seeing a classic Lady in White and even an older woman who likes to glare at trespassers.

Whether you believe in the territorial spirits lurking within Gurnsey Hollow or not, there's no denying that there is something eerie about it. Where many cemeteries offer a serene sense of peace, Gurnsey Hollow makes you feel isolated and alone… probably how that small child felt all those years ago when the townsfolk decided to end their life right where you stand in Gurnsey Hollow.

EXPERIENCE:

Cemetery

OPEN TO THE PUBLIC:

Yes

HANDICAP ACCESSIBLE:

No

HENCOOP SCHOOLHOUSE & CEMETERY

Hencoop Hollow Road, Ellicottville, New York, 14731
42.284532°, -78.708971°

Hidden among the snowy slopes of Holiday Valley and the quaint ski town of Ellicottville lies Hencoop Hollow Road. Similar to Delaware Road in Clarence and Pigman Road in Angola (both of which are coming soon, so stay tuned!), it appears as if the entire three-mile stretch of Hencoop Hollow Road is haunted.

> **FUN FACT:** The Ellicottville Historical Society is unable to find any evidence of a cemetery on Hencoop Hollow Road... yet the hauntings persist.

What was once the old Hencoop Schoolhouse is now a private residence, making it a bit difficult for paranormal enthusiasts to visit for themselves. However, that doesn't stop the stories of ghosts lurking in the home. According to the tales, the schoolhouse turned private home is haunted by the spirits of children. They are usually heard running around on the ground floor, laughing. They have also been spotted standing beside people's beds, watching them sleep.

Just down the road from the former schoolhouse is Hencoop Cemetery, situated safely in the woods. This cemetery dates back to the 1850s and is the final resting place for many children.

Motorists have reported seeing strange mists from the road as well as apparitions of children playing along the side of Hencoop Hollow Road. People brave enough to venture into the abandoned cemetery at night report strange occurrences such as cold spots, the sensation of being watched, and hearing noises coming from the surrounding woods, sounding an awful lot like children laughing and playing.

With Hencoop Schoolhouse closed to the public, we may never know why so many children haunt the land between the schoolhouse and the cemetery.

EXPERIENCE:

Cemetery/Private Residence/Haunted Road

OPEN TO THE PUBLIC:

Partial

HENRIETTA ROAD

Henrietta Road, Ashford, New York, 14141
42.474742°, -78.720163°

There is something spooky happening around Zoar Valley, quite possibly one of the most haunted pieces of land in all of Western New York (spoiler alert). What is now a favorite place among hikers and kayakers has always been considered haunted. This sentiment dates back to early European settlers, and the Native Americans who were here before them. And just beyond the hiking trails of Zoar Valley is a dead-end road (how fitting) that has its own haunting that will freak out any late-night driver.

The two-mile stretch of road will only take you about three minutes to drive down, just before you have to do a three-point turn and backtrack the way you came. But this narrow road that takes you through farmland is haunted by two male spirits who died along the innocent looking highway.

It is believed that a young boy once drowned in a nearby pond along the road (there are four ponds along this stretch of road as well as the nearby Cattaraugus Creek which adds to the validity of this claim). He has been seen wandering around ever since usually dripping wet with vegetation tangled all around him.

The spirit of a young man who died in a motorcycle accident has also been spotted walking along the road.

Neither of these entities interact with travelers. There are no stories of the spirits appearing in people's cars or trying to hitch a ride. There aren't even tales of unexplained noises or cold spots. Just two full-body apparitions walking silently, almost as if they're oblivious to anything else except the road where they died.

The stories surrounding the apparitions are anything but specific. Still, try not to think of them as you find yourself easing your way down Henrietta Road in the dark. If you see the shadow of a little boy up ahead, just beyond the glow of your headlights, just keep driving.

EXPERIENCE:

Haunted Road

OPEN TO THE PUBLIC:

Yes

HANDICAP ACCESSIBLE:

Yes

HINSDALE HOUSE

3830 McMahon Road, Hinsdale, New York, 14743
42.167377°, -78.342328°
www.hauntedhinsdalehouse.com

Alongside the Amityville Horror House, the Hinsdale House is possibly the most haunted house in all of New York State.

This modest white home is sometimes also known as the Dandy House. The former family home has been the subject of Discovery Channel's hit TV show, *A Haunting*, Destination America's *Paranormal Lockdown* with Nick Groff, as well as multiple books, including Clara Dandy's *Echoes of a Haunting*.

The home was built in 1853, and according to legend, the original owners were two brothers who murdered people along the stagecoach trail near their land. Despite this grisly beginning, the paranormal activity seemed to only start in the 1970s when the Dandy family moved in.

Family members were scratched, books flew off shelves, knives appeared to be thrown at family photos. And that was only the beginning. The Dandys heard chanting in the forest surrounding their home, received mysterious phone calls, saw an apparition of a woman in white, and even spotted demonic figures on the land and in their home. Father Alphonsus from the nearby St. Bonaventure University visited the family and the house before performing an exorcism on the premises. Sadly, the sacred ritual did nothing but upset the entities, and the paranormal activity came back stronger than ever. The Dandy family didn't last much longer and left the house for good shortly after.

The Hinsdale House sat vacant for some time and was scheduled for demolition when Daniel Klaes bought the home in 2015.

Today, the Hinsdale House acts as a paranormal research center where investigators can spend the night, starting at $50 per person (with a minimum of six people). With this money, Klaes is restoring the infamous Hinsdale House and hopes to turn it into a museum, and in exchange, researchers walk away with some incredible pieces of evidence. In recent years, there have been reports of shadow figures and full-body apparitions. On top of this, doors slam shut, footsteps come from the empty upstairs, and the sound of dogs barking can be heard. There have even been unexplained creatures captured on film.

> As seen on *A Haunting* season 2, episode 7 and *Paranormal Lockdown* season 1, episode 5.

Daniel Klaes and The Hinsdale House offer both private and public paranormal investigations as well as paranormal tours and meet-ups for those interested in seeing a piece of New York State's haunted history.

EXPERIENCE:
Ghost Hunt/Ghost Tour

> Contact:
> (716) 578-4586

OPEN TO THE PUBLIC:
Yes

HANDICAP ACCESSIBLE:
No

J.N. ADAM HOSPITAL

10317 County Road 58, Perrysburg, New York, 14129
42.449098°, -79.001302°

The J.N. Adam Hospital's story is like so many others in Western New York. Built over 100 years ago, it has since fallen into a state of abandonment, despite its incredible architecture, and supposed historical significance to Western New York.

> **~~FUN~~ FACT:** When tuberculosis was discovered in the late 1800s, it killed one out of every seven people in the US and Europe.

Though it isn't a problem in today's day and age, tuberculosis ran rampant in the first half of the 20th Century, leading sanitariums to open all around the country. The idea was to isolate the infected and remove them from society in the hopes of stopping the contagious disease from spreading. Patients were sent to sanitariums and tuberculosis wards all around the country, where they lived out their days—out of sight, and out of mind—until they died. And when the Great White Death came to Buffalo, Mayor James Noble Adam took action.

The J.N. Adam Memorial Hospital opened in 1912 in the small town of Perrysburg. The sanitarium managed to keep itself running with groundbreaking cures (at least for the time) for almost 50 years. Touting the incredible healing powers of the "sun cure," many patients were seen playing in the snow, practically naked. Such methods allowed the sick to get the two things required to heal tuberculosis: fresh air and sunshine. This treatment brought doctors and researchers to the hospital for decades, only falling out of style after World War II when the knowledge of antibiotics began to spread.

The J.N. Adam Hospital closed as a tuberculosis ward in 1960 but remained opened as a medical facility for local patients with developmental disabilities. But that, too, closed its doors in 1993, and the beautiful hospital has remained vacant ever since.

Even though it was listed on the New York State Register of Historic Places in 1985, and is still eligible for national status, the building continues to deteriorate. According to legend, the dining hall rotunda with its stained-glass dome was donated to the hospital by J.N. Adam, himself. Supposedly, it was once part of the Temple of Music where Leon Czolgosz assassinated President McKinley at the Pan-American Exposition. No evidence supports this claim, and the Parks, Recreation, and Historic Preservation office disagrees with such stories… but it manages to add to the creep factor of the empty complex.

FUN FACT: The Temple of Music was built for $85,000 (that's $2.6 million by today's standards).

For nearly 30 years, the hospital has sat alone, rotting on the side of the road, closed to the public. But that doesn't stop urban explorers and paranormal investigators from trespassing and wandering the halls with their peeling paint and broken windows.

Those who have managed to sneak inside tell stories of an abandoned building that is certainly not sitting quietly. There are reports of cold spots throughout the building and the sensation of someone watching you from down the hall. Many claim to hear the sound of footsteps echoing through the hospital, voices whispering in the darkness, and even screams. Full-body apparitions have also been spotted on the grounds.

With such a sick (pun intended?) and tragic history, the J.N. Adam Hospital is allegedly haunted by restless spirits of both patients and nurses who committed suicide there.

Sadly, the fate of the hospital is still unknown. After standing for 30 years in the harsh Western New York elements, it is beginning to rot and crumble. It would cost millions to rebuild and just as much to demolish, and so, she continues to sit.

The Friends of J.N. Adam Historic Landmark and Forest is the only group currently working to preserve what remains of the hospital, but with little support.

> **TIP:** Security has intensified recently, so be sure to get permission before visiting.

Will the J.N. Adam Hospital meet the same tragic fate as so many other historic buildings in Western New York? Or will we manage to rebuild her, repurpose her, and breathe new life into her? The Buffalo Psych Center managed to be reborn into the sprawling Hotel Henry, so perhaps there is hope for her yet.

EXPERIENCE:

Landmark

OPEN TO THE PUBLIC:

No

RANDY'S UP THE RIVER BAR & GRILL

3767 Nine Mile Road, Allegany, New York, 14706
42.089893°, -78.502674°
www.randysuptheriver.com

What has now become a favorite watering hole among locals to spend a night out with friends or watch a football game has been a staple just off of First Street in Allegany for over 150 years.

Built around 1869, it was originally opened as a hotel and stagecoach stop. When Prohibition began in 1920, the building supposedly became a speakeasy, and it has been quenching people's thirst and filling their bellies ever since.

The current owners, Randy and Debbie Korkowicz, purchased the place in 1988 and have turned it into a thriving restaurant and bar. They offer Monday night 65¢ wings, Wednesday clams and tacos (not exactly sure how those two go together, but I'm here for it!), a Thursday steak special, and the famous "Randy's Mom's Secret Beer Battered Friday Fish Fry."

As with many historic buildings turned tavern, it appears as if some spirits don't want to leave, and with almost 40 beers to choose from, who can blame them?

The most well-known spirit at Randy's Up the River is the full-body apparition of a man.

Always seen entering through a front downstairs door, staff have seen him so many times that they can even tell you what he likes to wear: blue jeans and a plaid shirt.

Aside from the plaid-wearing ghost, there has also been the sound of disembodied voices. In particular, a man's voice who likes to whisper staff members' names. There are also footsteps in an otherwise empty building, and even objects move on their own. This includes bottles of liquor, which is one of the most horrific claims I've ever heard… Be gone, you evil spirit! Keep away from our booze!

It's unknown if the haunting can be traced back to just the ghost in the plaid shirt, or if multiple entities are lurking in the bar. But the owner, Randy, insists that the presence is not evil in any way—they just like playing pranks on the living.

Randy's Up the River is open 365 days a year for you to experience their famous fish fry (Fridays only), jumbo chicken wings, as well as their impressive haunting.

EXPERIENCE:
Restaurant/Bar

OPEN TO THE PUBLIC:
Yes

HANDICAP ACCESSIBLE:
No

Important Info:
Hours of Operation:
Daily:
11:00-2:00am
Kitchen closes at midnight.
Contact:
(716) 372-9606

ST. BONAVENTURE

3261 West State Street, St. Bonaventure, New York, 14778
42.081777°, -78.484386°
www.sbu.edu

There are few things creepier than a haunting. Ghost monks? That can be creepy. A haunting after a black mass? I'd say that goes one step further and becomes slightly terrifying.

St. Bonaventure was founded in 1858 in the hopes of promoting Catholic-Franciscan education. It's grown over the years and is now the home of 2,000 students studying programs in liberal arts and sciences, business, education, journalism, and mass communication.

For a school that mixes spirituality with education, it should be no surprise that St. Bonaventure has at least three buildings on campus with an impressive array of hauntings.

Francis Hall which was initially called Christ the King Seminary is said to be haunted by the monks that once lived there. Students and staff report seeing full-body apparitions of the monks wandering through the halls when the building should be empty. You'd think ghost monks would be the pinnacle of any haunting, but they're just the beginning at St. Bonaventure.

> **FUN FACT:** Rumors of black masses date back to the 4th Century.

De La Roche Hall is the home of the university's science and computer classes. It is also said to be haunted by the spirit of a student who tragically died in a fire. According to legend, he was working on a paper when the fire broke out. To this day, he is still trying to finish his work. The third floor is where he is most active, continually turning the lights on and off.

But the most infamous haunt at the Catholic university has a very dark and twisted origin that seems like it belongs at the start of a horror movie.

Devereux Hall (also known as "the Dev") is the school's oldest residence hall, built in 1926. It houses almost 300 students on four floors. Even though it's one of the more popular dorms on campus, it has a dark past that seems to have tainted the energy in the building. The Dev is infamously known for its black mass that occurred in the 1960s. According to legend, students gathered in the residence hall in the hopes of conjuring a spirit. Before the ritual was complete, a staff member managed to stop the students, but many believe that the evil spirits conjured still lurk in the dormitory. The fifth floor of the Dev is under lock and key, making many believe that the black mass took place up there… the noises, bangs, and sounds of explosions coming from the upper floor only add to the mystery.

But it's not just evil spirits summoned to the Dev that haunt its halls. The most famous ghost haunting this dormitory is Willie Cooper, a World War II vet who is seen walking along the back wing where a war memorial once stood. A ghostly friar has also been seen jogging through the halls at night. According to legend, the Dev was also the sight of a murder in the 1930s.

TIP: If you're looking for Willie's name on the war memorial, you'll have to head to the Reilly Center's west entrance. It was moved from near the Dev to make room for the Donald F. Kenney Museum and art study wing.

Despite its desire to build up Catholic education, the University of St. Bonaventure has strangely always been connected to the paranormal with its black mass, murder, and even an exorcism at the nearby Hinsdale House.

When visiting, please keep in mind that the haunted locations are classrooms and two residence halls, so access may be denied.

EXPERIENCE:

School

OPEN TO THE PUBLIC:

Partial

SALAMANCA HISTORICAL SOCIETY MUSEUM

125 Main Street, Salamanca, New York, 14779
42.158957°, -78.714892°
www.salamancanyhistoricalmuseum.org

It might be a bit surprising to think that the unassuming Salamanca Historical Society Museum could be haunted. However, the building is filled with just as much history as other haunted museums in the region. So, why couldn't it be haunted?

The building that is now home to the historical society is the restored Salamanca Trust Co. Bank, which was built in 1882. In 2005, the impressive red brick building became the home of the Salamanca Historical Society Museum, and it has continued to be a part of Salamanca's community ever since.

FUN FACT: The building was leased to the Salamanca Historical Society for $1 a year.

In recent years, many volunteers have begun to suspect that parts of the building might be haunted, and several paranormal groups have been invited to visit the museum. There may not be much in the form of apparitions, moving objects, or unexplained voices. However, many of the groups have captured both EMF readings as well as voices on digital recorders. Could it be that the building, itself, is haunted or

could the paranormal activity be coming from one of the many artifacts the museum currently has on display?

The Salamanca Historical Society Museum is immense, with three floors of exhibits as well as a basement. Among the artifacts on display at the museum is an impressive safe from the building's days as a bank, antique sewing machines, school desks, a pump organ, church pews, and period clothes and photographs. Just one of these objects could lead to a haunting, so to have so many of them in one place could stir up some energy.

The museum is open and available for field trips, events, and meetings. They also open their doors to paranormal groups to see if they can capture anything else that might prove that the Salamanca Historical Society Museum is, in fact, haunted.

EXPERIENCE:
Museum

OPEN TO THE PUBLIC:
Yes

HANDICAP ACCESSIBLE:
Yes

Important Info:
Hours of Operation:
Tuesday, Thursday, and Saturday:
10:00am-4:00pm

WILDWOOD SANITARIUM

71 Prospect Avenue, Salamanca, New York, 14779
42.158196°, -78.692204°
www.wildwoodsanitarium.com

Wildwood Sanitarium was one of the first holistic hospitals in New York at the time of its establishment in 1909. At the time, it was revolutionary and state of the art with its bathhouse in the basement and programs that were designed to help patients struggling with alcoholism, drug addiction, and mental illness.

With 3600 square feet, Wildwood could comfortably hold 10 full-time patients and attempted to make its living conditions "as pleasant as possible." At the time of its opening, Wildwood did not accept anyone suffering from a contagious illness, but by 1923, that changed when it transformed into a tuberculosis ward.

As seen on *Paranormal Lockdown* season 3, episode 2.

Like many places that were touched by tuberculosis, ghost stories abound at the sanitarium, so much so that it attracted attention from Nick Groff of *Ghost Adventures* and *Paranormal Lockdown* fame. According to accounts, someone hanged themselves upstairs, no doubt the negative and sad energy leaving a psychic mark on the property. Tommy's Room is one of the more active locations in the house with the apparition of a little boy running around as well as shadows seen and voices heard. The spirit of a man named Charlie hides in the attic.

Today, Wildwood Sanitarium is a paranormal investigator's dream playground. Starting at $89 per person, groups can rent the space for a private ghost hunt overnight. The entire area is yours, from the attic to the bathhouse in the basement. And the best part (especially if you've investigated old or abandoned locations before)? It is heated and stocked with coffee and other comforts to make your hunt actually enjoyable.

EXPERIENCE:
Landmark/Ghost Hunt

Contact:
(716) 801-5270

OPEN TO THE PUBLIC:
Yes

HANDICAP ACCESSIBLE:
No

WING HOLLOW

Wing Hollow Road, Allegany, New York, 14706
42.127500°, -78.52317°

Wing Hollow is one of those locations that has succumbed to its bad luck and haunting (which is a total shame because we could use a haunted ski lodge around here!).

First opened in the 1950s as the Grosstal Ski Area, it was designed to rival even the finest ski resorts of the Alps. It was a fun, family-friendly resort that only lasted about 10 years. In 1968, a nine-year-old boy died from a freak ski lift accident, which closed the place down. Luckily for the avid skiers of Cattaraugus County, it was reopened shortly after as Ski Wing, and in 1975, it was renamed once more to Wing Hollow.

FUN FACT: There are haunted ski resorts all around North America found in New Hampshire, Vermont, Colorado, and Alberta.

For many citizens of Cattaraugus County, Wing Hollow is home to happy winter memories spent on the 11 runs up on the slopes. However, Wing Hollow is forever tainted by the 1978 double murder, which is a cold case even to this day.

Two overnight ski slope groomers were found murdered in the ski lodge. The unknown burglars shot the two men, execution-style, before making off with $18,000. Despite this tragedy, Wing Hollow continued to run for several years until it finally closed in the early 1980s.

Many people believe that because their murders have gone unsolved, the spirits of the two men still haunt the area. The ghost of the young boy who died in the chair lift is also said to haunt the former ski resort.

Today, it's impossible to experience the ski slopes for yourself. After the resort was closed in the 1980s, there was an effort to sell it to Holiday Valley which fell through. The 600 acres sold in 2007, yet the slopes have remained closed.

Despite this, people are still reporting paranormal activity along Wing Hollow Road, seemingly brimming over from Wing Hollow. Drivers making their way along Wing Hollow Road (which runs parallel to the abandoned resort), report seeing people dressed in ski equipment at all times of the year… even in the middle of summer.

Wing Hollow is one of those haunted locations that you have to seek out. It's an abandoned resort along a dead-end road… there's no reason for anyone to be there. But if you do find yourself just north of Allegany, look to the rolling hills along Five Mile Road, and you'll still see the outline of the slopes, now overgrown.

The unsolved murders, sudden deaths, and ghostly skiers are all a part of Wing Hollow's sad tale. Only time will tell if the abandoned slopes will be another addition to Wing Hollow's tragic story.

EXPERIENCE:

Former Ski Lodge

OPEN TO THE PUBLIC:

No

ZOAR VALLEY

Cattaraugus, New York, 14719
42.447506°, -78.865460°

Zoar Valley is an enigma when it comes to haunted places throughout Western New York. When you try to research paranormal claims, you won't find much aside from the universal belief that Zoar Valley is haunted. This claim is not unfounded. The park has a reputation and has an unusually high death toll with six confirmed deaths in the last 15 years, including Simon P. Griffis, the son of Griffis Sculpture Park founder, Larry Griffis, in 2010.

> **FUN FACT:** Zoar Valley is an old-growth forest, having gone relatively untouched for centuries.

Despite the lack of concrete evidence, Zoar Valley is still considered to be one of the most haunted places in Western New York, and it always has been. Algonquians initially inhabited the area during the Stone Age, and they left behind evidence of their time in the valley in immense burial mounds, some of them dating back 3500 years. Inside these mounds, archaeologists found spearheads, stone tools, and according to legend, nine-foot-tall skeletons. There is no evidence that these skeletons were actually found in Zoar Valley, but tales of similar giants are scattered throughout Western New York. Once the Algonquians left, the Seneca moved in, and stories of witches and wizards and a haunting continued through the years until European settlers arrived in the 19th Century.

The most famous story coming from Zoar Valley is that of the Clawfoot People. Someone cue the somber music as the tragic history of the Clawfoot People goes like this:

An English prostitute settled in the area, but she was unknowingly infected with syphilis and passed on a genetic abnormality to all of her male offspring. Over the decades, the deformity spread as the family continued to grow, and soon the Clawfoot People were shunned by the people of the town, leading to psychological impacts on the family. In the 1920s, the family wanted to put an end to their tragic line and decided not to have any more children. One by one, they died off, and today, no one remains of the Clawfoot People, an unnerving tale that has no doubt left an impact on Zoar Valley.

FUN FACT: The name comes from the biblical city of Zoar in the book of Genesis. It appeared in the tale of Sodom and Gomorrah.

Today, the valley acts as a state forest and is a favorite place among hikers, kayakers, and fishermen. But an increased number of visitors to the area means that more hikers go missing when they venture off the trails and remain in the forest after dark. One story of lost hikers managed to have a happy ending, with everyone found safe and sound. When the group was rescued, they informed the police that they followed another group of hikers in the hopes of asking for directions. Before they could ever catch up with them, the mystery hikers disappeared.

Could it be that the spirits of those lost to the valley continue to wander along the trails, leading hikers to safety?

EXPERIENCE:
Natural Wonder/Hiking Trails

OPEN TO THE PUBLIC:
Yes

HANDICAP ACCESSIBLE:
No

CHAUTAUQUA COUNTY

CHAUTAUQUA COUNTY

The westernmost county in New York is brimming with history and mysteries. Its name is said to be one of the few surviving remnants of the Erie language, lost during the Beaver Wars from 1629-1701. Its meaning is still unknown today. Founded in 1808, it is home to several Utopian-esque societies including the Chautauqua Institution and Lily Dale Assembly, as well as UFO and Bigfoot sightings. Some of Western New York's most famous citizens are from Chautauqua, including Lucille Ball and Backstreet Boy, Nick Carter (cue the fangirl screams).

1. Assembly Hall
2. Athenaeum Hotel
3. Bemus Point Village Casino
4. Bennett House
5. Dewittville Cemetery
6. Dunkirk Lighthouse
7. Hollenbeck Cemetery
8. Holy Cross Seminary Site
9. Hotel Lenhart
10. House of Seven Secrets
11. Igoe Hall
12. Inspiration Stump
13. Jacquins Pond
14. Jefferson Middle School
15. Lady in Glass
16. Lucille Ball Little Theatre
17. Maplewood Hotel
18. Reg Lenna Civic Center
19. Sherman Beast
20. Stockton Hotel
21. White Inn

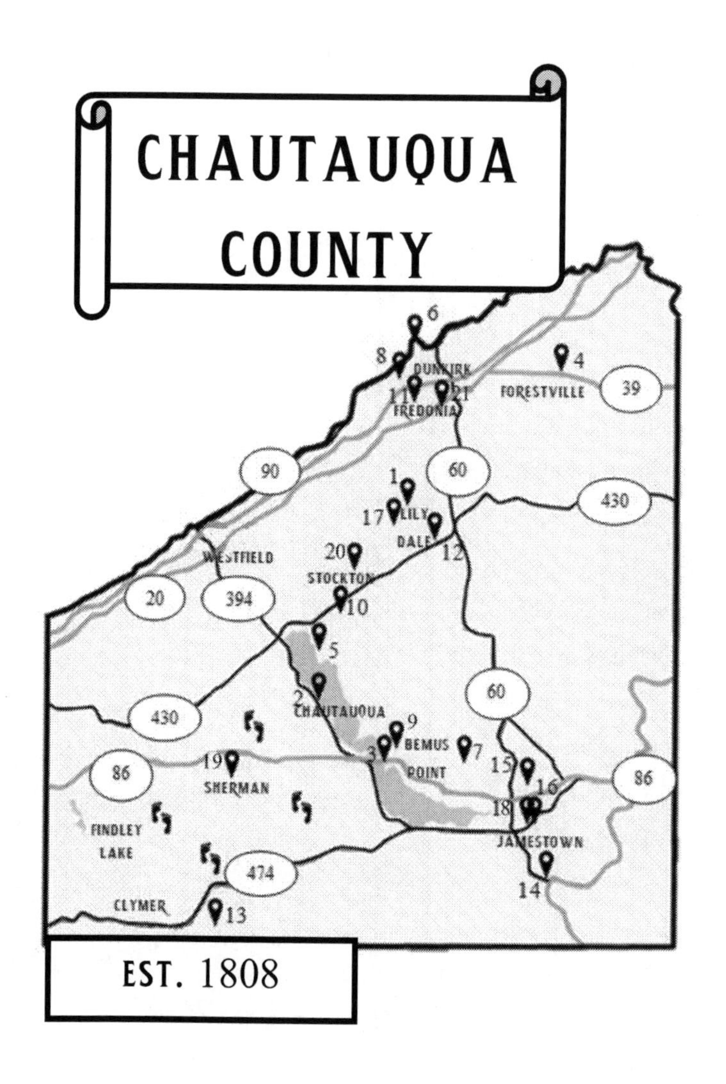
CHAUTAUQUA
COUNTY
DUNKIRK
FREDONIA
FORESTVILLE
LILY
DALE
WESTFIELD
STOCKTON
CHAUTAUQUA
BEMUS
POINT
SHERMAN
FINDLEY
LAKE
JAMESTOWN
CLYMER
EST. 1808

ASSEMBLY HALL

11 Cleveland Avenue, Lily Dale, New York, 14752
42.3528667°, -79.3248412°
www.lilydaleassembly.org/venue/lakeside-assembly-hall

> **FUN FACT:** Maggie and Kate Fox (the younger Fox Sisters) used "rappings" to convince their older sister, Leah, that they were communicating with spirits. They experienced success until Maggie admitted it was a hoax.

Spiritualism took Europe and America by storm in the mid to late 19th Century, fueled by the popularity of the Fox Sisters. After the American Civil War, families were left to mourn the deaths of their sons. Spiritualism offered those grieving families a chance to communicate with their deceased loved ones. Harry Houdini spent years trying to debunk the works of Spiritualists and psychic mediums like the Fox Sisters. Despite Houdini's best-laid efforts, the community of Lily Dale has thrived even into the 21st Century.

When most people visit Lily Dale, they think of the not quite poetically named Inspiration Stump (page 155). Many associate the stump as the hub of the Dale's connection with Spirit. However, the Lily Dale Assembly Hall has been just as helpful to mediums for nearly as long as the famous stump in Leolyn Woods.

Built in the early days of Lily Dale in the 1880s, the Assembly Hall has been used for workshops, lectures, and demonstrations of Spiritualism for over a century.

There aren't nearly as many stories surrounding the Assembly Hall as other places in Lily Dale. However, the hall has managed to snag a few paranormal claims of its own.

Aside from the usual (and somewhat expected) cold spots, the Assembly Hall is supposedly haunted by the spirit of a man. He's been seen by both residents of Lily Dale and visitors and is described as a bearded gentleman with glasses, wearing Victorian-era clothes. Well, that certainly does narrow things down for us!

Lily Dale is open year-round for visitors. However, most of the lectures, workshops, and services are held in the warmer months of the year. From the end of June (usually just after the summer solstice) to September 1st, a gate pass is required. With your gate pass, you get access to free parking, morning meditations, healing services, Inspiration Stump message services, a service at the Auditorium, and a Forest Temple message service.

EXPERIENCE:

Community/Hiking Trails/Psychic Mediums

OPEN TO THE PUBLIC:

Yes

HANDICAP ACCESSIBLE:

Partial

Admission:
(During Peak Season)

Adults: $15 per day
Seniors: Free
Veterans: Free
Children under 17: Free
Weekly Pass: $93
Season Pass: $238

ATHENAEUM HOTEL

3 South Lake Drive, Chautauqua, New York, 14722
42.208202°, -79.463414°
www.chq.org/athenaeum-hotel

The Chautauqua Institution seems to be an enigma in and of itself—some people see it as a cult where others describe it as a perfect society.

Dating back to 1874, the Chautauqua Institution was founded for religious purposes. Thanks to the Chautauqua Literary and Scientific Circle which began in 1878, it has managed to weave religion and education into the small town that has gone relatively untouched since the 19th Century.

> **FUN FACT:** Some famous artists who have performed here are John Philip Sousa, Ella Fitzgerald, Duke Ellington, and even Michael Jackson.

7,500 summer residents live on 750 acres on the shore of Chautauqua Lake in pastel Victorian houses, riding their bikes, and living the "highest ideal for spiritualism and intellect." Four US presidents visited the institution—Ulysses S. Grant, Theodore Roosevelt, Franklin D. Roosevelt, and Bill Clinton. The community has its own newspaper, orchestra, theatre, opera, and ballet company. It offers Catholic masses and Jewish services, as well as courses on ethics and even bridge. The population tends to be heavily Caucasian and over 50, just adding to its Stepford appearance.

And at the heart of the Chautauqua Institution is the Athenaeum Hotel.

This 158-room structure was built in 1881 and was the world's first hotel with electric lights. Since then, the wooden Victorian hotel has welcomed guests to Chautauqua Lake, offering a beautiful place to stay.

With a hefty $360 price tag on a standard room in the summer, it's easy to say that you'll stay at the motel just down the road. But with those three Ben Franklins you might get to experience a piece of Chautauqua's history… its haunted history to be precise.

> **TIP:** Lakeside rooms cost more than your average room, so if the views don't matter to you, put that money towards a king-sized bed.

If you ask the staff at the Athenaeum Hotel if it is haunted, they'll just smile and say, "No. The hotel is not haunted." But if you listen carefully, they refer to the hotel as if it is alive (cue *The Shining* theme), making many paranormal enthusiasts take note of the ghost stories surrounding the historic hotel.

According to legend, a little girl was staying at the hotel many years ago. While she was riding her tricycle through the halls, she rode it into the elevator shaft and tragically died. Her tricycle bell can still be heard chiming through the hotel today.

There are also reports of poltergeist activity in some of the hotel rooms, including beds shaking.

Depending on the time of year you decide to visit, everyone 13 years old and older must purchase a gate pass. Sadly, this includes visiting the haunted Athenaeum Hotel, making this a pricier place to visit.

But, hey, if you get woken up by a little girl's tricycle bell in the middle of the night, it's totally worth it, right?

EXPERIENCE:
Hotel

> Contact:
> (716) 357-4444

OPEN TO THE PUBLIC:
Yes

HANDICAP ACCESSIBLE:
Yes

Admission:
(For anyone 13 and over)

Overnight (10:00pm-10:00am): $10
Afternoon (12:00-8:00pm): $15
Morning (7:00am-2:00pm): $25
Morning/Afternoon (7:00am-8:00pm): $40
Afternoon/Evening (12:00pm-12:00am): $60
All day (7:00-12:00am): $85
Weekend (Friday 4:00pm-Monday 10:00am): $160

Gate pass does not include parking pass.

BEMUS POINT VILLAGE CASINO

1 Lakeside Drive, Bemus Point, New York, 14712
42.157490°, -79.396176°
www.bemuspointcasino.com

When summer arrives on Chautauqua Lake, the small town of Bemus Point comes alive. The Bemus Point Village Casino has been a part of entertaining tourists for almost a century, and its history dates back even further.

There is recent evidence that Native American tribes would gather in the early 19th Century where the village casino now sits. But it wasn't until the 1930s that it opened as the casino, and it's remained an entertainment mecca for the Chautauqua region ever since.

> **FUN FACT:** The Village Casino set a Guinness World Record for most chicken wings served in 24 hours!

The Bemus Point Village Casino has hosted big bands and Vaudeville acts including icons such as Billie Holiday and Frank Sinatra. Over the decades, the village casino has been many things to the people of Chautauqua, including a beach house, a ballroom, and even a bowling alley. Today, it is a casual restaurant and pub, and still the entertainment capital of the area.

The most famous ghost haunting the casino is Chef Jordan Basile. Sadly, young Basile died in an explosion due to a malfunctioning oven. Today, patrons and staff report that food goes missing and dancers have been seen tripping over nothing. Unique to the Bemus Point Village Casino, Chef Jordan is seen every two years on August 16th—the anniversary of his death—working hard in the kitchen, usually cooking lobster.

If you're hoping to spot the ghost of Jordan Basile or try some of the casino's chicken wings keep in mind that the Bemus Point Village Casino (and much of Chautauqua Lake for that matter) is only open between Memorial Day and Labor Day.

EXPERIENCE:
Restaurant/Bar

OPEN TO THE PUBLIC:
Yes

HANDICAP ACCESSIBLE:
Yes

Important Info:
Hours of Operation:
Daily:
11:00-2:00am
Only open Memorial Day through Labor Day.
Contact:
(716) 386-1247

THE BENNETT HOUSE

11051 Bennett State Road, Forestville, New York, 14062
42.482215°, -79.167186°

> As seen on *Haunted Collector* season 2, episode 8.

No, this isn't a Jane Austen novel so don't even waste your time looking for Mr. Darcy. This Bennett family home is located in Forestville, a small hamlet just outside Hanover with a population of under 700 people… and a few ghosts thrown in just to keep things interesting.

What was once one of Chautauqua County's oldest structures has now fallen into a state of disrepair, left for nature to repossess.

Built in 1820, Reverend James Bennett and his family once owned the house. But the family did not experience the best of times in their new home. In 1852, their son, Jerome, fell ill and was diagnosed with the White Death—tuberculosis. Luckily, the young man wasn't sent to one of the many sanitariums in the region. Instead, he was isolated in his family home, where doctors treated him with bloodletting (an ancient practice of drawing blood from an afflicted person in the hopes of healing them… usually with leeches). Sadly, Jerome died in the house, and he is buried next door in the Forestville Pioneer Cemetery along with several other members of his family.

Over the decades, families who moved into the home reported strange disturbances and unexplained phenomenon. They heard footsteps through the house and mysterious voices. There was muffled music playing somewhere in the house. People also reported hearing disembodied screams and even what sounded like claws scratching on the floor.

> **FUN FACT:** New York State law does not require a seller to inform potential buyers that a house could be haunted.

The house sold for $25,500 in 2016, but not before it was featured on *Haunted Collector* in 2012. In the episode, John Zaffis and his team captured an EVP that said, "Jerome," and found a leech jar up in the attic.

Many believe the leech jar was the catalyst for the haunting. But with the structure now sitting vacant, there's no telling if the spirits of the Bennett family are still wandering around their family home, or if they're finally able to rest in the nearby Pioneer Cemetery.

EXPERIENCE:

Private Residence

OPEN TO THE PUBLIC:

No. But Pioneer Cemetery is.

BIGFOOT

The legend of Bigfoot has fascinated both believers and skeptics for centuries. Almost every culture has a creature such as Bigfoot in their folk history. While most people associate Bigfoot with the Pacific Northwest, it seems the hairy cryptid has made a few appearances in Western New York, particularly in Chautauqua County.

In recent years, there have been over 30 reports from different people living throughout Chautauqua County. This led Peter Wiemer to begin the Chautauqua Lake Bigfoot Expo in 2012. Bringing together eyewitnesses and experts, the Chautauqua Lake Bigfoot Expo offers a safe environment for people to share their findings, physical evidence, and experiences. Patrons can also attend lectures from experts, view films about Bigfoot, and for a lucky few, even go on a Bigfoot trek.

With no clear photos and only a few tufts of hair and some molds of Bigfoot's feet, there isn't much to go off of aside from eyewitness accounts. But everyone who has seen Bigfoot in the region tends to agree: they are between six and seven feet tall with reddish-brown hair covering their entire body. More often, people don't see Bigfoot, but rather smell them. Some people report hearing them screaming in the distance, including the area surrounding Chautauqua Lake and even southwest around Findley Lake.

Wiemer has spoken with nearly 40 people from Chautauqua County and eight people from Cattaraugus County about their Bigfoot sightings. According to the Bigfoot Field Research Organization, there have also been sightings in Allegany, Orleans, Erie, and Niagara Counties.

More than 63% of New York State is wooded, and just Chautauqua, alone, has over 17,000 acres of forests, making it a viable habitat for a Bigfoot.

Today, more than 30% of Americans believe in the possibility of Bigfoot. In this fast-paced, high tech world, we have no hard physical evidence of the creature's existence. But call it Bigfoot, Sasquatch, Uluk, Yeren, Kikomba, or the Yeti… it doesn't matter. People all over the globe need a bit of mystery in the world. It looks like Bigfoot is giving it to us, right here in Chautauqua.

FUN FACT: According to researchers, there are over a dozen types of Bigfoot just in the United States.

EXPERIENCE:

Cryptid Sighting

DEWITTVILLE CEMETERY

Meadows Road, Dewittville, New York, 14728
42.245264°, -79.442435°

Located on the picturesque shores of Chautauqua Lake just down the road from the equally haunted Bemus Point, is the Dewittville Cemetery. Also known as the Chautauqua County Poorhouse Cemetery, the cemetery was active from 1833 to 1918. Located on over 440 acres of land, the poorhouse offered shelter to the poor and destitute, and its cemetery provided a final resting place for hundreds of poor unfortunate souls.

> **FUN FACT:** Grave markers weren't used here until 1869.

It's dwindled in size over the years with the poor house and farm closing long ago, leaving a small roadside cemetery on Dewittville Creek.

As one might expect with a tragic past revolving around the potter's field, some ghost stories are floating around the hallowed ground. The restless spirits of Dewittville have begun to manifest themselves as orbs of light and strange noises.

EXPERIENCE:

Cemetery

OPEN TO THE PUBLIC:

Yes

HANDICAP ACCESSIBLE:

Yes

DUNKIRK LIGHTHOUSE

1 Lighthouse Point Drive, Dunkirk, New York, 14048
42.493571°, -79.353797°
www.dunkirklighthouse.com

Let's just admit it: there's something a little eerie about lighthouses. People live in almost complete isolation (depending on the lighthouse, of course) to tend the lamp in the hopes of saving sailors from a watery grave. No pressure.

Lighthouses have both fascinated us and haunted us since the world's oldest—the Lighthouse of Alexandria—was erected between 280-247BCE. Western New York may not be able to boast the biggest or the oldest lighthouses, but, we do have around 20 of them along Lake Erie, both active and inactive. And the most famous one is situated just off of I-90 and has been safely guiding ships into Dunkirk Harbor for almost 200 years.

Dunkirk Lighthouse was first established in 1827 on Point Gratiot on the shores of Lake Erie. But just 50 years later, the lighthouse had fallen into a state of disrepair. From 1875-1876 a new lighthouse was built on the site of the original, as well as a home for the lighthouse keeper. And that same structure is what you see today when you visit Dunkirk Lighthouse and Veterans Park Museum.

FUN FACT: The first shot of the War of 1812 was fired near the west bank of the lighthouse.

The lighthouse and museum are open from May through October and welcomes guests of all ages. Patrons can visit the museum, which includes an extensive collection of military artifacts. Tours allow you to walk through the restored lighthouse keeper's home and even climb the stairs to the observation deck of the lighthouse, itself.

Not much has changed over the centuries for the Dunkirk Lighthouse, including the Fresnel (pronounced "Fraynel") lens and lantern that was refitted in 1857. Because the lighthouse has experienced little change even in the 21st Century, many people believe it has created a warm and welcoming environment for both the living and the dead.

Like so many lighthouses in the country, Dunkirk Lighthouse is considered to be haunted by previous lighthouse keepers. Visitors have reported being touched while on the walking tour of the lighthouse and grounds. There are also claims of unexplained sounds such as someone walking up the stairs to the light when no one else is around, as well as disembodied talking and humming. It's also thought that the museum is haunted due to the military memorabilia. Residual energy is said to attach to objects, and we see this in military artifacts more than anything else.

TIP: The last tour of the day leaves one hour prior to closing.

The Dunkirk Lighthouse gives visitors every opportunity to visit the nautical landmark and not just through their historic walking tours. Events are held each summer on the grounds from boat races on Lake Erie to reenactments of the French and Indian War and the Civil War. And, of course, the lighthouse is always open to sharing its ghost stories.

Public ghost hunts are offered several times through the summer and into October to allow those curious about the lighthouse's haunted history to take a look behind the veil. Tickets are just $30 per person (which, if you've checked out other ghost hunts in the area, you'll know is a steal) but space is limited and sells out fast. If you're looking for a more

TIP: Walking shoes are preferred on the lighthouse tower tour.

intimate experience with the spirits of the lighthouse, private ghost hunts are available at $100 for the first three participants and an additional $30 per person after that (again: a steal). Tickets for the public ghost hunts can be purchased directly through the lighthouse's website. However, you will have to call the office directly for private investigations.

EXPERIENCE:
Museum/Landmark/
Ghost Hunt

OPEN TO THE PUBLIC:
Yes

HANDICAP ACCESSIBLE:
Partial

Important Info:
Hours of Operation:
May-June:
10:00am-2:00pm
July-August:
10:00am-4:00pm
September-October:
10:00am-2:00pm
Contact:
(716) 366-5050

Admission:
(Walking Tour)

Adults: $10
Seniors: $8
Veterans: $8
Students: $8
Children (4-10): $3

Free to walk the grounds.

HOLLENBECK CEMETERY

Moon Road, Ellicot, New York, 14701
42.1405892°, -79.2472993°

Hollenbeck is one of the lesser-known haunted cemeteries in Western New York. But the paranormal claims are just as impressive as the more infamous final resting places in the region. Situated on the side of Moon Road just 10 minutes outside of Jamestown, Hollenbeck is tiny with only 25 graves, and many of the tombstones have disappeared over the years.

In July 1995, most of the 19th Century grave markers were stolen and have been replaced by a single memorial erected by the town of Ellicot.

Perhaps the haunting stems from the fact that the graves were disturbed when the markers were taken. No matter the reason, the souls of Hollenbeck are doing anything but resting peacefully.

Along with claims of orbs captured in photos and the sound of knocks and screams, there are also more exciting stories coming from Hollenbeck. Visitors have reported hearing an unseen baby crying along with a ghostly woman in white. But the most impressive reports tell of a headless horseman a la *The Legend of Sleepy Hollow* chasing people

FUN FACT: Headless horsemen have appeared in mythology since the Middle Ages.

from the hallowed ground.

EXPERIENCE:

Cemetery

OPEN TO THE PUBLIC:

Yes

HANDICAP ACCESSIBLE:

No

HOLY CROSS SEMINARY SITE

4680 West Lake Road, Dunkirk, New York, 14048
42.471721°, -79.368330°

The Holy Cross Seminary may no longer stand on the shores of Lake Erie, but it seems as if no one has told the spirits haunting the area that their home was demolished decades ago.

The Catholic Church's Passionist congregation found its start in Europe in 1720. The group moved to Dunkirk in 1860, and in 1913, the Passionists purchased 72 acres of land along West Lake Road. On September 22, 1920, Holy Cross Passionist Monastery and Preparatory College were opened.

The college was included in Dunkirk's city directory over the years, but it slowly fell out of the public's eye. It disappeared from most lists in 1944. The school was officially closed in 1968 and remained abandoned until it was demolished in the 1980s.

All that remains of the Holy Cross Seminary Site is the ruins of the chapel and the driveway… oh, and a ghost.

The most common paranormal claim that has been reported is the apparition of a priest. People have reported seeing the man in broad daylight with his head bowed in prayer. As soon as he realizes someone is watching him, he disappears without a trace.

EXPERIENCE:

Ruins

OPEN TO THE PUBLIC:

No

HOTEL LENHART

20-22 Lakeside Drive, Bemus Point, New York, 14712
42.158545°, -79.394717°
www.hotellenhart.com

The four-story yellow Hotel Lenhart looms over Chautauqua Lake directly next door to the Bemus Point Village Casino.

Built in the 1880s, the hotel has been owned and operated by the same family ever since. This is saying something because the Lenhart had a pretty rough time over the last century. Only 10 years after the Lenhart opened its doors, it was destroyed in a fire and needed to be rebuilt. After 50 years, in 1941, the hotel was destroyed in yet another fire and needed to be rebuilt once more.

Today, it is a boutique hotel that offers guests a chance to experience a simpler time in the historic hotel on the shores of Chautauqua Lake. With 53 rooms (and several community bathrooms), the Hotel Lenhart functions on a cash-only basis in both the hotel and their onsite cocktail lounge called the Lamplighter Room.

TIP: Rooms in the back of the building tend to be quieter while rooms in the front of the building offer views of the lake.

But amidst their lovely veranda complete with rocking chairs and old-world charm, something a bit more sinister lurks in the shadows. Many locals claim that something negative resides inside the hotel. There is no ghost story linked to the hotel, but it seems to be haunted nonetheless.

The mysterious entity has been known to open doors as well as slam them shut, and it has a nasty habit of pulling people's hair.

To experience the history and haunting of Hotel Lenhart for yourself, you can enjoy a cocktail in the Lamplighter Room, take part in a traditional Victorian tea, or even spend the night in one of their many rooms (starting at $90 a night).

TIP: Be sure to order their signature cocktail: the Lenhart Rocker!

EXPERIENCE:
Restaurant/Bar/Hotel

OPEN TO THE PUBLIC:
Yes

HANDICAP ACCESSIBLE:
No

Important Info:
Only open Memorial Day through Labor Day.
Contact:
(716) 386-2715

HOUSE OF SEVEN SECRETS

6001-6101 Coe Road, Stockton, New York, 14784
42.289523°, -79.397148°

The House of Seven Secrets was considered by many to be one of the most haunted places in Western New York before it came down in the early 2000s. Despite its infamous reputation, there isn't much known about the old house, only legends.

Some stories claim that a family was murdered in the house, leading to the dark and evil haunting. Other tales come from people who broke in and found scorch marks on the floors, suggesting black magic was practiced inside the house, again, leading to a negative haunt or possibly even a curse. Either way, the house was a beacon for daredevil teens and ghost hunters alike. If there is any truth to the stories, the House of Seven Secrets was an active and terrifying place to visit.

According to one claim, when a group of explorers entered the abandoned house, the kitchen table was set for a family of four, and the refrigerator was fully stocked with food, leading people to think that the tales of a murdered family might be right. Others claim that the phone on the wall would have a voice on the other end, telling the intruders to, "Get out!" even though it wasn't hooked up. Doors would slam shut, the sound of footsteps would echo through the house, and lighters would explode.

But the most famous legend says that the House of Seven Secrets was filled with (you guessed it!) seven secrets. No one knows what these secrets were, but supposedly they were hidden in places like the attic, bathroom, and basement, and if you managed to find all seven of them, you would die in the house.

Luckily, those seven secrets were never found, and now there is no hope of ever discovering them. Around 2002, the house came down. To add to the mystery of the House of Seven Secrets, no one knows how or why it came tumbling down. Was it torn down by the state, or did it burn to the ground? Either way, today the House of Seven Secrets is nothing more than an empty lot on Coe Road, but it still haunts those who braved the cursed house all those years ago.

EXPERIENCE:

Ruins

IGOE HALL

280 Central Avenue, Fredonia, New York, 14063
42.453236°, -79.340746°
www.fredonia.edu/student-life/residence-life/igoe

SUNY Fredonia, one of Western New York's most popular universities, experienced a bout of tragedy in the death of one of their students. Known initially as Building E when it opened in 1970, the residence hall was renamed Igoe Hall in memory of James Robert Igoe. Sadly, Igoe drowned in Lake Erie while out on a fishing trip.

> **~~FUN~~ FACT:** There have been nearly 800 drownings in the Great Lakes since 2010.

Over the last few years, there has been a drop in Fredonia's student enrollment, leading to empty rooms and floors in many of the residence halls… including the haunted Igoe Hall.

It is believed that young James haunts the building that was named after him, making himself known to fellow students since his death. He's been known to slam doors and change the television channels. He'll turn the lights on and off as well as the faucets in the bathroom. He even makes the elevator move on its own.

Although your television turning on in the middle of the night or your shower being mysteriously turned off might cause even the bravest college student to run back home to mommy and daddy, very few residents report feeling threatened or scared of Igoe.

EXPERIENCE:

School

OPEN TO THE PUBLIC:

Partial

INSPIRATION STUMP

Leolyn Woods, South Street, Lily Dale, New York, 14752
42.348974°, -79.322874°
lilydaleassembly.org/place-to-see-points-of-interest/inspiration-stump

Being the home of the infamous Fox Sisters as well as one of the longest-running Spiritualist communities in the country, New York was (and still is) an integral part of Spiritualism.

First incorporated in 1879 as the Cassadaga Lake Free Association, Lily Dale was home for Spiritualists, suffragists, and freethinkers. The name was changed in 1903 to the City of Light and finally transformed to Lily Dale Assembly in 1906. Since its initial establishment, Lily Dale has been a community for psychic mediums and those hoping to further the science and religion of Spiritualism. Today, over 20,000 visitors come through the gates of Lily Dale annually, and the community is home to over 50 registered psychic mediums. Workshops and church services are held where guests and mediums tap into Spirit.

FUN FACT: Nearby is one of the country's oldest pet cemeteries. There's even a horse buried here!

Lily Dale is not your usual haunt. You won't hear stories of grisly murders or deadly battles. There's no word on whether there are any poltergeists or malevolent spirits haunting the historic buildings and surrounding woods. However, it is one of the most interesting locations you might visit. The community taps into the spiritual world in every aspect of life, and that can be felt even by someone who doesn't consider themselves "sensitive."

The hub of the energy is Inspiration Stump, which is believed to be a vortex. Guests are no longer permitted to stand on the stump because of medical problems many experienced (seizures, fainting spells, nausea, etc.). However, the daily service (public psychic reading) is held there, and it is beautiful if nothing else. Lily Dale might be considered more of a spiritual experience, and not a paranormal one. The level of activity you might experience will depend on how sensitive you are.

EXPERIENCE:
Community/Hiking Trails/ Psychic Mediums

OPEN TO THE PUBLIC:
Yes

HANDICAP ACCESSIBLE:
Yes

Important Info:
Message services at Inspiration Stump are held daily in the summer at 1:00pm and 5:30pm.

Admission:
(During Peak Season)

Adults: $15 per day
Seniors: Free
Veterans: Free
Children under 17: Free
Weekly Pass: $93
Season Pass: $238

JACQUINS POND

Caflisch Road, Clymer, New York, 14724
42.013347°, -79.590543°

Jacquins Pond is 30 acres of wetlands along the Pennsylvania border, southwest of Chautauqua Lake. The Department of Environmental Conservation bought it in 1977, and today, it is popular among hikers, hunters, and fishermen. It is also home to one of the more tragic ghost stories of Western New York.

According to legend, a man named George was a bus driver in the area. One day, his bus was involved in an accident that killed a young boy. George was so overwhelmed with grief that he committed suicide at Jacquins Pond, and supposedly, his spirit still haunts the area.

There are three bridges in the wetlands, and all of them are said to be haunted by George's ghost. But it is the third bridge that has the most stories surrounding it, as well as its own paranormal dare. If you're brave enough to stand on the bridge and say George's name three times, you might see his spirit. He's also been known to lock your car doors on you, so make sure to bring your keys with you.

Another legend surrounding the road running through the wetlands tells of a fork in the road, with the "Light Path" and the "Dark Path." In recent years, the "Dark Path" has been a popular site for local teens to commit suicide.

If you find yourself walking along the "Dark Path" and contemplating suicide, please reach out to a friend, loved one, or call the Suicide Prevention Hotline at 1-800-273-8255 where you can talk to anyone 24 hours a day.

EXPERIENCE:

Hiking Trails

OPEN TO THE PUBLIC:

Yes

HANDICAP ACCESSIBLE:

Partial

JEFFERSON MIDDLE SCHOOL

The unassuming middle school has some dark stories attached to it, including the tale of a young girl and her untimely death.

According to legend, a little girl wandered into the school back in the 1950s, searching for her brother. Some stories claim there was an accident that led to her death in the school. Other tales like to add dramatic flair and say that she was stalked and chased into the school where she was then murdered. Whichever you believe, the young girl died in the school and now haunts the halls in a white dress, still searching for her brother for all eternity.

In the 1990s, students of Jefferson Middle School reported seeing a girl in a white dress roaming the halls. Along with full-body apparitions of little girls, there are other claims of items falling in the classrooms as well as unexplained loud bangs.

Unfortunately (or rather, I should say fortunately), there is no evidence of a young girl dying in the school, and especially not in the 1950s. Jefferson Middle School was constructed in 1976, making many people doubt these tales are true.

There may be paranormal activity in the classrooms of Jefferson Middle School. However, it's doubtful that a little girl in a white dress was killed there (unless she could time travel by about 20 years).

EXPERIENCE:

School

OPEN TO THE PUBLIC:

No

THE LADY IN GLASS

907 Lakeview Avenue, Jamestown, New York, 14701
42.113091°, -79.239922°

It seems as if the legend surrounding the Lady in Glass grows more dramatic with each generation. Some stories claim that she was a tragic bride who died on her wedding day of a broken heart. In the 1950s, the bride transformed into a prom date gone wrong. Other tales tell of a forbidden love affair with an heiress and her chauffeur. My personal favorite claims that the young bride was left at the altar. She was so overcome with grief, she turned to stone, and her father decided to protect her with a glass case. No matter how colorful these local legends are, not a single one of them are anywhere close to the truth.

The beauty behind the glass case overlooking Lake View Cemetery is Grace Galloway. The only daughter of John and Sara Galloway, Grace enjoyed a comfortable life and made a name for herself as a gifted singer. She graced the stage of the Chautauqua Institution on more than one occasion and even traveled to Boston to further her studies. Sadly, that is where her charmed life suddenly took a turn.

FUN FACT: Grace Galloway isn't the only famous resident of Lake View Cemetery... Lucille Ball is buried here too!

'Twas not a broken heart that killed the young lady, but rather, tuberculosis.

She died in Pittsburgh on November 2, 1898, at the age of 27 years.

Her father, overcome with grief, spent over $2,000 to erect a marble statue of his beloved daughter. The likeness is uncanny—all five-feet-six-inches of her—and it should be because, by today's standards, this statue would cost over $60,000 to create.

The marble visage of young Grace has sparked countless urban legends and ghost stories throughout the years. Some people report spotting a woman wandering through the cemetery in a wedding dress. Locals who like to break into the cemetery at night have also reported seeing the glass case empty, only adding to the wandering bride tale.

It doesn't look like the Jamestown locals care to tell the difference between fact and fiction. So where do these wild ghostly tales come from, when we know almost all there is to know about Grace Galloway?

Some blame a newspaper article in the *Jamestown Evening Journal* back in 1924. The newspaper tells of a ghostly woman in black who appeared near the Lady in Glass. According to reports, the woman leaped in front of a trolley. Luckily for the traumatized trolley driver and passengers, she vanished, leaving only the stench of sulfur.

> **TIP:** You can find Grace Galloway nestled between Cypress Section and North Main Street.

Perhaps the tale of the woman in black and our young Miss Galloway have merged throughout the last century to create one hell of a tragic ghost story.

EXPERIENCE:

Cemetery

OPEN TO THE PUBLIC:

Yes

HANDICAP ACCESSIBLE:

Yes

LUCILLE BALL LITTLE THEATRE

18 East Second Street, Jamestown, New York, 14701
42.095553°, -79.240109°
www.lucilleballlittletheatre.org

The citizens of Jamestown enjoyed the luxuries of a first-class theatre as early as 1874 when Allen's Opera House opened, offering a variety of quality vaudeville acts. Sadly, a fire destroyed the structure in 1881, but another theatre promptly took its place. The theatre passed through several hands until it was sold in 1919 and became Shea's Theatre (not to be confused with Shea's in the city of Buffalo on page 47). Little Theatre of Jamestown purchased the theatre to act as their home in 1968 and in 1989, it was named after Jamestown's most famous citizen, Lucille Ball.

Today, the Lucille Ball Little Theatre is still an operating theatre with five productions put on each year, and like so many theatres, it's haunted.

Full-body apparitions have been seen lurking throughout the theatre—not just backstage but also center stage in the limelight. According to claims, a man has been seen taking the stage when the theatre should be empty of performers. Children visiting the theatre have heard voices, and there have been various accounts of people's names being called out when no one else is present.

The most famous claims of the Little Theatre come from the shoe room. The door of the costume room has been known to slam shut, locking poor unsuspecting performers and crew members inside. The temperature will also rise and drop rapidly without any reason.

We know Jamestown is famous for Lucille Ball and the beloved show *I Love Lucy*, but being locked in a freezing cold room is no laughing matter.

EXPERIENCE:
Theatre

OPEN TO THE PUBLIC:
Yes

HANDICAP ACCESSIBLE:
Yes

Important Info:
Box Office Hours of Operation:
Tuesday-Friday:
12:30-4:30pm
Contact:
(716) 483-1095

MAPLEWOOD HOTEL

11 Cottage Row, Lily Dale, New York, 14752
42.352396°, -79.325271°
https://lilydaleassembly.org/general- information/accommodations/lily-dale-hotels/

Considered to be the heart of the modern-day Spiritualist movement and religion, you shouldn't be surprised to see Lily Dale listed here yet again. With every aspect of life tapping into the spirit world, of course, different apparitions would come and go throughout the last century. It seems like many ghosts have gravitated to the heart of Lily Dale itself: the Maplewood Hotel.

Built around 1888, the Maplewood Hotel is one of two hotels that host the 20,000 visitors to Lily Dale each year. Keeping with the 19th Century charms, the owners deny their guests modern-day amenities such as telephones, televisions, air conditioning, and an elevator. However, it offers an expansive porch filled with rocking chairs overlooking Cassadaga Lake, where many guests can unwind and tap into Spirit.

But Maplewood Hotel is a bit different from other vintage hotels in Western New York, as one might expect from Lily Dale. Paintings hang on the walls, supposedly created with help from the spirit world, and there is even a sign in the front lobby that reads *No séances, readings, or healings allowed.* Only in Lily Dale!

Throughout the 40 guest rooms, there is said to be activity everywhere—particularly the third floor which is haunted by the spirit of a former maid. In many of the rooms, guests have also reported seeing shadow figures and apparitions. They also claim to hear the sound of footsteps walking up behind them. Many have been woken up in the middle of the night by an unseen entity. Patrons also claim to sense someone in the room with them.

It is unknown whether these spirits are good or bad—no one knows who they are or why they haunt the Maplewood Hotel. Is this ghostly activity just another run of the mill haunt? Or is it as active as it is because guests checking in are sensitive to the spirit realm? There's only one way to find out:

TIP: Not all rooms have a private bathroom, so it might be worth it to add the additional $10 for your own comfort.

Book a room at the Maplewood Hotel with rooms starting at just $50 a night for a basic single room with a twin bed, a sink, and a shared bathroom (you'll have to pay extra for a private bath).

EXPERIENCE:

Hotel

OPEN TO THE PUBLIC:

Yes

HANDICAP ACCESSIBLE:

No

Contact:
(716) 595-8721

REG LENNA CIVIC CENTER

116 East Third Street, Jamestown, New York, 14701
42.096590°, -79.239404°
www.reglenna.com

Since it is the famed hometown of the one and only Lucille Ball, it shouldn't surprise anyone that Jamestown has an impressive arts scene. One of the many places in the city that supports the performing arts is the Reg Lenna Civic Center.

> **FUN FACT:** The center is home to a 1,165 seat theatre, a multi-media arts studio, an event space, a conference room, 3rd on 3rd art gallery, and WRFA-LP 107.9 community radio.

Its full name is the Reg Lenna Center for the Arts (sometimes simply the Reg), but it was originally known as the Palace Theatre in 1923. Like so many places in Jamestown, it has one degree of separation from (no, not Kevin Bacon) Lucille Ball. The theatre hosted the world premiere of *Forever, Darling* in 1956 which starred Lucille Ball and Desi Arnaz. After that, though, the theatre sadly fell into the dreaded dark ages that many theatres in Western New York faced. After the Reginald and Elizabeth Lenna Foundation made an impressive $1 million donation (which also bought them the name of the building), it was restored in 1987 and reopened in 1990.

Today, the Reg hosts a wide variety of events including blockbuster movies, concerts, and (of course) stand-up comedians. On occasion (especially around Halloween), the Reg has been known to host public ghost hunts for those curious about the paranormal side of the historic building.

Speaking of which…

According to legend, the land that the theatre now stands on was once a hotel. And at one point in time, that hotel caught on fire. During this tragedy, five people are said to have died: a woman, her two children, their nurse, and an African American gentleman.

Whether there was a tragic fire on the site or not, there is an impressive collection of paranormal activity at work inside the theatre.

Children's voices are heard coming from the dressing rooms while unexplained noises are also coming from the balcony of the theatre. A man dressed in black has been seen roaming through the theatre, and a small boy has been known to play tricks on tour groups.

The majority of the activity has been reported during rehearsals when the theatre is otherwise closed to the public. However, the Reg is open on a fairly regular basis, continually bringing the public opportunities to experience what their beautiful building has to offer. Tickets for "Movies @ The Reg" start at just $5, making the Reg Lenna Civic Center one of the most affordable theatres to visit in all of Western New York.

EXPERIENCE:
Theatre

OPEN TO THE PUBLIC:
Yes

HANDICAP ACCESSIBLE:
Yes

Important Info:
Box Office Hours of Operation:
Tuesday-Friday:
10:00am-12:00pm
And one hour prior to movies and events.
Contact:
(716) 664-2465

SHERMAN BEAST

Sherman, New York, 14781
42.1294575°, -79.5856169°

If Chautauqua is known for any cryptid, it's Bigfoot (mostly thanks to the Chautauqua Lake Bigfoot Expo). But there's an area nestled between Chautauqua Lake and Findley Lake that is the home to some stories that will make even the most avid amateur cryptozoologist scratch their heads.

Spotted mostly in the 1960s and 1970s, the creature was described by a 15-year-old boy as being large and white. This sounds somewhat like the Spring Valley Road monster in Allegany County (page 88). However, as he described the cryptid in greater detail, it's clear that there are two different types of hairy, albino creatures lurking in Western New York.

The "white monster" stands between 12 and 18 feet tall, it's hairy, and always white. Some people have seen its massive claws, and they say it can move on both four feet and two. As bizarre as it sounds, this creature has been described several times as a giant sloth.

You don't have to be a zoologist to know that sloths don't live in Western New York, much less gigantic ones. However, this isn't the first time such a creature has been spotted in the world. It sounds an awful lot like the Mapinguari: a cryptid believed to be hiding in the Amazon rainforest.

> **FUN FACT:** Stories of the Mapinguari are so widespread and consistent that scientists have actually begun searching for it in the Amazon.

Mapinguari are described as hairy meat-eaters (the stories differ on whether they're man-eaters or stick to a livestock-only diet) with backward feet and one eye. Some stories go even further to say these creatures have a second mouth on their stomach (sometimes it's a beating heart instead). These creatures are so ingrained in South American lore, that, even though there is no physical evidence of such a beast, hundreds of people come forward each year with new sightings.

Many experts believe the Mapinguari could be a legend that stemmed from the previously extinct Megatherium (giant ground sloth) from the Miocene Epoch that only ended 10,000 years ago. Inhabitants of South America may have come into contact with a ground sloth and told stories that evolved into the Mapinguari over thousands of years.

The Megatherium explains the Mapinguari... but what about our Sherman Beast? Well, North America had its own giant sloth called Megalonyx, and it roamed most of the continent, including Western New York.

Researchers aren't entirely sure if the locals in Sherman are seeing a formerly extinct giant sloth. Some have suggested that the albinism could be a result of inbreeding with such a small and isolated population. Without any physical evidence, there's no way of knowing for sure. But that doesn't stop eyewitnesses from sharing their incredible stories. From the 1960s to today, these creatures have been spotted, most recently just down the road from Mount Pleasant State Forest in 2015.

Next time you find yourself hiking through Chautauqua County, if you don't see a Bigfoot, don't lose hope—you might cross paths with a previously extinct beast. Either way, you might want to back away slowly...

EXPERIENCE:

Cryptid Sighting

STOCKTON HOTEL

7293 South Main Street, Stockton, New York, 14784
42.316884°, -79.355850°
www.stocktonhotelny.com

The Stockton Hotel has been a staple for the town of Stockton and Chautauqua County for over a century.

In 1812, a man named Abel Thompson purchased the land that the Stockton Hotel now sits on, and quickly built a tavern for weary travelers and local revelers. Sadly, a fire destroyed one of Thompson's buildings, and today, the foundation of that building is part of the Stockton Hotel.

> **TIP:** If you're visiting Western New York, order their WNY sampler. It comes with chicken wings, mini beef on wecks, fries, and mini fish fry bites... All the food that we're obsessed with around here.

Built in 1899, the Stockton Hotel hasn't changed much, having served Stockton as a hotel and restaurant ever since. The establishment has passed through several hands in recent years but still acts as a restaurant, bar, and banquet hall. They offer local Chautauqua Lake wines as well as an impressive collection of chicken wing sauces and "dry shakes." The Stockton Hotel is also home to a long history of ghost stories that staff members are excited to share with patrons.

Unfortunately, because the current owners acquired the Stockton Hotel recently, many of the paranormal claims have been lost in the transition. Still, the staff members are open to the idea of a haunting and encourage conversations about it.

According to legend, a young man attempted to commit suicide up in the attic by hanging (and strangely enough, a rope still hangs up there). A woman in an old fashioned dress has also been seen in the bathroom on the upper floor. Some staff members believe that the area was once a brothel. The sound of footsteps can be heard in the empty building. Some of the

staff even refuse to go into the basement after one waitress had a spooky encounter in the cooler with several items moving on their own.

If you have any tales from the Stockton Hotel, be sure to share it with the staff and current owners… they're hungry to know more!

EXPERIENCE:
Restaurant/Bar

OPEN TO THE PUBLIC:
Yes

HANDICAP ACCESSIBLE:
Partial. No access to the upper floor.

Important Info:
Hours of Operation:
Sunday:
11:00am-10:00pm
Monday-Tuesday:
4:00-10:00pm
Wednesday-Thursday:
11:00am-10:00pm
Friday-Saturday:
11:00-12:00am
Contact:
(716) 595-3505

WHITE INN

52 East Main Street, Fredonia, New York, 14063
42.441526°, -79.329595°

Before the White Inn was one of the more elegant places to stay in Fredonia, it was the private home of Chautauqua County's first doctor.

Squire White built his home in 1811, but his son was the one that created the White Inn that we see today with its veranda and columns. In 1868, an extension was added on to the main structure, and again in 1919, another wing was added. While the entire inn seems to have paranormal claims, it is the 1868 section of the house that appears to be the most active. In fact, paranormal investigators and staff at the inn have managed to pinpoint where the activity is the strongest.

The White Inn is supposedly home to the ghost of Isabel White who sold the inn in 1919. She was bitter that her family home was transformed into a hotel, and her grumpy spirit haunts rooms 314 and 264. Around here, appliances don't work correctly, furniture moves on its own, and an apparition of a young girl has also been spotted.

Possibly one of the more tragic stories that haunt the building is the murder-suicide of the married innkeepers. The couple was the innkeepers of the White Inn from the 1940s through the 1960s. Known alcoholics, the two died tragically in the 1960s supposedly in room 272. Today, their restless spirits haunt the entire inn, though they are never seen together.

Unfortunately, the 24-room boutique hotel owned by Jeff Gambino went into foreclosure in 2018. But the White Inn wasn't sentenced to decades of abandonment like so many other historic buildings throughout Western New York. The inn was purchased by Josh Grunzweig, the president of JG Funding in March 2019. Currently, no one knows for sure what the future looks like for the White Inn. When asked what his plans were for the historic hotel, Grunzweig simply said, "Time will tell."

FUN FACT: Dr. White had a restaurant named after him in the White Inn called Squire's Table.

At the time of publication, the White Inn is still closed to the public. However, if you find yourself visiting any other haunted attractions in Fredonia, it's worth it to pull to the side of the road to see the impressive building that has been an essential piece of Fredonia's history for over a century. And if we're lucky, the White Inn might open its doors to the public once more, which will probably only frustrate Isabel White even more… Worth it.

EXPERIENCE:

Hotel

OPEN TO THE PUBLIC:

No

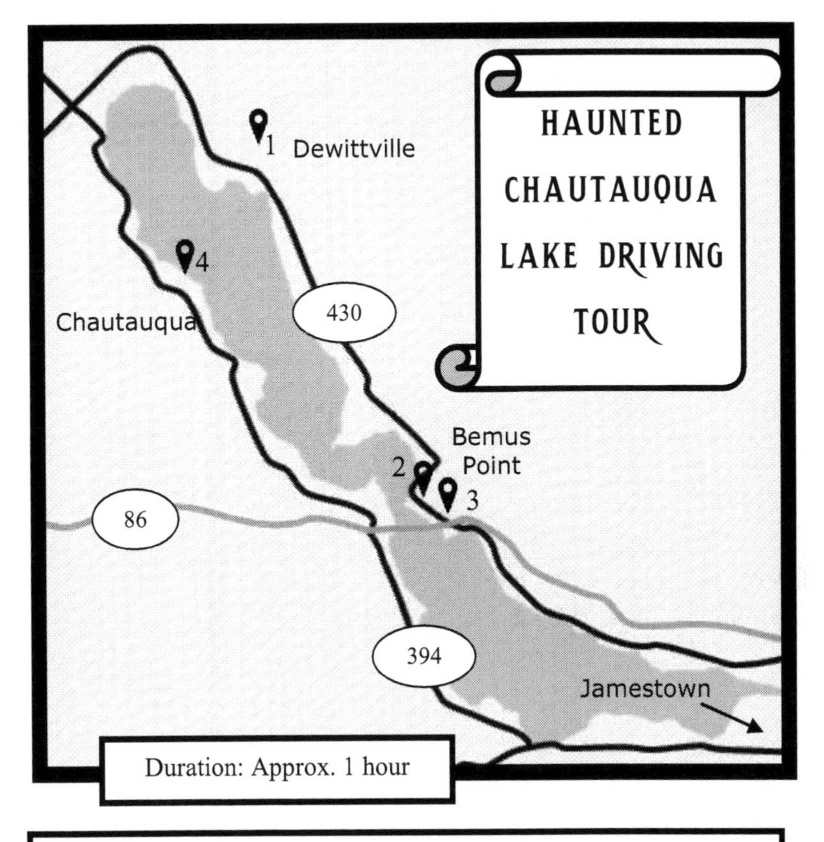

Chautauqua Lake offers a scenic drive at any time of the year and this driving tour will take you to all of its haunted locations. Heading south on I-90 from Buffalo, take Exit 59 onto NY-60S and stop at the Stockton Hotel on your way down! Your first stop is **Dewittville Cemetery (1)** just down the road from the shore of Chautauqua Lake. Head south and turn left onto NY-430E toward Bemus Point. With **Hotel Lenhart (2)** and **Bemus Point Village Casino (3)** next to each other, park your car and walk around the quaint village and consider having a drink at the hotel or a quick snack at the casino. [If you'd like to add the Jamestown tour, continue south on NY-430E.] To cross Chautauqua Lake, follow NY-430E and merge onto I-86W. Take Exit 8 to NY-394W until you reach the Chautauqua Institution and the **Athenaeum Hotel (4)**. [NOTE: You will have to pay to enter.]

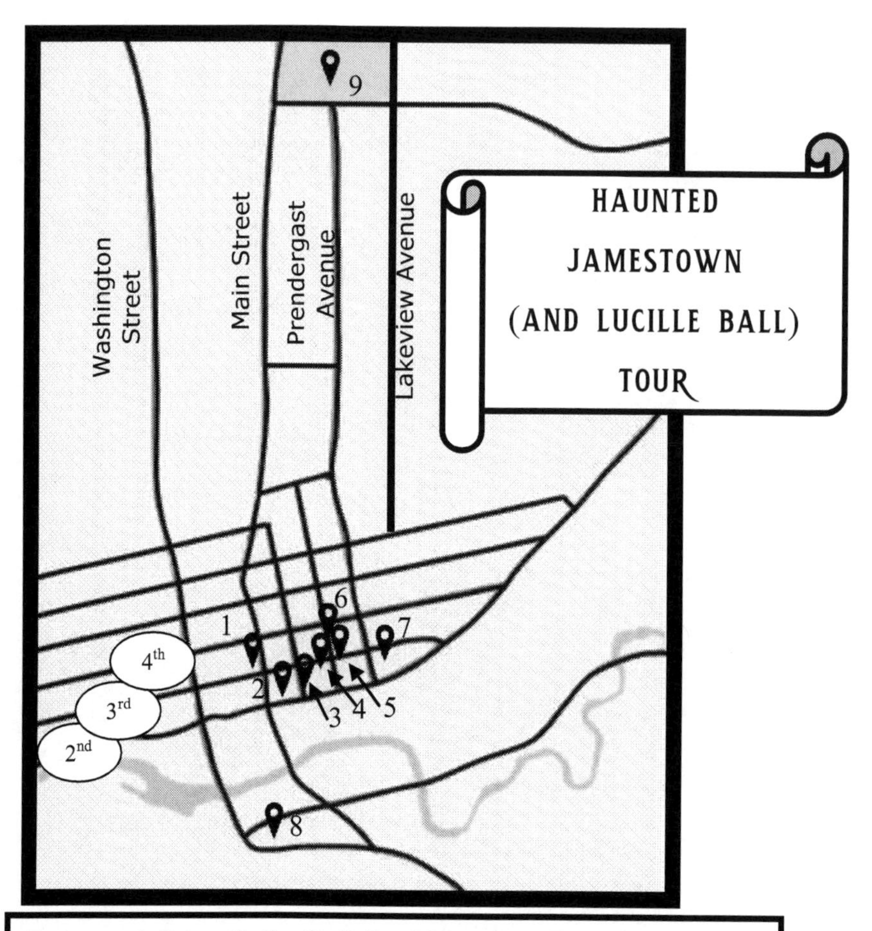

Jamestown is famous for Lucille Ball and *I Love Lucy*. Each haunted location has a connection to Lucy, and for fun, I added the famous *I Love Lucy* murals to the Jamestown tour. Some locations are a bit too far to walk and some are so close together, there's no need to drive. Here's a list of the locations in Jamestown for you to choose your own adventure, be it spooky, silly, or a little bit of both!

If you're a true fan of Lucy and Desi, stop by the **Lucille Ball & Desi Arnaz Museum (1)**. On Second Street, you'll find the haunted **Lucille Ball Little Theatre (2)** and the **Candy Factory mural (3)**. Around the corner from the mural on Third Street is the haunted **Reg Lenna Civic Center (4)**. Continue down Third Street to see the **Vitameatavegamin mural (5)** on the side of the parking garage and the **Postage Stamp mural (7)** on the side of the post office. Just north of the Vitameatavegamin mural is a **Lucy/Desi mural (6)** on Fourth Street. Venture over the Chadakoin River to **the world's largest Lucy mural (8)** at 34 Harrison Street. For the taphophile in your life, head north up Main Street to **Lake View Cemetery (9)**. It's here you'll find the Lady in Glass as well as Lucille Ball (follow the red heart path to her grave).

NIAGARA COUNTY

NIAGARA COUNTY

Formed from Genesee County in 1808, the name Niagara comes from the Iroquois word *Onguiaahra,* meaning thunder of waters. It is home to the "Seventh Wonder of the World" as well as Old Fort Niagara, the Niagara Wine Trail, and the Honeymoon Capital of the World. The town of Lewiston borders the Niagara River and Canada, making it the end of the Underground Railroad in the area. Today, there is a monument dedicated to the former slaves escaping to freedom on the banks of the river and many homes contain evidence connecting them to the Underground Railroad.

1. Aunt Hannah's Grave
2. Black Nose Spring Road
3. Clet Hall
4. Cold Springs Cemetery
5. Cold Springs Road
6. Devil's Hole State Park
7. Dick Block
8. Echo Club
9. Frontier House
10. Ghostlight Theatre
11. Graestone Manor
12. Hall's Apple Farm
13. Historic Holy Trinity Church
14. Kenan House & Center
15. Legends Bar & Grill
16. Lewiston Public Library
17. Lockport Cave
18. Marjim Manor
19. Oakwood Cemetery
20. Old Fort Niagara
21. Rapids Theatre
22. Red Coach Inn
23. Riviera Theatre
24. Thirty Mile Point Lighthouse
25. Van Horn Mansion

NIAGARA
COUNTY
EST. 1808
SOMERSET
BURT
APPLETON
YOUNGSTOWN
LEWISTON
SANDBORN
GASPORT
LOCKPORT
NIAGARA
FALLS
NORTH
TONAWANDA
18
78
104
104
31
190
62
1
2
3
4/5
6
7
8
9
10
11
12
13
14
15
16
17
18
19
20
21
22
23
24
25

AUNT HANNAH'S GRAVE

207 Payne Avenue, North Tonawanda, New York, 14120
43.029842°, -78.869067°

There's not much known about Aunt Hannah Johnson (also known historically as Black Hannah). Over the years, she has become more of a legend in North Tonawanda than an actual historical figure. She was born sometime around the turn of the 19th Century and grew up as a slave. Some stories have her born in New York State while others say she made her way north through the Underground Railroad. Either way, by 1834 she settled in North Tonawanda, a free woman, living on land owned by a man named John Chadwick.

FUN FACT: Some believe Aunt Hannah practiced hoodoo, a form of folk magic that originated in West Africa.

From the moment Hannah arrived, she seemed to capture the interest and imagination of the citizens of the area, quickly winning them over. She was a part of a small community of former slaves living along Tonawanda Creek and managed to make a living off of telling fortunes for the ladies in the town. She was particularly gifted at reading tea leaves, casting love spells, and selling potions, as well as offering herbal remedies for ailments.

According to legend, after her death in 1883, flowers that are not native to North Tonawanda grew all around her cabin in what became known as Black Hannah's Woods.

But the tales of Aunt Hannah did not end with her death.

In the years that followed, legends spread of the woods where Hannah had lived and how the old fortune teller's spirit continued to haunt the forest.

Unfortunately, Hannah's forest no longer stands. Between the 1960s-1980s most of the woods were cut down to build houses throughout North Tonawanda. Before much of the forest was developed into housing, local children would claim to experience strange events which helped bring the legend of Aunt Hannah back into the 20th Century. Based off of a 1927 description in the *Tonawanda News*, Hannah's Woods were located "north of Sweeney Street and about directly east of the end of Tremont Street." Historians have placed it along South Meadow Drive near East Goundry Street. And with the passage of over 130 years and the destruction of Aunt Hannah's woods, any evidence of Hannah's life and home are long gone. The only thing left of Aunt Hannah, it would seem, is her grave in Sweeney Cemetery.

Just like the earlier parts of her life, there are different stories about just where Aunt Hannah's final resting place is in Sweeny Cemetery. According to the most popular claims, she is buried in an unmarked grave. There is a Hannah Johnson who died in 1883 buried there, as well as a Johnson couple with dates close enough to Hannah's death that it could be her. Whichever version of the story you choose to believe, Sweeney Cemetery is believed to be haunted by the spirit of Aunt Hannah. Unexplained lights have been seen floating through the gravestones as well as strange noises, and people experience the sensation of someone watching them.

TIP: When you enter from the Payne Avenue entrance, bear to the left and head down the first complete row of graves. There is a limestone grave marker beside a bush with the name Johnson. This is supposedly Hannah's final resting place.

If you visit Sweeney Cemetery, please be aware of the residences surrounding it. Oh, and the North Tonawanda police station across the street…

EXPERIENCE:
Cemetery

OPEN TO THE PUBLIC:
Yes

HANDICAP ACCESSIBLE:
Yes

BLACK NOSE SPRING ROAD

Black Nose Spring Road, Sanborn, New York, 14132
43.179591°, -78.930281°

There is nothing entirely out of the ordinary about this one mile stretch of road: just the clashing of cultures as European settlers arrived on the native Iroquois's land.

Now situated on the Tuscarora Reservation in Sandborn, Black Nose Spring Road connects Upper and Lower Mountain Roads along the land of Bond Lake Park. This now beautiful and serene part of Niagara County was once the sight of an ambush that many believe has tainted the area even to this day.

According to legend, the Native American occupants of the land attacked and killed the newly arrived European settlers. They then disposed of the settlers' bodies by throwing them into a nearby lake (most likely Bond Lake or Myers Lake West). However, shortly after these murders, the faces of the settlers would appear to the Seneca in the muddy waters, haunting them. It is hard to say if this tale is simply a legend or if the attack was part of the effects of the War of 1812. Either way, the faces of the settlers seem to still appear to anyone passing through Black Nose Spring Road.

Drivers have reported seeing the ghostly white faces of strangers in their mirrors as they drive along the road, passing the lake. There are also claims of unexplained noises being heard from inside the cars. It's as if something is tapping on the moving vehicle or somehow managing to run alongside it (going about 40 miles per hour mind you).

Many believe the spirits of the settlers still haunt the land where they met their end. There have been several other murders reported in the 1990s that occurred along the same road, so it is possible that souls from both the 19th and 20th Centuries haunt the land today.

EXPERIENCE:

Haunted Road

OPEN TO THE PUBLIC:

Yes

HANDICAP ACCESSIBLE:

Yes

CLET HALL

5795 Lewiston Road, Niagara University, New York, 14109
43.138749°, -79.039374°
www.niagara.edu

Formerly known as the Seminary of Our Lady of Angels, Niagara University is one of the leading colleges in Western New York, situated at the highest point of the Niagara Gorge. Founded in 1856, Clet Hall was built in 1860, making it the oldest building on campus. Today, Clet Hall is a residence hall and also home to Leary Theatre.

TIP: Clet is pronounced "clay."

If you've been one of the poor unfortunate freshmen to move into Clet Hall, you've been privy to the ghost story of Thomas Hopkins. It's a tale that upperclassmen seem to use to torture new students.

Only four years after Clet Hall was constructed, a horrific fire broke out and destroyed much of the building. Thomas Hopkins, a young seminary student from Brooklyn, is said to have run back to his room to save some of his textbooks. Fellow students reported seeing Hopkins from his window on the upper floors of the building, pleading for help before a wall collapsed on top of him.

Since that tragic day, there have been reports of paranormal activity. Doors will slam on their own, lights will turn off and on, and faucets in many of the bathrooms will turn on with no logical explanation. It is said that Hopkins's spirit resides in the attic, and many students venture there to test their courage.

Today, a white obelisk stands outside the dorm, memorializing the young seminary student who lost his life in 1864. But that doesn't seem to be enough for the young man's spirit. He's been making his presence known to fellow students for over 150 years, and there's no sign he'll be stopping anytime soon.

FUN FACT: The NU coat of arms includes symbols for Niagara Falls, the Immaculate Conception, the 19th Century, and Saint Vincent de Paul.

Niagara University's motto is *Ut Omnes Te Cognoscant*… "That all may know you." It appears that the ghost of Thomas Hopkins has taken his beloved school's motto to heart, even if making himself known to all is merely slamming a door or two.

EXPERIENCE:

School

OPEN TO THE PUBLIC:

Partial

COLD SPRINGS CEMETERY

4849 Cold Springs Road, Lockport, New York, 14094
43.183906°, -78.657474°
www.coldspringscem.weebly.com

Cold Springs Cemetery was incorporated in 1841 with the first civilian burial dating back to 1815. Before the cemetery's first official burial, 12 soldiers were laid to rest in what is now Lockport's oldest cemetery.

According to legend, during the War of 1812, the 12 soldiers were traveling from Batavia to the Niagara Frontier. They decided to rest at the cold springs—natural springs that still trickle through the cemetery today—and by the next morning, they were dead. There are several theories about what happened to this unlucky group of soldiers. Some think they enjoyed a bit too much whiskey while others believe they succumbed to an illness. Either way, the men were buried beside the cold spring. Over the years, more and more citizens were buried alongside the soldiers, successfully turning the natural spring into the National Historic Place we see today.

A prime example of a rural Victorian cemetery, Cold Springs is made up of 50 acres of rolling hills and is the final resting place to some of Niagara County's historical elite. Inventor and initial owner of the Lockport Cave, Birdsill Holly, and Jessie Hawley, first advocate for the Erie Canal, both call the cemetery their eternal home. But the most mysterious resident may not be buried on the grounds. However, according to stories, she died there.

A local urban legend tells the story of a young girl who was hitchhiking through the area. Sadly, she decided to hop into the wrong car, and she was brought to the cemetery where her abductor murdered her. There is no evidence that this tragedy ever took place. However, many believe the ghost of the young hitchhiker still haunts the place of her death.

> **TIP:** The cemetery is most beautiful in the spring when the Japanese cherry blossoms are in bloom.

Cold Springs Cemetery is open year-round, but the owners ask that you use common sense when navigating the rough paths during winter and spring.

EXPERIENCE:

Cemetery

OPEN TO THE PUBLIC:

Yes

HANDICAP ACCESSIBLE:

Yes

COLD SPRINGS ROAD

Cold Springs Road, Lockport, New York, 14094
43.181934°, -78.659014°

Cold Springs Road might only be half a mile long, but it runs directly next to Cold Springs Cemetery, making it one spooky stretch of road.

Legends surrounding the road in the middle of Lockport date back to the 1960s and tell of a witch lurking in the shadows. The aptly named Cold Springs Witch has been haunting drivers along the road for generations.

There are no traditional claims such as cold spots, the sensation of someone watching you, or even unexplained sounds coming from in or around your car. This haunting goes straight to the full-body apparition… and this "witch" likes to reveal herself to weary travelers in different ways.

Some say that she is a witch like her nickname suggests. Others consider her an elusive phantom hitchhiker (all good haunted roads need a hitchhiking ghost, after all). Some claim that she is a child or a young woman. Others have reported seeing her on the side of the road as a middle-aged woman. While others, still, claim to have seen a haggard old crone sitting in the car with them as they drive down the street.

FUN FACT: Vanishing hitchhikers can be traced back to at least 1870 and are seen all over the world including Europe, Korea, and even tsarist Russia.

If we connect the dots (like all good investigators should—even paranormal ones), legend tells us that a young woman was murdered in the nearby cemetery while trying to hitchhike (you should remember… it was only two pages ago). Perhaps she is the phantom hitchhiker so many have reported seeing over the decades.

We may never know the true identity of the Cold Springs Witch. But one thing is for sure: there is something strange happening at Cold Springs Cemetery in Lockport, and it looks as if the ghost stories have flooded out onto the roads. My word of advice: Don't pick up any hitchhikers along Cold Springs Road, especially if they look like a witch (whatever that might be).

EXPERIENCE:

Haunted Road

OPEN TO THE PUBLIC:

Yes

HANDICAP ACCESSIBLE:

Yes

DEVIL'S HOLE STATE PARK

Robert Moses Parkway, Niagara Falls, New York, 14305
43.133179°, -79.046173°
www.parks.ny.gov/parks/42

There are two types of people from Western New York: the ones that love hiking through Devil's Hole State Park and those who panic at just the mention of the name. Of course, Devil's Hole State Park is breathtakingly beautiful with 42 acres of trails that overlook the lower Niagara Gorge and offers access to the Lower Whirlpool rapids. But something is unnerving about the park. Some think that the violent history of Devil's Hole is to blame, while others believe that the land is cursed.

The reputation of Devil's Hole dates back to the days before European settlers arrived. According to Native American legends and lore, an evil spirit haunts the caves, especially the Devil's Den. Many people report sensing a dark aura inside that cave, and some have even witnessed the remnants of animal sacrifice and black magic rituals.

The infamy of Devil's Hole was engraved in the history books of Western New York when, in 1763, 80 British soldiers were killed and scalped by a tribe of Native Americans. This ambush would become known as the Devil's Hole Massacre, and many believe that the spirits of those soldiers still haunt their bloody final resting place.

Tourists gravitate towards the hiking trail with its tales of disembodied voices, full-body apparitions, and unexplained noises. The most famous visitor learned quickly that the curse of Devil's Hole State Park was no joke: President William McKinley. While visiting Buffalo during the Pan-American Exposition in 1901, it is said McKinley visited Devil's Hole just hours before he was assassinated in the Temple of Music by Leon Czolgosz. And he isn't the only one who met an untimely demise after daring to step foot in Devil's Hole. There have been countless murders, suicides, and simple accidents along the 410 steps leading down to the gorge below.

TIP: Devil's Hole State Park is adjacent to Whirlpool State Park and shares many of the same trails.

It's always safe to bring a buddy while you're hiking. At Devil's Hole State Park, it's no exception. You'll need a companion for one of two reasons: to offer you a bit of bravery if/when you cross paths with a scalped 18th Century spirit or if you just need someone to help you climb back up those awful stairs.

TIP: The Devil's Den is off the official Devil's Hole Trail (#6). Bear to the right when the path forks. Approximate coordinates are:
43.134780°, -79.044834°

EXPERIENCE:

Natural Wonder/Hiking Trails

OPEN TO THE PUBLIC:

Yes

HANDICAP ACCESSIBLE:

No

DICK BLOCK

62 Webster Street, North Tonawanda, New York, 14120
43.023556°, -78.877563°

If you walk down Webster Street in North Tonawanda, you'll see a prime example of that classic Western New York revival. What was once considered the rough part of town has experienced a renaissance over the last few years. Webster Street is now an entertainment district with the Riviera Theatre, Dwyer's Irish Pub, Webster's Bistro, and the historic Erie Canal just down the road. It's an eclectic mix of buildings with the taller brick structures standing out. And they should since they're over a century old and one of them is a bit on the haunted side.

The Dick Block was built in 1891 and placed on the National Register of Historic Places in 2012. Today, the three-story brick building is home to a variety of businesses including Canal Club 62, an upscale taproom and eatery on the bottom floor, and Escape Room Adventures on the third floor.

Both businesses experienced some spooky activity during renovations in 2016, leading many employees to think that there is more to their historic building than meets the eye.

According to stories, the upper floor of the building was a speakeasy during Prohibition. They (the ever omniscient "they") say there is even a secret room you can see today where the bootleggers used to hide the ladies and liquor when the police arrived.

Employees and customers have reported ghostly activity including feeling uneasy in the women's bathroom on the upper floor, doors opening and closing on their own, items flying through the air, names being called out, and even the apparition of a young boy.

TIP: Ask to see the secret room on the upper floor to see a piece of North Tonawanda's hidden history.

There is little known about the haunting such as who it is or why they might be there. But it looks like the spirits are finally waking up to see what all that noise is down on Webster Street.

EXPERIENCE:

Landmark/Restaurant/Bar

OPEN TO THE PUBLIC:

Yes

HANDICAP ACCESSIBLE:

Partial. First floor only.

Contact:
Escape Room Adventures:
escaperoomadventures@outlook.com
Canal Club 62:
(716) 260-1824

ECHO CLUB

341 Portage Road, Niagara Falls, New York, 14303
43.088085°, -79.043245°

With such a colorful haunted history, it is a shame that the Echo Club currently sits empty. Even though it was featured on *Haunted Collector* in 2012 and was supposedly where William McKinley enjoyed his final meal, the 19th Century mansion was put on the market in 2018 for $999,999. If you're looking to invest in the historic property in Niagara Falls, a word to the wise:

According to former employees, the Echo is nothing but chaos—not a negative haunt, just chaos.

The 24-room home was used as a restaurant, bar, and dinner theatre up until recently, with stories of a nasty ghost who liked to smash plates, move furniture, and scream at guests.

> As seen on *Haunted Collector* season 3, episode 1.

The most famous ghost story surrounding the Echo is the spirit of a little girl. She is seen most often in the bathroom, crying. Most recently, she was seen at a high school reunion only to disappear when the patrons came near her. She is believed to be the daughter of a worker who died in the basement. And it seems she continues to mourn for her father even in the afterlife.

To add a bit of darkness to this sad tale, one of the previous owners had a jail in the basement where he would hold people unable to repay their debts.

Other paranormal claims tell of rooms shaking on the upper floors, unexplained noises, as well as objects flying across the rooms. Sadly, at the time of publication, it's impossible to experience the activity of the Echo first hand. But if anyone has $1 million lying around, I think we'd all be grateful that a piece of Western New York's haunted history could be restored to its spooky glory.

FUN FACT: According to stories, both President Woodrow Wilson and Marilyn Monroe visited the club.

EXPERIENCE:

Restaurant/Bar/Event Venue

OPEN TO THE PUBLIC:

No

FRONTIER HOUSE

460 Center Street, Lewiston, New York, 14092
43.172903°, -79.042350°

Although the Frontier House has had one of the more fascinating histories in Western New York, it now sits empty with no one celebrating its past, haunted or otherwise.

Built in 1824, the Frontier House was considered to be the best hotel west of Albany and hosted William McKinley, Mark Twain, Charles Dickens, and Jenny Lind. It transformed from a hotel to a private residence and finally into a fine dining restaurant. In 1973, it suffered from a devastating fire before it was transformed into (strangely enough) a McDonald's. The fast-food restaurant remained open until 2004 before it was abandoned. It was obtained by the village of Lewiston in 2013 and finally sold in February 2019, but the historic building remains vacant… for now.

Many places in Lewiston try to hide their hauntings, and even though the Frontier House is empty, it is full of ghost stories. Doors and windows open and close on their own and tools and equipment would go missing while the house was being renovated into the fast-food chain. An older man has been seen in the pantry while a woman has been spotted on the upper floors. Supposedly, the house is also haunted by a bricklayer who hated the Freemasons… and it just so happens that they held their secret meetings on the uppermost floor.

The most macabre legend associated with the Frontier House dates back to its earliest days when it was being built in the 19th Century. Supposedly, one of the men constructing the house fell from the third floor down to the basement. Instead of reporting the death, his coworkers took his body and buried him inside one of the walls of the Frontier House.

> **FUN FACT:** William Morgan (the anti-Masonic gent from page 68) was kidnapped and held behind the house before being sent to Fort Niagara.

Unfortunately, this piece of Lewiston history is still barred from visitors at present. Plans for the building and grounds will be revealed in the coming months. But for now, those curious about the Frontier House's activity will have to continue to wait (im)patiently.

EXPERIENCE:
Landmark

OPEN TO THE PUBLIC:
No (at least at the time of publication)

GHOSTLIGHT THEATRE

170 Schenck Street, North Tonawanda, New York, 14120
43.031138°, -78.873983°
www.starrynighttheatre.com

The Ghostlight Theatre was not always the home of Starry Night Theatre, Inc. Up until 2001, it was the home of the Evangelical Friedens Church of North Tonawanda. According to legend, the cornerstone was laid on a dark and stormy Halloween night in 1889. The church was a part of the North Tonawanda community, standing tall on the corners of Schenck and Vandervoort for over 110 years. In the early 2000s, the building was given to L. Don Swartz, and it was renamed the Ghostlight Theatre.

Since Starry Night Theatre, Inc. moved into the old church, volunteers both on stage and off have reported unusual and unexplained activity. These reports come from all over the building. The "Early America" room in the basement. The costume room on the second floor. The prop room backstage.

Even up in the balcony. The most haunted place in the entire theatre is the infamous spiral staircase. Inside, EVPs have been captured saying people's names, the sound of phantom footsteps are heard, and most who venture up the stairs share a feeling of uneasiness.

Supposedly, several spirits are haunting the old church now turned theatre, the most famous of them being the Lady in Red. No one knows who she is or why she still lingers at the Ghostlight Theatre. Usually, the Lady in Red appears to volunteers as a full-body apparition. She seems so life-like that people don't realize who (or should I say what?) she is until she's gone.

Photo courtesy of L. Don Swartz

Aside from full-body apparitions (though that is impressive in and of itself), the spirits of the Ghostlight Theatre like to make themselves known in other ways. Sometimes, they run around and move hangers in the costume room. They speak in both English and German in EVPs. And they've even appeared in photographs. The most famous photo taken at the Ghostlight was during a 2004 performance of *A Christmas Carol* where a figure can be seen standing behind the actor playing Jacob Marley (see image).

In recent years, the theatre has opened its doors to guests for their annual ghost hunt. This event offers amateur paranormal investigators the chance to explore parts of the theatre usually off-limits to guests—including the bell tower where the 2,800-pound bell still hangs. Incredible photos and EVPs have been captured throughout the last three years on these hunts. One such photograph is of former theatre member, Jedidiah Woomer, as he appeared at 11 years old (just eight years before his death in 2015). With the photo, they captured a companion EVP of his voice in the same location of the basement. His words

TIP: Aside from the five productions, the theatre also holds fundraisers throughout the year including a radio show in the spring. It's a fun, entertaining way to support the restoration of the historic theatre.

haunt his family as well as the members of the theatre, his voice echoing a reassuring, "I'm fine."

The Ghostlight Theatre seems to be alive with spirits coming and going as they please. Some are from over a century ago, and others only departed this world within the last few years. But no matter when or where they're from, it is clear that their presence is felt all throughout the theatre, as they silently watch the performers on stage (and sometimes even make a cameo).

EXPERIENCE:
Theatre/Ghost Hunt

OPEN TO THE PUBLIC:
Yes

HANDICAP ACCESSIBLE:
Partial. Chair lift to theatre. Basement and second floor not accessible.

Important Info:
Performances Include:
Fall Thriller
Christmas Show
Winter Classic
Spring Comedy
Summer Musical

Thursday:
7:00pm
Friday-Saturday:
8:00pm
Sunday:
2:00pm
Contact:
(716) 743-1614

Admission:
Musical & Christmas/General

Adults: $18/15
Seniors: $16/13
Veterans: $16/13
Students: $16/13
Children: $16/13

Season tickets are available for $60 and includes all five productions.

GRAESTONE MANOR

4049 Root Road, Gasport, New York, 14067
43.211307°, -78.545155°
www.graestonemanor.com

There are so many haunted locations in Western New York closed to the general public or (even worse) with owners who refuse to acknowledge the haunting. It is a relief to find that one of the most active locations in Niagara County is owned by a psychic medium and is ready to open itself up to anyone curious about the historic building.

Graestone Manor was built in 1865 by Curtis Root and was home to the Root family and their thoroughbreds until 1923. Since then, two other families have called the manor home until Bob Mattison and Heather Rease Mattison purchased the property in 2017. The house has been open for both private and public ghost hunts, and the couple has been hard at work transforming Graestone into a bed and breakfast.

The most haunted B&B in Western New York can hold six people, three rooms with double occupancy. The Mattisons are hoping to transport guests back to a simpler time, offering all the charm of the Victorian era, from the food to the furnishings. Guests will just have to be okay with sharing the place with a

> **TIP:** For people with allergies, please be aware that the manor is also home to four friendly cats: Erik, Salem, Jim, and Doug.

few ghosts.

Graestone Manor has some of the most extraordinary claims in all of Western New York. Visitors report hearing the sound of horse hooves (remember the Roots bred horses), a man's voice, and whistling. People smell perfume and see a nonhuman entity in the upstairs hallway. The apparition of a woman has been seen looking out a window, and she also seems to enjoy following people.

TIP: Owner Heather Rease Mattison offers psychic services during your stay as well as paranormal investigations and wine tours.

Shadow figures have been spotted in the house and on the property. There are also reports of a portal in the basement and upstairs in the children's bedroom. Some believe these portals are a result of the Victorians' obsession with séances and Ouija boards.

With so many different reports, Graestone Manor is a mecca for anyone interested in the paranormal. Public ghost hunts are held throughout the year at $35 per person (prices for investigations through second party groups range from $25-75 per person). Private hunts cost $300, running from 6:00-11:00pm or 7:00pm-12:00am, and can accommodate five to 10 people.

To experience all that Graestone Manor has to offer, you can book a room starting at just $99 per night (which is pretty darn good as far as bed and breakfasts go). Each of the three bedrooms has its own paranormal claims:

TIP: Just a minute from the manor, you'll hit the Slayton Settlement fork. Take the road on the left and cross the single lane bridge over the canal to get to Root Road. Most GPS will miss this and take you to the right.

If you're looking for full-body apparitions, why not try The Red Room where an older woman has been seen? If you like objects moving and capturing ghostly images on camera, then The Gold Room is perfect for you. If you're looking for someone watching you while you sleep, as well as the smell of cigar smoke and the sensation of ghostly hands touching you, then you should definitely check out The Green Room. It's the room where Curtis Root died after an accident involving his beloved racehorse, Playboy.

You can book a night at Graestone Manor through either their website or AirBnB. No matter which room you book, though, you're likely to have an incredible experience in one of Western New York's (openly) haunted bed and breakfasts.

EXPERIENCE:
Hotel/Ghost Hunt

OPEN TO THE PUBLIC:
Yes

HANDICAP ACCESSIBLE:
No

Contact:
(716) 481-6097

HALL'S APPLE FARM

6100 Ruhlmann Road, Lockport, New York, 14094
43.150800°, -78.703587°
www.hallsapplefarm.com

Hall's Apple Farm is just as much an integral part of Lockport as the Erie Canal or its Locks. Famous in Western New York for their homemade pies, traditionally pressed apple cider, and their wide selection of old-fashioned hard candies, Hall's has also made a name for itself in the paranormal community with a few ghost stories of its own.

Founded in 1892 by William T. Hall, the business is now in its sixth generation, and still going strong. When you visit, you can see where the old meets new with a modern storefront near the road and an antique farm (dating to 1912) hiding back by the orchard. Whether you're in the older part of the farm or the more modern section, no place is safe when it comes to ghostly activity.

Employees and even the owner have reported seeing "something odd." A full-body apparition has been spotted walking through the store, and people have reported hearing their names called out to them. Objects seem to like to move on their own, and EVPs have been captured in the barn.

The owners are healthy skeptics, but there's no denying that something unnatural is going on at Hall's Apple Farm.

As seen on *My Ghost Story* season 4, episode 12.

If nothing else, it could be how unbelievably delicious their apple caramel walnut pies are.

EXPERIENCE:
Store

OPEN TO THE PUBLIC:
Yes

HANDICAP ACCESSIBLE:
Yes

Important Info:
Hours of Operation:
Sunday:
Closed
Monday-Saturday:
9:00am-5:30pm
Contact:
(716) 434-0838

HISTORIC HOLY TRINITY CHURCH

1419 Falls Street, Niagara Falls, New York, 14303
43.086775°, -79.043962°
www.historicht.org

On October 27, 1901, Holy Trinity Church was founded with just 21 members. It offered the Polish-speaking community of Western New York a place to worship at Pasek's Bar and Grill on the corners of Falls and 13th Street. The small parish built their church in 1905 with a rectory added in 1907 and a convent in 1910. The final addition to Holy Trinity was the school that opened its doors in 1914, and it remained a part of the church until it closed in 1974. The church was bought by the not-for-profit group, "Niagara Heritage of Hope and Service" in 2009, and today it acts as a community center, hosting family-friendly events.

After having such an active role in the community of Niagara Falls, the historic Holy Trinity Church has become a beacon for paranormal activity over the years. People smell perfume and fresh-cut flowers throughout the complex. Such fragrances were used for Catholic wakes and funeral services, making many people believe this could be a part of a residual haunting. There is also the sound of disembodied voices, including the sound of a woman singing hymns. The most famous story belongs to the spirit of a little girl in a white dress. She runs through the church, and if you're lucky, you might feel her ghostly fingers playing with your hair.

Holy Trinity Church is open to the public for various community events, including historical tours on Fridays in the summer. They also have a thrift store open on Saturdays from 10:00am-1:00pm. You may not necessarily spot a phantom girl playing in the former church, but you could walk away with a good deal or a kitschy treasure (you tell me which is better).

> **TIP:** You can access the thrift store through entrance #2 off of 14th Street.

EXPERIENCE:

Community Center/Former Church

OPEN TO THE PUBLIC:

Yes

HANDICAP ACCESSIBLE:

Partial

KENAN HOUSE & CENTER

433 Locust Street, Lockport, New York, 14094
43.158117°, -78.682337°
www.kenancenter.org

What is now the Kenan Center of Lockport was once just a single brick home built in 1853. Sadly, the house was almost destroyed in a fire the following year, and it wasn't until 1858 that George W. Rogers rebuilt it. It was given the name of Kenan House when Mr. and Mrs. William Rand Kenan moved in in 1912. Since then, the 25 acres of the Kenan land has been transformed into the Kenan Center complete with an arena, theatre, garden, education building, and even an art exhibit.

While people are enjoying the Kenan Center's festivities, it is easy to forget the history surrounding the complex and the ghost stories that have survived for over a century. A strange white light is seen throughout the house and grounds. Sometimes it also appears in photographs. There have been full-body apparitions spotted, including that of a little boy running through the house.

TIP: The art and photography exhibits are always free.

The Kenan Center is open to the public and hosts various events each year, including their Wine and Beer Tasting Fest (my personal favorite), Holiday Craft Show, and the 100 American Craftsmen craft show.

EXPERIENCE:

Community Center/Landmark

OPEN TO THE PUBLIC:

Yes

HANDICAP ACCESSIBLE:

Yes

Important Info:
Gallery Hours of Operation:
Sunday: 2:00-5:00pm
Monday-Friday: 12:00-6:00pm
Saturday: Closed
Check the center's website for special events.
Contact: (716) 433-2617

LEGENDS BAR & GRILL

Quality Inn, 240 First Street, Niagara Falls, New York, 14303
43.08564°, -79.062117°
www.qualityniagarafalls.com/dining.php

Legends Bar and Grill may be one of the more unassuming haunts throughout Western New York. It isn't the site of a bloody battle. There's no evidence of witchcraft or curses. It isn't even in a creepy old building. Legends is situated in the Quality Inn Hotel right in Downtown Niagara Falls.

Located within walking distance to the Falls and the Seneca Niagara Casino, Legends is in the heart of Niagara Falls. With weekly events, over 50 beers to choose from, and an outdoor patio in the summer, it's hard to think that this bustling sports bar could be haunted in any way. But that's where you'd be wrong.

Famous for their fried pickles, Legends is also infamous for their most renowned spirit. Known only as Jack, this full-body apparition appears dressed in a long black coat (possibly in the highwayman style) and wanders through the main dining room after hours. He doesn't interact much with staff who have only reported seeing him from a distance before he disappears.

No one knows who the heck Jack is, but he manages to add a bit of charm to what would otherwise be just another sports bar in the middle of a budget hotel.

EXPERIENCE:

Restaurant/Bar

OPEN TO THE PUBLIC:

Yes

HANDICAP ACCESSIBLE:

Yes

Important Info:
Hours of Operation:
Sunday:
12:00-8:00pm
Monday-Thursday:
4:00pm-12:00am
Friday-Saturday:
12:00pm-1:00am

LEWISTON PUBLIC LIBRARY

305 South Eighth Street, Lewiston, New York, 14092
43.169105°, -79.037089°
www.lewistonpubliclibrary.org

The Lewiston Public Library is the perfect example of haunted items, rather than a haunted space. The building that is now home to the Lewiston Public Library dates back to only the 1990s. However, the library, itself, dates back to 1901. The town's library found its start at the Men's Club of Lewiston's New Year's party. Every member brought two books to the party with them, and the rest is history.

Even though the building is new as far as haunted locations go, there is a surprising amount of paranormal activity reported by visitors, custodial staff, and librarians. Many people report feeling or hearing things that they cannot explain. They sense a presence in the history section of the library, and shadow people have been spotted moving through the shelves of the adult nonfiction area.

> **FUN FACT:** Theodore Roosevelt was invited to the Christmas party but was unable to attend. He still sent a book to add to the library which is on display in the local history room.

The most famous (and heartbreaking) ghost haunting the rows of books is a former librarian. Back in the 1970s, the woman committed suicide, and it seems as if her restless spirit has followed the books of her beloved library ever since.

People have reported smelling perfume, and a reading therapy dog marched intently to a grandfather clock donated by the late librarian's children. Many believe the dog was following her ghost, and it is she who continues to make herself known throughout the library.

If there's any place that would be perfect for an impromptu paranormal investigation, it's a library. If nothing else, you know it will be quiet.

EXPERIENCE:
Library

OPEN TO THE PUBLIC:
Yes

HANDICAP ACCESSIBLE:
Yes

Important Info:
Hours of Operation:
Sunday:
Closed
Monday-Tuesday:
10:00am-8:00pm
Wednesday-Thursday:
10:00am-5:00pm
Friday:
12:00-5:00pm
Saturday:
10:00am-3:00pm

LOCKPORT CAVE

5 Gooding Street, Lockport, New York, 14094
43.171941°, -78.692531°
www.lockportcave.com

If you grew up in Western New York, you probably visited the Lockport Locks on a school field trip. The town of Lockport is famous for its historical importance in the construction of the Erie Canal in 1825. But Lockport is also known for another quirky tourist attraction: the Lockport Cave.

Surprisingly, only one of these caves is natural while the other was constructed from 1858-1900. During this time, these caves provided hydraulic power to much of the town of Lockport, including nearby mills.

The young inventor, Birdsill Holly, was placed in charge of the hydraulic mill along the Erie Canal, and Holly Manufacturing was born. With Holly Manufacturing and the underground hydraulic race tunnel, Holly was able to supply clean drinking water to domestic homes as well as pressurized water to things such as fire hydrants throughout the town. But Holly wasn't just an inventor. He was also a friend of the Fox Sisters who had a hand in founding the religion of Spiritualism.

As seen on *Ghost Hunters* season 8, episode 21.

Running water helps to create energy, and many paranormal investigators believe that this could stir up ghostly activity.

The Lockport Cave has quite a reputation among paranormal investigators. According to claims by tour guides and visitors, faces are seen in the water from the boats in the underground cave tours. Shadows are cast along the rock walls, mists have been seen floating through the tunnels, and people also hear the sound of ghostly footsteps and moaning. It is also believed that a young man named Bertram drowned after being pushed into the canal, and today, he haunts the tunnels.

> **FUN FACT:** After being revealed as frauds, the Fox Sisters vanished into alcoholism, poverty, and obscurity until their deaths in the 1890s.

If you'd like to become your very own Ghost Hunter and see if you can capture evidence of Bertram or any of the other spirits, the Lockport Cave offers private ghost hunt experiences with four hours of access to the subterranean caves. For more information on booking the Ghost Hunters Experience, you can call the Lockport Cave at (716) 438-0174.

For a not so spooky experience, you can sign up for the classic tour: The Lockport Cave and Underground Boat Ride. From May through October, you can enjoy a 70-minute walking tour through the cave and ride along the underground river.

EXPERIENCE:
Natural Wonder/Ghost Hunt

OPEN TO THE PUBLIC:
Yes

HANDICAP ACCESSIBLE:
No

> **Important Info:**
> Tours vary based on time of year and popularity. Visit their website to view their calendar, tour options, and times.

Admission:

Adults: $17.50 +tax
Children (6-13): $12.25 +tax
Children 5 and under: $3.50 +tax

MARJIM MANOR

7171 Lake Road, Appleton, New York, 14008
43.348262°, -78.639135°
www.marjimmanor.com

The Legend of Appleton Hall does have the habit of steering from historical fact. However, that doesn't stop the hauntings of the Winery at Marjim Manor.

Appleton Hall was built in 1854 by Shubal Scudder Merrit for his wife, Sophia. For the next few years, they lived there happily with their children Phebe Sophia, Cordelia, and Lewis. Sadly, their happiness didn't last too long.

Over the last 160 years, Shubal's beloved Appleton Hall has gone through many different owners. From the tragic Merritt family to the director of the Buffalo Psych Center, Dr. Charles A. Ring and his two wives, Hannah and Estelle Morse, and finally the Sisters of St. Joseph who lived in the manor until 1993. Multiple deaths were recorded on the property, including Sophie and Lewis Merritt as well as Hannah Ring. And there have been even more hauntings recorded over the years.

According to claims made by both staff and customers, the ghosts of Shubal, Sophie, and Lewis Merritt are all present in what was once their family home. Some believe that Sophie still haunts the manor because it was built especially for her during the height of the family's prosperity. Others fear that Lewis's spirit is still present because of his tragic and unexpected death. Legend tells us that as Lewis entered through a pair of French doors (see image), he frightened his father who accidentally shot him in the middle of the house. Of course, no evidence supports this tragic tale, but that does nothing to explain why these doors like to open on their own.

The three members of the Merritt family are not alone in eternity. Charles and Hannah Ring have been seen as well as Estelle Morse and even the Sisters of St. Joseph's dog, Duke. Hannah is seen standing behind the employees in the tasting room, almost as if she is supervising their work. Estelle (who was known to be a shrewd businesswoman in life) has been spotted standing at the main entrance, greeting guests.

Today, Appleton Hall has been converted into a winery where the legend of the Merritt family is alive more than ever. Many of the wines are named after the ghost story, such as Lady of the Manor, Cordelia's Desire (my favorite… especially heated up on a chilly autumn day), and Thursday Afternoon at Three.

Speaking of Thursdays at three…

The Legend of Appleton Hall claims that every death on the premises happened at precisely three o'clock in the afternoon on a Thursday, from Lewis Merritt to Duke, the dog. And it seems as if the strange and mysterious afternoon happenings haven't stopped at Marjim Manor. From phantom footsteps, lights turning on and off, and wine bottles falling off shelves (what a travesty!), the activity seems to peak at three o'clock on Thursdays.

As seen on *Ghost Hunters* season 4, episode 20 and *Most Terrifying Places in America part 7*.

Of course, many skeptics believe that the Legend of Appleton Hall originated from an article that Estelle Morse wrote to cover up the fact that she convinced Dr. Ring to change his will so that she would inherit the house in the case of his death. I wonder what time he died? I'm willing to bet it was on a Thursday afternoon at three…

EXPERIENCE:
Winery

OPEN TO THE PUBLIC:
Yes

HANDICAP ACCESSIBLE:
Yes

Important Info:
Hours of Operation:
Sunday:
12:00-6:00pm
Monday-Saturday:
10:00am-6:00pm
Contact:
(716) 778-7001

THE 1920 INCIDENT

North Tonawanda, New York, 14120
43.038783°, -78.864155°

The relatively quiet town of North Tonawanda was once home to an apparition that is still a mystery even 100 years later.

North Tonawanda was incorporated along the shores of the Mighty Niagara River and the Erie Canal in 1897. Despite its relatively peaceful history, for 10 days, citizens of the town were tormented by what many described as a flying scarecrow.

In the 1920s, reports came in of a giant humanoid form flying through the streets of North Tonawanda, sometimes managing to stop traffic entirely. The entity was spotted by multiple witnesses, including a local policeman.

As the days wore on and the monster continued to appear, the local bicycle club vowed to put an end to the chaos and try to catch the creature. According to reports, members of the bicycle club managed to surround the apparition for a moment before it flew straight up and disappeared into the clouds never to be seen again.

Many people have tried to come up with an explanation for these 10 days of terror in North Tonawanda. Some claim it was this region's very own Mothman. Others cling to the flying scarecrow claims, while others also reported it appeared to wear a headdress similar to local Native American tribes.

No matter what flew through the streets of North Tonawanda over 100 years ago, its mystery still haunts the more curious citizens even to this day.

EXPERIENCE:

Unexplained Phenomenon/Cryptid

OAKWOOD CEMETERY

763 Portage Road, Niagara Falls, New York, 14301
43.097131°, -79.047416°
www.oakwoodniagara.org

A sanctuary nestled in the middle of the city, Oakwood Cemetery is made up of more than 18 acres of trees and graves—over 22,000 of them for that matter. The cemetery was established in 1852 and is still active. For history buffs, it is the final resting place to some of Niagara Falls' most famous residents, including Annie Edson Taylor, the first person to go over Niagara Falls in a barrel (and live to tell the tale).

While it's difficult to find any real stories about the cemetery's haunting, Oakwood does offer an event around Halloween time called "Spirits with the Spirits." For one body, it's $30, and for two bodies, it's $50. Either way, you get to enjoy four hours in the cemetery with wine, beer, and cider from the region as well as appetizers, a tour of the cemetery, and a chance to meet a psychic medium.

> **TIP:** To find Annie Edson Taylor's grave, bear to the right when you enter. You'll find her in the "Stunter's Rest" section in a small triangle of grass at a fork in the road.

The lack of ghost stories surrounding this supposed "haunted" cemetery might be a bit disappointing. But after a few drinks at their "Spirits with the Spirits" event, I doubt you'll really care.

EXPERIENCE:

Cemetery

OPEN TO THE PUBLIC:

Yes

HANDICAP ACCESSIBLE:

Yes

OLD FORT NIAGARA

102 Marrow Plaza, Youngstown, New York, 14174
43.262662°, -79.063230°
www.oldfortniagara.org

If you didn't make it to the Lockport Locks in elementary school, then hopefully your teachers at least took you to Old Fort Niagara. It is one of the oldest structures in the greater Niagara region and has seen over 300 years of history, both tumultuous and peaceful.

Originally a French post in 1679, it was known as Fort Conti back in the day. In 1755 it was expanded and built to the size that it is today, and throughout the following centuries, changed hands multiple times.

The fort played a significant role in the French and Indian War. The Battle of Fort Niagara lasted 19 days in July of 1759. Eventually, the fort fell into the hands of the British and would remain under their control for the next 37 years. Because of this, it served as a fortress for the Loyalists in New York during the American Revolution. Once the Americans won their independence in 1783, it was ceded to them. Again, the fort saw action in the War of 1812 (basically American Revolution 2.0) and was recaptured by the British in December of 1813. Luckily for local elementary school students, the fort was returned to the Americans and was an active military site even into the 20th Century.

As seen on *Ghost Hunters* season 7, episode 17 and *Ghost Lab* season 2, episode 2.

With all the bloodshed and fighting Old Fort Niagara has seen, of course, there would be some ghostly tales surrounding the French Castle, the barracks, the gun towers, and the battery. The most famous of all these stories is that of Henri LeClerc, a French soldier who is said to haunt the Castle hundreds of years after his untimely death.

According to legend, Henri engaged in a sword fighting duel with another man for the affections of a Seneca woman named Onita. Sadly for him, he lost said duel and also lost his head in the process. He was decapitated, and his head was supposedly thrown into the well. His headless ghost first appeared to his beloved Onita, and he has been seen wandering the grounds of the fort ever since.

Many historians claim this ghost story is nothing more than that: a story. There is no proof that such a duel ever occurred, and if it did, no one would have thrown a bloody head into their drinking water. But that doesn't matter for visitors—to many, the headless French soldier is more a part of Old Fort Niagara's history than the Revolutionary War!

TIP: Ticket sales end 30 minutes prior to closing.

That being said, staff and guests alike, report strange activity such as shadows running across the walls of the French Castle, doors slamming shut, and even orbs of light seen in photographs as well as with the naked eye.

Old Fort Niagara doesn't shy away from its ghost stories. Around Halloween, they offer Haunted Fortress tours for $20 per person. The fort is open all year round aside from Christmas, Thanksgiving, and New Year's Day.

For history buffs, the fort offers reenactments throughout the year starting in the spring. For paranormal enthusiasts, a cemetery is also on-site, dating back to 1755, making it one of the oldest in the region.

Whether you're looking for history or mysteries, Old Fort Niagara has it all, offering a day of fun and education (don't tell the kids) for the whole family.

EXPERIENCE:

Landmark/Ghost Tour

OPEN TO THE PUBLIC:

Yes

HANDICAP ACCESSIBLE:

Partial

Important Info:

Hours of Operation:
January-June:
9:00am-5:00pm
July-August:
9:00am-7:00pm
September-December:
9:00am-5:00pm
Contact:
(716) 745-7611

Admission:

Adults: $13
Seniors: $12
Veterans: $12 (with ID)
NYS Parks Discovery Pass: $12 ($8 for children)
Children (6-12): $9
Children 5 and under: Free

The fort is maintained by a not-for-profit organization so donations are always accepted.

RAPIDS THEATRE

1711 Main Street, Niagara Falls, New York, 14305
43.105154°, -79.052644°
www.rapidstheatre.com

The Rapids Theatre is one of the more famous haunted locations in Niagara Falls and even offers guests a chance to experience their ghostly activity for themselves.

What is now the Rapids Theatre was once the Bellevue Theatre. Initially opened in 1921 as a silent movie theatre and a vaudeville venue, the Bellevue is said to have hosted great acts through the decades including the Three Stooges. At the time of its opening, a ticket to one of their matinee movies would cost 28¢. Today, tickets are a bit pricier, but the impressive acts are still going strong, including Dropkick Murphys, Snoop Dogg, and even SyFy's *Ghost Hunters* back in 2011.

According to stories, a young woman hanged herself backstage, and since then, her restless spirit has been haunting the theatre, making her presence known. Employees and patrons have reported seeing her as well as hearing footsteps in empty halls. There are also stories of objects moving on their own and disappearing altogether.

One claim that is unique to the Rapids Theatre among the other theatres in the area is the sound of whistling. In theatre culture, whistling is considered bad luck. Historically speaking, stagehands would whistle to have different rigs rise and fall. When backdrops would move, sandbags balanced them out, sometimes landing on unsuspecting victims. Modern-day thespians believe that if you whistle in a theatre, something will fall on you. We all know theatre people are a superstitious lot, leading many to believe that the whistling is coming from somewhere beyond the grave.

The Rapids Theatre has embraced their spooky phenomenon and even opens its doors to those curious about the ghostly activity. They held their first public ghost hunt in 2012, just three years after reopening. The events are so popular the theatre now offers both private and public hunts.

As seen on *Ghost Hunters* season 7, episode 19.

Public events are limited to 50 people and allow guests to explore the front and rear tunnels, the stage and theatre area, the balcony, and the green room. Private hunts are also available for a bit of a steeper price. For the minimum number of people, it costs a whopping $150 per person, and for the maximum group capacity of 50 people, it costs $75 per person.

If you're just starting out exploring the paranormal, it might be better to participate in cheaper hunts before tackling the Rapids Theatre.

EXPERIENCE:
Theatre/Ghost Hunt

OPEN TO THE PUBLIC:
Yes

HANDICAP ACCESSIBLE:
Yes

Important Info:
Box Office Hours of Operation:
Wednesday-Saturday:
12:00-5:00pm
Contact:
(716) 205-8925

RED COACH INN

2 Buffalo Avenue, Niagara Falls, New York, 14303
43.084189°, -79.063025°
www.redcoach.com

Niagara Falls was declared the Honeymoon Capital of the World right around the time that the Red Coach Inn opened its doors on the shores of the mighty Niagara River.

The original owners, William Schoellkopf and Charles Peabody, spared no expense when constructing the Inn. They built it in the architectural Tudor style, fashioned after the Bell Inn in England (which also happens to be haunted). The Inn was open for business in 1923 and, according to legend, the Red Coach Inn's most famous guest checked into the hotel in 1925.

There are several competing stories in regards to the hotel's most famous ghost, simply known as The Bride. Some legends say that the bride and groom committed suicide on the night of their wedding. The other claim (and far more popular among the wait staff of the restaurant on the lower floor) is much more grisly, involving a violent murder with a candlestick. Either way, a young bride died while staying in the Victoria Suite, and she's been haunting the third floor ever since.

As seen on *Celebrity Ghost Stories* episode 69.

If you don't get a chance to stay in the Victoria Suite (which will cost you over $300 a night) to see the infamous Bride, there are other tales surrounding the boutique hotel and restaurant. They may not be tales of murder via candlestick, but it might still make it worth your while to check-in and pay around $200 a night for the less extravagant rooms. Guests staying in the hotel have experienced the sound of phantom footsteps as well as music playing softly. Ghostly images appear in photographs, and jewelry sometimes moves across tables in many of the suites.

TIP: If you'd like a view of the Niagara River while spending the night, request a room on the second or third floor.

If you're not looking to check into one of the elegantly furnished rooms, there are still plenty of places for you to check out in the restaurant. Choose to sit in the Grill Room with its stone fireplace, the patio in the summer, or the Rapids Room which offers incredible views of the Niagara River. This award-winning restaurant offers breakfast, lunch, and dinner for both locals and tourists as well as a few spirits from the bottle. Might I recommend the Red Coach Punch, a rum-based cocktail that will transport you to the Caribbean even in the middle of our awful winters?

The Red Coach Inn isn't going out of its way to advertise its haunting. But if you ask any member of the wait staff in the restaurant, they will have stories to share with you. Whether or not they believe in The Bride, you'll find that most of them tend to avoid the Victoria Suite and the entire third floor for that matter.

EXPERIENCE:

Restaurant/Bar/Hotel

OPEN TO THE PUBLIC:

Yes

HANDICAP ACCESSIBLE:

Partial.
Finedon Room is accessible and available to book.

Important Info:
Restaurant Hours of Operation:
Open daily for breakfast, lunch, and dinner, except for Christmas Day.
Contact:
(716) 282-1459

RIVIERA THEATRE

67 Webster Street, North Tonawanda, New York, 14120
43.023586°, -78.876866°
www.rivieratheatre.org

One of the anchors of North Tonawanda and the core of the entertainment district of Webster Street is the Riviera Theatre. Aside from being a part of Buffalo's vast and diverse theatre scene, it is also home to the Mighty Wurlitzer: one of a few still active pipe organs in the country.

The 1,140 seat theatre was built in 1926 and welcomed vaudeville acts and screened silent films (the first one ever shown was *Upstage* starring Norma Shearer). During the Great Depression, it was sold to Shea's Theatre Co., and since then it has changed hands a multitude of times. Over the years, it's hosted dance recitals and community theatre productions, shown movies on Saturday mornings, and today it presents various musical acts that tour the country.

The Riviera isn't only home to the Wurlitzer organ and impressive French crystal chandelier. It is also the eternal home to a little spirit, lovingly known as Mary.

The stories surrounding the young woman tell of a tragic accident that occurred on the stage. Before there were the safety measures that exist today, a sandbag fell from a stage rig and came crashing down on Mary, killing her right where she stood center stage.

Since then, Mary has made herself known in different ways to volunteers and patrons. People hear noises from the balcony, and a ghostly apparition of the young woman has been seen watching performers from the seats. Items throughout the theatre—from tools to props—have also gone missing and have even moved on their own. Of course, all of these things only occur when Mary feels that it's time to clean her beloved theatre.

TIP: Look to each side of the stage. It's there you'll find the chambers where the Wurlitzer's pipes are hidden.

No one knows precisely who Mary was or when she died, but it's safe to say that she loves the theatre just as much as the volunteers keeping the lights on. And she'll be around, reminding them of her presence for years to come.

EXPERIENCE:
Theatre

OPEN TO THE PUBLIC:
Yes

HANDICAP ACCESSIBLE:
Partial. No elevator to the balcony.

Important Info:
The Riviera's busy schedule is always changing. For an updated list of events and acts, visit their website.

THIRTY MILE POINT LIGHTHOUSE

Lower Lake Road, Golden Hill State Park, Barker, New York, 14012
43.374890°, -78.486049°
www.parks.ny.gov/parks/143/details.aspx

The land surrounding Thirty Mile Point Lighthouse is extremely isolated from the rest of Western New York. Today, it is situated in Golden Hill State Park. Long before a lighthouse even stood on the shores of Lake Ontario, the land (or rather, the water) was wrought with misfortune. Thirty Mile Point is not a guiding light to a safe harbor, but rather, a warning to mariners against shoals and sandbars. The lighthouse was only constructed in 1875, almost a century after the most tragic shipwreck in the area (out of at least four recorded).

The *HMS Ontario* was leaving Fort Niagara for Montreal on Halloween night (of course) in 1790. Onboard were 88 passengers and $15,000 in gold and silver. The vessel was caught in a storm, and when the *Ontario* sank, there were no survivors. Oh, and the gold fell to the bottom of Lake Ontario (valued at nearly $275,000 today, so I'd say it's time to bust out your SCUBA equipment).

Constructed in 1875, its light was first lit in 1876 and it safely guided ships along the southern shore of Lake Ontario until the 1950s. By 1958, the treacherous sandbar had diminished, making Thirty Mile Point Lighthouse obsolete. She was officially decommissioned on December 17, 1958.

> **TIP:** Lighthouse tours are available for only $1.

Today, the lighthouse and keeper's cottage are part of the Golden Hill State Park along with 50 other campsites and yurts. For those looking for a thrill along the waters of Lake Ontario, the lighthouse is available to rent. I say "thrill" because there is a guestbook inside the lighthouse filled with people's paranormal experiences while staying there.

The #1 claim is of people capturing orbs of light in photographs. Of course, the age-old debate of whether this proves the existence of ghosts or the need to invest in dusting spray makes this not the most impressive claim. But the stories don't stop there. Both employees and visitors report the sound of children running and laughing. Footsteps are heard pacing up and down the empty halls. Doors slam shut and the TV has the bad habit of turning on and off all on its own. People have even reported the sensation of someone sitting on the edge of the bed while they're trying to sleep.

In 2006, a psychic medium visited the lighthouse and claimed that the space is haunted by no less than 24 spirits, including a former keeper. Visitors to the lighthouse have reported seeing an older man dressed as a lighthouse keeper with many spotting him in the kitchen of the cottage.

If haunted hotels are passé and you're looking to up your haunted overnight stay game, why not consider booking the old lighthouse? Reservations can be made through Reserve America. A night will set you back $200, but it holds up to six of your bravest friends.

There are no reports of any negativity coming from this haunt, so you'll likely have a good night's sleep. That is unless one of the passengers lost on the *HMS Ontario* show up and tell you where you can find a boatload of cash (pun intended) at the bottom of Lake Ontario.

EXPERIENCE:
Landmark

OPEN TO THE PUBLIC:
Yes

HANDICAP ACCESSIBLE:
No

Important Info:
You can reserve the lighthouse cottage (or a campsite or yurt) through Reserve America:

www.parks.ny.gov/parks/143/details.aspx

Admission:

Park entrance fee is $6 per car.

TONAWANDA ISLAND GIANTS

Tonawanda Island, North Tonawanda, New York, 14120
43.028161°, -78.88248°

Centuries before European settlers arrived in Western New York, the Seneca inhabited Tonawanda Island. During their time on the small island off the shore of North Tonawanda, the indigenous people erected a burial mound about 10 feet tall.

> **FUN FACT:** Mounds found in Bougon, France date back to 4500BCE, making them some of the oldest in western European culture.

Burial mounds are nothing out of the ordinary. They've appeared throughout human history all over the world. From the cairns in Great Britain and Viking burial mounds in Scandinavia to the ancient civilizations along the horn of Africa, mounds go hand in hand with humanity. However, it's what was buried inside the Tonawanda Island mound that has perplexed historians, cryptozoologists, and paranormal investigators over the years.

According to legend, when Stephen White built Beechwater in the mid-19th Century, he tore down the mound and unearthed two skeletons that could only be described as giants. In fact, they were measured at eight feet tall.

But just like the mounds, giants are not nearly as rare an occurrence as one might think. As far back as ancient times, there have been tales of giants (the most famous story being that of David and Goliath from the Bible). There have even been several archaeological discoveries over the years, unearthing skeletons that seem larger than life. In 1991, the first complete giant skeleton was discovered in Rome, and others from Poland and Egypt have been reported along with the thousands of claims throughout North America.

Many historians attribute these giant skeletons to the aptly named disease, gigantism, a condition that begins during childhood when a pituitary gland malfunctions, causing extreme growth. It's a rare disease, leading some researchers to believe that not all the skeletons unearthed are humans suffering from gigantism. The bizarre skulls don't hurt their argument either.

If the early reports are true, the two skulls pulled from the mound on Tonawanda Island were said to have "protruding lower jaws and [a] canine forehead." Some believe this could be an evolutionary "missing link" such as Gigantopithecus, a now extinct primate that existed until about 100,000 years ago (give or take a day). However, evidence of Gigantopithecus has only been found in what is now India, Vietnam, China, and Indonesia, which rules out that theory. Others use these archaeological finds to try to prove the existence of Bigfoot.

Whether you believe in giants and Bigfoot, or not, there is no denying that something weird was once present on the otherwise quiet Tonawanda Island.

Today, the island has been taken over almost entirely by feral cats, a marina, and the Shores restaurant where you can sit and watch the sunset, oblivious to the giants that were once buried right beneath your feet.

EXPERIENCE:

Burial Ground

OPEN TO THE PUBLIC:

Partial. The restaurant is open, the marina is not.

HANDICAP ACCESSIBLE:

Yes

VAN HORN MANSION

2165 Lockport-Olcott Road, Burt, New York, 14028
43.311885°, -78.714361°
www.newfanehistoricalsociety.com

The Georgian style mansion was built in 1823 by James Van Horn Sr., but today it is most known for the ghost of Malinda Niles Van Horn.

Malinda married James Van Horn Jr. in 1836, and after just one year of wedded bliss, Malinda died. Her cause of death is still unknown. She was buried in the rose garden, where her tombstone can be seen today. Perhaps it was because she died under questionable circumstances or maybe it is because she died at such a young age. Either way, Malinda has made her presence known in the mansion for over 180 years.

Some of the claims tell of Malinda appearing throughout the mansion in a blue dress, particularly in the upper windows. There are even tales of a young woman running from the house and into traffic on the street.

FUN FACT: The mansion was the first brick house in the area.

Malinda doesn't seem to be the only spirit haunting the halls of the beautiful Van Horn Mansion. The maid's bedroom door has been known to open and close on its own as does the attic door. The smell of tobacco comes from the smoking room on the second floor, and there are also claims of someone looking out the kitchen window when the building is supposed to be empty. Construction crews that were hired to help restore the home claimed to see faces watching them from the windows. And psychic mediums have confirmed the presence of restless spirits wandering through the Van Horn family home.

FUN FACT: The stained glass skylight in the foyer was imported from Paris.

Today, the Newfane Historical Society owns the Van Horn Mansion. Open on Sundays from April to November, the historical society also offers tours, tea, and ghost hunts.

EXPERIENCE:

Museum/Landmark/
Ghost Hunt

OPEN TO THE PUBLIC:

Yes

HANDICAP ACCESSIBLE:

Partial.
No elevator to second floor or attic.

Important Info:
Hours of Operation:
April-November:
Sundays
1:00-4:00pm
July-August:
Sundays and
Wednesdays
1:00-4:00pm
Contact:
(716) 778-7197

Admission:

$5 for the tour (free for members).

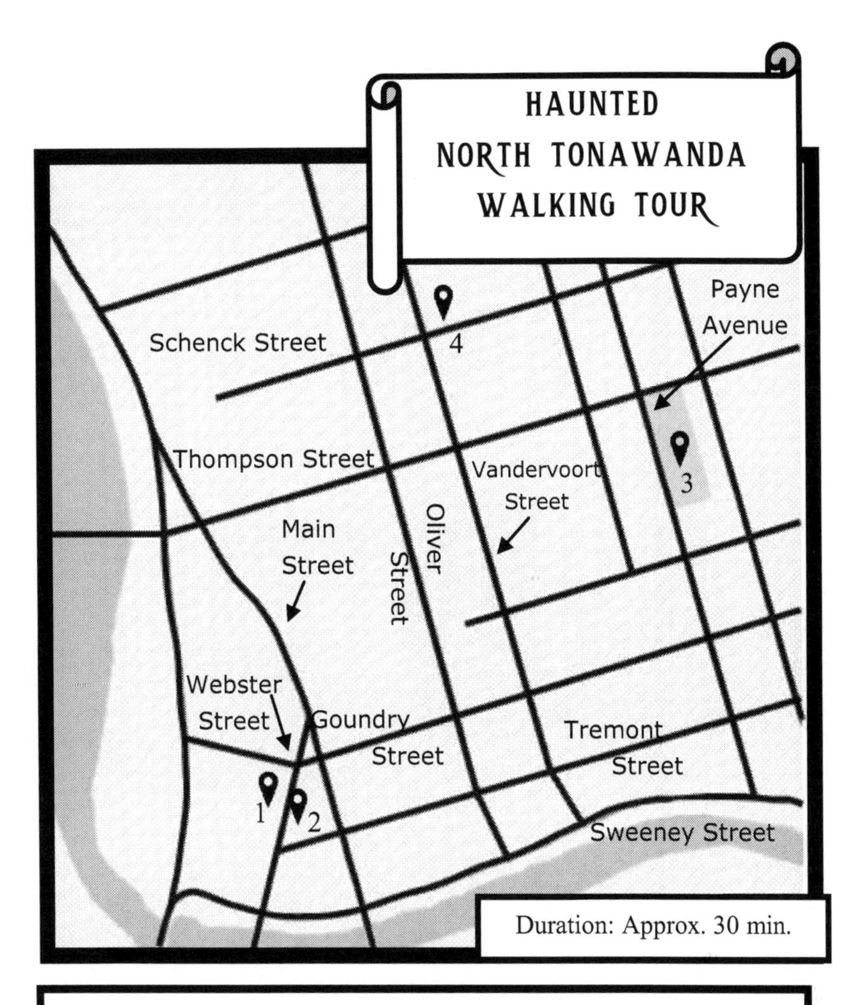

Begin on Webster Street. Lock yourself in the escape room or eat at Canal Club—both are inside the **Dick Block (1)**. Just across the street is the home of the Mighty Wurlitzer organ, the **Riviera Theatre (2)**. Before you journey deeper into North Tonawanda, stop at Pulp 716 for a bubble tea or a signature hot chocolate. Now that you have sustenance, make your way to Payne Avenue. For a scenic route along Tonawanda Creek, take Sweeney Street. For a more direct (and far less appealing) path, take Tremont or Goundry Street. Turn left onto Payne Avenue and **Sweeney Cemetery (3)** will be on your right side. Stop to pay your respects to Aunt Hannah before walking two more blocks to Schenck Street. Turn left and eventually the towering white **Ghostlight Theatre (4)** will be on your right. To finish your tour, head inside for a performance or journey a bit further to Oliver Street and enjoy a pint at Witter's.

ERIE

COUNTY

ERIE COUNTY

Even though Erie was one of the last counties formed in Western New York (founded in only 1821), it is now the home of the second-largest city in New York State. Named for Lake Erie and the Erie tribe that lived in the region before 1654, the first towns formed in Erie County were Clarence and Willink (eventually renamed East Aurora). In 1861, a hamlet within Lancaster seceded from the Union and sent $5 to the Confederate Army. They did not rejoin the Union until 1946.

1. Aurora Player's Pavilion
2. Curtis Hall
3. Delaware Road
4. Dos on the Lake
5. Elmlawn Cemetery
6. Erie County Home
7. Eternal Flame Falls
8. Former Amherst Synagogue
9. Former Holiday Inn
10. Gardenier House
11. The Globe Restaurant
12. Goodleburg Cemetery
13. Hull Family House
14. Lackawanna Basilica
15. Lancaster Opera House
16. Lindbergh Elementary
17. Murder Creek
18. Mystery Goo
19. New Era Field
20. Old Main Cemetery
21. Pigman Road
22. Roycroft Inn & Campus
23. Snyder Bar & Grill
24. Vidler's
25. Western House
26. Whitehaven Cemetery

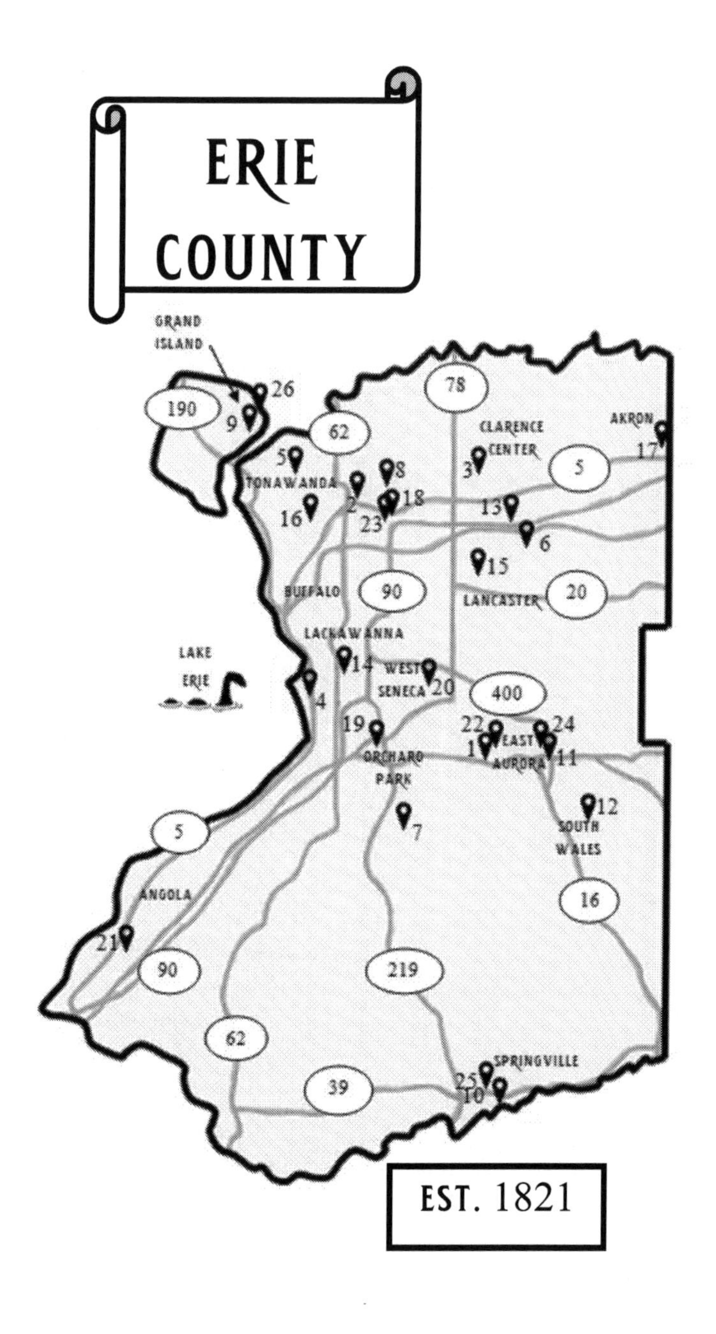
ERIE
COUNTY
GRAND ISLAND
190
26
9
62
78
CLARENCE CENTER
AKRON
17
5
3
5
TONAWANDA
8
2
18
16
23
13
6
15
BUFFALO
90
LANCASTER
20
LACKAWANNA
LAKE ERIE
14
WEST SENECA
20
4
400
19
22
24
EAST AURORA
1
11
ORCHARD PARK
12
SOUTH WALES
7
5
ANGOLA
16
21
90
219
62
SPRINGVILLE
25
39
10
EST. 1821

AURORA PLAYERS PAVILION

480 Prospect Avenue, East Aurora, New York, 14052
42.763509°, -78.616810°
www.auroraplayers.org

Consider this your official warning: when you visit East Aurora, there is no escaping the Roycrofters. From the font you see on most of the village's signs to the quotes on the garbage cans, and even the Roycroft itself, it should be no surprise that the Aurora Players Pavilion was once (and sometimes still is) called the Roycroft Pavilion.

Built in 1903 as a gift from the Roycroft to the town of East Aurora, it was the site of Elbert and Alice Hubbard's funeral services after their tragic death on the Lusitania in 1915 (spoiler alert). Today, it is home to one of the nation's oldest community theatre groups: the Aurora Players.

Founded in 1934, the Aurora Players moved into the Roycroft Pavilion in 1941 and they have been performing there ever since. Offering three productions a year including a drama, a comedy, and a musical, the Aurora Players provide another thing for the Western New York theatre scene: a ghost.

Props will move on their own and disappear entirely. Lights will turn on and off on their own, and the curtain has also been known to open and close when no one else is around. But the most common report is of a female apparition.

No one has ever given her a name, but performers have seen her often enough to come up with a relatively good description of her. She is a middle-aged woman, with dark hair, and she seems to enjoy sitting and watching the performances of various productions. She isn't frightening, but cast members report feeling strange when rehearsing and performing, usually meaning that the unknown entity is watching from somewhere nearby.

TIP: A free show is offered in the summer months at the outdoor stage.

The Aurora Players Pavilion is situated in Hamlin Park just down the road from the Roycroft Inn and Campus (don't say I didn't warn you).

EXPERIENCE:
Theatre

OPEN TO THE PUBLIC:
Yes

HANDICAP ACCESSIBLE:
Yes

Important Info:
Performances Include:
Two Plays
One Musical
Thursday-Saturday:
8:00pm
Sunday:
2:30pm
Contact:
(716) 687-6727

Admission:

Adults: $15
Seniors (62+): $14
Students (18 and under): $14

BESSIE

Lake Erie
42.867161°, -78.895483°

Every region of America deserves at least one good cryptid, and Western New York is no exception.

Bessie AKA South Bay Bessie AKA the Lake Erie Monster has been lurking in the waters of (you guessed it) Lake Erie for centuries.

> **FUN FACT:** Monster serpents have been part of folklore for millennia with the Hydra of Ancient Greece and Jörmungandr of Norse mythology.

The very first reported sighting of the lesser-known cousin of the Loch Ness Monster was in 1793 by a boat captain, and she has been making waves ever since

She is described as being snake-like, running about 30-40 feet long, and dark gray or black.

There have been sightings of the elusive beast as recently as 1993, but it's been over 100 years since Bessie was seen close to home.

On May 5, 1896, four eyewitnesses watched the monster swimming just off the shore near Crystal Beach for over 45 minutes. They described it as a 30-foot long creature with a dog-shaped head and a pointy tail. After splashing around in the water for nearly an hour, the monster dove down and disappeared beneath the waves.

This sighting so close to Western New York is an exciting one for believers of the mysterious Bessie. Nearly every sighting of the cryptid has been reported in the southwest section of Lake Erie near Ohio.

> **FUN FACT:** Bessie was first named in *Creature Chronicles* #14 in 1991.

At 240 miles, Lake Erie is 10 times the size of Loch Ness, making it nearly impossible to ever find a shred of proof of the monster's existence. Despite virtually no evidence aside from eyewitness accounts dating back hundreds of years, the legend of Bessie lives on and doesn't show any sign of dying out any time soon.

EXPERIENCE:

Cryptid Sighting

CURTIS HALL

4380 Main Street, Amherst, New York, 14226
42.964472°, -78.791333°
www.daemen.edu

One of the many colleges sprinkled throughout Western New York, Daemen College, began in only 1947 as an all-girls school, known initially as Rosary Hill College. Men joined in the 1960s, and by 1976, the name was officially changed to Daemen in honor of the Sisters of St. Francis of Penance and Christian Charity founder, Mother Magdalene Daemen.

> **FUN FACT:** The sisters are not cloistered nuns but are active in the world usually working as teachers.

The Coplon family built Curtis Hall in 1918, and despite its brief history, it has a colorful haunting.

According to the legend of Daemen College's ghost story, Joseph and David Coplon were living together in what is now Curtis Hall with their parents. After a fierce argument, the two brothers parted ways, each of them committing suicide by hanging themselves unbeknownst to the other. Today, their restless spirits are said to haunt the office building. Those visiting Curtis Hall report hearing voices in the attic and seeing books fly from their shelves, aimed directly at people.

There are some conflicting stories when it comes to this haunting. Many people claim it wasn't the Coplon brothers, but rather the Waite brothers. The dispute goes further to say that the two brothers didn't kill themselves, only one—George Waite. According to records, though, the Crouch-Waite Mansion was home to George Waite before being sold to the Sisters of St. Francis, which today is known as Rosary Hall.

The different stories, don't take away from the eerie feeling people report when they visit Curtis Hall.

EXPERIENCE:

School

OPEN TO THE PUBLIC:

Partial

DELAWARE ROAD

Delaware Road, Clarence Center, New York, 14032
43.058114°, -78.622808°

Not nearly as famous as Angola's Pigman Road, Delaware Road has just as many urban legends surrounding it, some even more disturbing than the killer butcher, the Pigman (if you're sick of me alluding to it, you can skip ahead to page 291 to finally read about Western New York's most haunted road).

> ~~**FUN**~~ **FACT:** The Ku Klux Klan has had a presence in WNY since the 1920s and has somehow managed to survive into the 21st Century.

According to local stories, Western New York members of the Ku Klux Klan would meet in the woods surrounding Delaware Road. There's a reason why: Delaware Road is hardly a road. With no lines and no lights shining down to show the way, not many people venture down there at night. Except for thrill-seekers and those curious about the tales surrounding the stretch of road, that is.

The most famous claim surrounding the Clarence Center road is that of an older man carrying a lantern. Some think he was a member of the KKK and was sent to protect the secret meetings. Whether he was part of the local gang or not doesn't matter: he appears to weary travelers in the middle of the night, crossing the road with his lantern. Sometimes he's alone and sometimes he's with a little girl. No one knows who the old man or the child might be, and there are even conflicting stories about the girl. Some claim she looks beaten and bloody, and others say she looks perfectly normal as if she was alive.

Others who are brave enough to visit at night have reported seeing phantom headlights appear behind them only to vanish without a trace.

But what makes Delaware Road unique from some other haunted roads in Western New York are the claims of cryptids crossing the street. There is something strange and unusual lurking in the woods of Clarence Center, and it's described as looking like half a horse and half a dog. Of course, there is no physical evidence of this, but that never stopped Bigfoot!

> **FUN FACT:** There are mythical creatures that are half-dog, half-monkey (the shug monkey) and half-man, and half-horse (at least five to be precise), but half-dog and half-horse is a new one.

EXPERIENCE:

Haunted Road

OPEN TO THE PUBLIC:

Yes

HANDICAP ACCESSIBLE:

Yes

DOS ON THE LAKE

3800 Hanover Road, Blasdell, New York, 14219
42.781935°, -78.855088°
www.dos716.com

What is now Dos on the Lake is most commonly known among Western New Yorkers as the Dock at the Bay restaurant. It is one of the oldest buildings in the Buffalo area, some of the sections of the structure dating back to 1804, and many of its paranormal claims are from the War of 1812.

Since it is situated on the shores of Lake Erie, Dos on the Lake—formerly known as Dos Amigos on the Lake, the Dock at the Bay, The Dock, Bay View House, and Willink Hotel—was a prime location during the War of 1812. It may not have seen any action during the war, but it is believed that it was the final stop for many soldiers before they were shipped off to the front lines. With such energy connected to war, trauma, and the classic "final happy moments," Dos on the Lake is filled with paranormal activity.

The most famous ghost story surrounds Captain James Byrd, a soldier during the war, serving under Colonel Perry. According to the legend of "The Captain," Byrd continuously snuck off his ship to rendezvous with his lover in the Willink Hotel. Sadly, their love story did not have a happy ending, and eventually, Byrd was caught, court-marshaled, and executed by firing squad. And it looks like his spirit has never left his beloved hotel.

Although it has transformed from a hotel into a restaurant and experienced multiple name changes over the last 200 years, the ghost of Captain Byrd is still seen and felt on the premises. People report phantom footsteps and objects moving on their own. There is even a full-body apparition of a man in a cloak and a wide-brimmed hat. Many assume that the phantom is that of James Byrd, and he is still referred to as "The Captain."

> **FUN FACT:** Willink was also the name of one of Erie County's oldest towns. It was renamed East Aurora.

Today, Dos on the Lake is one of the best waterfront restaurants on Lake Erie, offering Southern California cuisine and a wide variety of seafood dishes, as well as colorful cocktails including prickly pear margaritas.

But while the spirits are flowing freely in the bar, Dos on the Lake isn't talking about the history of their incredible building, haunted or mundane. I suppose we can drown our sorrows in a margarita flight.

EXPERIENCE:
Restaurant/Bar

OPEN TO THE PUBLIC:
Yes

HANDICAP ACCESSIBLE:
Yes

> **Important Info:**
> Hours of Operation:
> Sunday-Thursday:
> 4:00-9:00pm
> Friday-Saturday:
> 4:00-10:00pm
> Contact:
> (716) 823-8247

ELMLAWN CEMETERY

3939 Delaware Avenue, Kenmore, New York, 14217
42.99305°, -78.86419°
www.elmlawncemetery.com

As cemeteries in Western New York go, Elmlawn is a relatively new addition to the region's hallowed grounds. Established in only 1901, it is a functioning cemetery and crematorium with nearly 45 acres left to expand. It's impossible to drive down Delaware Avenue and not take in its massive size. And while there aren't any famous graves or notable eternal residents, Elmlawn has managed to catch a few ghost stories over the last 100 years.

Drivers making their way down Delaware Avenue report seeing orbs and other flashes of light within the cemetery's grounds, almost always between the hours of midnight and 3:00am.

Elmlawn's most famous paranormal resident isn't just a simple ball of light, however. It's the full-body apparition of a young lady… a bride to be precise.

According to legend, after her wedding in the cemetery's chapel, the young bride was making her way to her carriage when another runaway carriage crashed into her, killing her instantly. Today, people have witnessed the tragic bride trying to run across the street. Many believe that the "Little Chapel in the Elms," which was built in 1903, is that very chapel where this tragic event took place.

While the cemetery doesn't officially acknowledge the existence of their bride, her story adds to the gothic architecture of the Little Chapel and the rolling acres of graves nestled along the busy avenue.

Elmlawn Cemetery is open daily from 8:00am until the ever specific "dusk." Please show the proper respect when visiting, keeping in mind that it is still an active cemetery with funerals occurring and families mourning.

EXPERIENCE:

Cemetery

OPEN TO THE PUBLIC:

Yes

HANDICAP ACCESSIBLE:

Yes

ERIE COUNTY HOME

11580 Walden Avenue, Alden, New York, 14004
42.938680°, -78.554699°

Now almost impossible to access due to a pesky chain-link fence, the Erie County Home was built in 1928. The imposing structure remained open (most recently as a nursing home), until it finally closed its doors for good in 2005, with most of its staff and residents moving to ECMC.

The now-abandoned nursing home is made up of five buildings total and sits on over 150 acres of land along Walden Avenue. Not much has changed over the decades since it opened, aside from the FOR SALE sign now plastered out front.

With large abandoned buildings (and a hospital to boot), there are bound to be a few ghost stories lurking in the empty halls.

According to reports from when the nursing home was still in operation, the third floor is haunted by an unidentified man. He doesn't seem to interact with the living too much because aside from the apparition, there isn't too much activity.

Since the Erie County Home closed down in 2005, there have also been reports made by local residents of mysterious lights coming from inside the abandoned building. Of course, there's no way to know if these lights are a sign of paranormal activity or curious teenagers hoping to stumble upon a good ghost story.

FUN FACT: In 2003, an auction sold everything in the building including a Steinway piano and an organ.

In 2013, plans were announced to demolish the expansive complex over the next five to 10 years. However, not much progress was made, and in July 2018, the FOR SALE sign went up. The Erie County Home could be repurposed just like Hotel Henry, but until a buyer appears, it continues to sit empty.

The Erie County Home is an impressive sight. But keep in mind to stay on the correct side of the chain-link fence. It is the wisest and safest way (not to mention the only legal way) to experience the beautiful but abandoned building, home to almost a century of memories, asbestos, and a nameless man still pacing the third floor.

EXPERIENCE:

Landmark

OPEN TO THE PUBLIC:

No

ETERNAL FLAME FALLS

Eternal Flame Hiking Trail, Orchard Park, New York, 14127
42.701046°, -78.750279°

Western New York is home to some pretty incredible natural sights and wonders—and not just Niagara Falls. This region is blessed with scenic drives, natural beauty, and impressive earthworks thanks to the glaciers of the Ice Age. But one of our many hiking trails in the area has scientists scratching their heads… and it all has to do with a tiny dancing flame.

Eternal Flame Falls is located on the Shale Creek Reserve (part of Chestnut Ridge Park) just outside of Orchard Park. The hiking can be a bit rugged and dangerous. But if you manage to make it to the waterfall, you'll be treated to one of nature's little peculiarities: the eternal flame.

Hidden behind a waterfall, it's believed the flame was lit by Native Americans thousands of years ago. Now at first, there doesn't seem to be anything too bizarre about this. There are naturally fueled fires found all around the world. The most famous one is the Darvaza gas crater (more colorfully known as the Door to Hell) in Turkmenistan which has continuously been burning since 1971. However, there is something peculiar about our little eternal flame: no one can explain how it's there. According to scientists, the rocks at

> **TIP:** To guarantee you see the eternal flame, bring a lighter with you in case you have to reignite it.

Eternal Flame Falls should be near the boiling point of water to break down carbon molecules in the shale to create the natural gas. However, the rocks surrounding the flame are nowhere near that hot (but still hot, so please don't touch them).

This unexplained phenomenon is accompanied by a few ghost stories too. While standing near the flame, many hikers claim that if you stand still and listen carefully, you can hear the sound of chanting, humming, and drums somewhere in the distance. Those foolish enough to visit at night report seeing shadow figures darting around the flame and also on top of the waterfall. [Note: I do not recommend visiting Eternal Flame Falls at night.]

Despite Eternal Flame Falls once being an obscure attraction in Western New York, it has become a popular hiking trail for locals. While visiting, please be respectful of your fellow hikers and nature. Don't litter, don't venture off the trails (especially in spring when flooding is more prevalent), and leave no trace.

> **TIP:** For a longer hike, park on Seufert Road instead of the parking lot (see above photo).

EXPERIENCE:

Natural Wonder/Hiking Trail

OPEN TO THE PUBLIC:

Yes

HANDICAP ACCESSIBLE:

No

FORMER AMHERST SYNAGOGUE

504 Frankhauser Road, Amherst, New York, 14221
42.98458°, -78.788379°

Though it was only built in the 1980s, the old Amherst Synagogue has managed to create quite a name for itself among Western New York paranormal investigators. The building, itself, has a unique design reminiscent of the quirky decade it was constructed in. Yet most people who dare to visit it after dark claim it is one of the scariest places in the world. The synagogue (well, a church now), itself isn't haunted, but the undeveloped field behind it is another story entirely.

According to the lore of the former synagogue, three men died while the structure was being built. A wall collapsed on top of them, killing them instantly. And those three tragic deaths aren't the only bloodshed this place has seen. Legend says that the land was once a dumping ground for a child killer in the area, and the paranormal activity seems to support this claim.

Ghostly images have appeared in photos over the years, and people exploring the field surrounding the building have reported being touched and hearing howling. Shadow people and full-body apparitions are seen in the darkness as well, including the figure of a man. Some reports claim that he is carrying an ax, while others say he is moving a body. But everyone agrees that the restless spirits of children are haunting the fields surrounding the holy place of worship.

The former synagogue has gone through several hands over the years, and as of 2012, it is the home of Restoration Church. Lucky for them, all of the activity is behind their building and not inside.

> ~~FUN~~ **FACT:** The field and wooded area behind the church is supposedly where the children's graves are located.

The former Amherst Synagogue, now Restoration Church, is located on Frankhauser Road in the middle of a neighborhood. Because it is a place of worship (and because trespassing is frowned upon), please be respectful when you visit, and acquire the proper permission before heading over to the haunted field.

EXPERIENCE:

Church

OPEN TO THE PUBLIC:

No (unless you want to sit in on a church service)

FORMER HOLIDAY INN

100 Whitehaven Road, Grand Island, New York, 14072
43.021633°, -78.896112°
www.radisson.com/grand-island-hotel-ny-14072/usagrny

The former Holiday Inn on Grand Island is one of Western New York's most famous haunted locations. Built in 1973, it has been called Holiday Inn, Byblos, and today, the Radisson (though there's no guarantee that this name will stick either). And ever since it opened its doors to guests, there have been paranormal claims. The most famous ghost haunting the hotel on the shores of the Niagara River is little Tanya.

Tanya has been making herself known in the hotel for decades now. She is a playful, noisy spirit who enjoys jumping on beds and running through the halls. Her favorite haunt is the swimming pool where she's been seen and heard many times. Her wet footprints were even left behind when the pool was under construction. As if all of those claims aren't enough to whet your appetite, many believe that Tanya was captured in a photograph in 1994 (see image), making it a must on any paranormal buff's bucket list.

> **TIP:** Room 422 is supposedly the most active room in the hotel.

Multiple guests over the years have reported seeing a little girl in their rooms. Sometimes she is standing at the foot of their bed while they sleep, and other times she plays with their children. Doors lock on their own and glasses of water fly through the air. The elevators will stop on floors even though no one pressed that particular button, and others have heard their names called out by a little girl. Many staff members were skeptics before working at the hotel, but little Tanya has managed to make a believer out of them.

Photo courtesy of the Toy family

No one knows who Tanya is. According to legend, Tanya is the daughter of John Nice. Nice was the supervisor of a logging community in the Whitehaven Settlement on Grand Island in the mid-19th Century. The legend claims that there was a fire in the Nice family's home, killing little Tanya.

A dramatic fire and the tragic death of a little girl makes for a great story. However, according to the Grand Island Historical Society, there is no proof of a fire or Tanya. Yes, John Nice did have 10 children, but none of them were named Tanya, and none of them died in a fire. Some may be disappointed, but that adds to the mystery of Tanya and the haunting at the former Holiday Inn.

For people who don't relish the idea of being kept up all night by a playful spirit, you can check out Currents. This on-site restaurant offers delicious American cuisine and even a breakfast buffet during their peak season. More importantly, Happy Hour runs from 5:00-7:00pm Monday through Friday.

TIP: All rooms have a balcony, so be sure to request a river side room to sit and enjoy (with a glass of wine).

EXPERIENCE:

Restaurant/Bar/Hotel

OPEN TO THE PUBLIC:

Yes

HANDICAP ACCESSIBLE:

Yes

Contact:
(716) 773-1111

GARDENIER HOUSE

105 East Main Street, Springville, New York, 14141
42.507945°, -78.663542°

It might be hard to believe, but the history surrounding the Gardenier House is almost more interesting than its haunting!

What is now a multi-family home was originally built in 1876 by John P. Myers. Better known as JP Myers, he served in the 104th Regiment New York State Volunteers in the American Civil War. After being captured in the Battle of Gettysburg, Myers was sent to the infamous Andersonville Prison… and lived to tell the tale.

> ~~FUN~~ **FACT:** Of the 45,000 POWs in Andersonville, 13,000 died most commonly from scurvy, diarrhea, and dysentery.

Fast forward to 10 years later, Myers is living happily in the Gardenier House, making his fortune off of buying and selling real estate. But one day, JP Myers left his home telling his wife and coworkers that he was bringing an inheritance to a client. He left town with about $25,000 in cash (that's over $750,000 by today's standards), but Myers never made it to his destination.

He disappeared along with the money. Some think he ran off with the inheritance, while others say he was murdered and robbed. Whatever the truth may be, no one knows what happened to Myers even to this day.

After JP Myers' disappearance, the house was sold to Isaac Gardenier whom the house is named after. He lived there peacefully enough with his wife, Hattie, and their daughter, Alice. Alice lived in the house until her death in the 1940s. After that, it was transformed into apartments, which is how it has remained until today.

If the drama of the living was colorful in the Gardenier House, you can be darn sure it's technicolor in the afterlife. Many people who move into the apartments don't seem to last very long. Animals don't fare well inside or around the house with many dogs reacting to what appears to be an invisible psychic presence. But most interestingly, people have spotted a young woman in the tower, looking down on the people walking by on the street. Some think she might be Myers' daughter. However, more people suspect that it is Alice, the daughter of Isaac Gardenier, who lived in the house her entire life.

The Gardenier House is a private residence, making it difficult for paranormal investigators to get inside. However, it's a beautiful home to appreciate from the sidewalk, and that's where you're most likely to spot Alice as she stands in the upper window of the tower.

EXPERIENCE:

Private Residence

OPEN TO THE PUBLIC:

No

THE GLOBE RESTAURANT

711 East Main Street, East Aurora, New York, 14052
42.767626°, -78.608202°
www.theglobeea.com

There must be something in the water in East Aurora because this little village is overflowing with paranormal activity and ghost stories. Just down the street from the Roycroft Inn and Campus and around the corner from the Aurora Players Pavilion is East Aurora's longest-running business that has been a part of Main Street for almost 200 years.

Opened in 1824, The Globe was once a general store, a stagecoach stop, a hotel, and today it serves as one of East Aurora's main watering holes. With a colorful history filled with good food and booze, it's no shocker that The Globe is the eternal haunt for some spirits, including the ghost of its former owner.

The paranormal claims coming from 711 East Main Street start in the usual fashion: unexplained noises, tools going missing, and the sense that you're not alone. From there, the reports get a bit more interesting. The two upper floors which are now used for storage and offices are said to be the most haunted with the ghost of a small child seen running around, playing with a ball. The sound of

> **TIP:** The current owner is a former pastry chef so save room for dessert!

music can be heard from the third floor, which was once a speakeasy and now all but abandoned. Molly Flynn, the current owner, has reported hearing a woman humming on the second floor, but only if she is entirely alone in the building. When Flynn mentioned this to the previous owner, he confirmed it, saying that the singing woman also haunted Victor Balthasar, the man who owned the place until his death in 1975.

FUN FACT: Stories claim there are tunnels beneath The Globe leftover from the Underground Railroad. Sadly, that is simply a rumor started by a previous owner.

Speaking of Victor Balthasar…

The most famous ghost of The Globe isn't lurking up on the top two floors or even down in the basement. This ghost has been spotted so many times the staff recognize him as Balthasar and have dubbed the apparition Old Vic. You'll find the former owner wandering through the bar and dining room, keeping an eye on things, reveling in the ongoing success of The Globe.

You likely won't see the spirits running around the upper floors or in the basement—you need special access for those two spots. However, for just the cost of a pint of beer, you might catch a glimpse of Old Vic on the main floor. While you're sitting looking for the ghostly owner, why not order a cup of The Globe's famous French onion soup or one of Molly Flynn's 711 cookies?

If you can't quite afford the Roycroft Inn and you're looking for a place to eat in East Aurora with some history and a whole lot of ghost stories, The Globe is an excellent choice. It's got a cozy environment, cold beer, and a few spirits thrown in too.

EXPERIENCE:

Restaurant/Bar

OPEN TO THE PUBLIC:

Yes

HANDICAP ACCESSIBLE:

No

Important Info:
Hours of Operation:
Sunday:
3:00-8:00pm
Monday:
11:00am-10:00pm
Tuesday:
Closed
Wednesday-Thursday:
11:00am-10:00pm
Friday-Saturday:
11:00am-11:00pm
Contact:
(716) 652-4221

GOODLEBURG CEMETERY

12119 Goodleburg Road, South Wales, New York, 14139
42.714109°, -78.537602°

Goodleburg Cemetery has a reputation throughout Western New York as being quite possibly the most haunted place in the entire region. It's had a dark past throughout its 200-year history, making it a favorite spot for both ghost hunters and those merely curious about Western New York's most infamous cemetery.

No longer in use, the cemetery was active from 1811 until 1927 and is the final resting place for two veterans: one from the Civil War and another from the American Revolution. It remained relatively quiet and undisturbed until the late 1990s when paranormal tales began to spread surrounding the village cemetery. Sadly, since then, it has become victim to vandals, rowdy teenagers, and ghost hunters leading to many of the graves' destruction and even the tragic death of a paranormal investigator in 2003.

Death seems to surround Goodleburg, much more than your average cemetery. The morbid history of Goodleburg began in the early 19th Century in a small shack that once stood near the entrance. It was there that a local doctor performed illegal abortions on young women. The story claims that the doctor would take the aborted fetuses and bury them in unmarked graves. And when the operations were botched, and the young mothers died in the process, he would dump their bodies in the nearby pond.

It seems both the mothers and their babies continue to haunt the old cemetery. Visitors have reported seeing the mothers wandering through the graves before vanishing into thin air. Babies are heard crying and even seen crawling along the ground. Sometimes people see a low hanging fog, and they also hear the sound of faint music playing somewhere in the distance. And it isn't just the mothers and babies felt, seen, and heard at Goodleburg—the doctor has been spotted as well. Supposedly, on the first Friday of every month, the doctor can be seen hanging from the very tree that he hanged himself from all those years ago.

If you're expecting an intimidating and haunting cemetery, ye be warned: Goodleburg has had a rough time in recent years. Vandals are destroying headstones and leaving broken bottles and trash all around the haunted hill. There are even bullet holes in the signs surrounding the hallowed ground. It is still a must-visit for any paranormal or history enthusiast (the Revolutionary War veteran's grave is impressive to see), but don't build up your expectations too much.

> **TIP:** The cemetery is located at a blind curve. It's safest to visit during the day.

EXPERIENCE:
Cemetery

OPEN TO THE PUBLIC:
Yes

HANDICAP ACCESSIBLE:
No

HULL FAMILY HOUSE

5976 Genesee Street, Lancaster, New York, 14086
42.944981°, -78.622606°
www.hullfamilyhome.com

It's the only surviving stone house from the 19th Century in Erie County, and it has seen a majority of Western New York's history through the centuries.

Revolutionary War veteran, Warren Hull, and his wife, Polly, migrated from Killingworth, Connecticut to the wilderness of Western New York in 1804. By 1810, the Hull Family House was completed for the Hulls and their 12 children. During the years the Hull family lived in the Federal-style home, they witnessed the War of 1812 and the construction of the Erie Canal, as well as early pioneer life, the Abolitionist movement, and the Underground Railroad.

Today, several members of the Hull family are buried in the family cemetery just 800 feet behind the house. Sometimes also known as the Wheelock Cemetery and the Wolf Cemetery, most of the Hull children lived and died in Lancaster.

Today, the Hull Family House opens its doors to visitors for special events throughout the year. It's here that guests can witness the 200-year-old house with its original woodwork, fireplaces, windows, and stairways. Special events include tea, animal adoption events, historical tours, and in June 2019, it hosted its first ghost hunt.

Strangely enough, with such a long history, a cemetery on-site, and ghost hunts, there aren't too many ghost stories surrounding the Hull House. For paranormal enthusiasts looking for some good, juicy stories, this might be a bit of a bummer. Here's hoping with an increase in investigations, we get a better idea of the haunting of the Hull Family House. In the meantime, we can sit back and enjoy the history of the place… that's impressive in and of itself.

EXPERIENCE:

Landmark/Ghost Hunt

OPEN TO THE PUBLIC:

Yes

HANDICAP ACCESSIBLE:

No

Contact:
(716) 681-6451

LACKAWANNA BASILICA

767 Ridge Road, Buffalo, New York, 14218
42.825429°, -78.823147°
www.ourladyofvictory.org

If you grew up in the Catholic Church, you've probably been threatened with being sent to Father Baker's at least a few times. Of course, Father Baker's incredible Our Lady of Victory National Shrine and Basilica hasn't always towered over Ridge Road. Saint Patrick's Parish once stood there, but after it was destroyed in a fire, Father Baker opened the basilica in 1925. Now the basilica may not be exactly haunted. But I think we can admit that some supernatural things have occurred there in the past.

According to legend, Father Baker recreated the miracle of the "fish and loaves" and managed to feed droves of hungry people during the Great Depression. He was known to have birds flock to him, and he healed the blind and restored sight. There has been a multitude of miracles associated with Father Baker, though the Catholic Church hasn't officially acknowledged any of them. Because of this, Father Baker is still not recognized as a saint. But that doesn't stop local members of the church from admiring the man who created a hospital, opened a boys' orphanage, and managed to help countless people throughout Western New York.

Possibly the most intriguing story surrounding the mysterious Father Baker was when his remains were moved from Holy Cross Cemetery to the basilica in 1999. When his body was moved to the basilica's Grotto Shrine to Our Lady of Lourdes, three vials of his blood were still liquid more than 60 years after his death. Many of Father Baker's faithful followers consider this one more reason why the Catholic Church should canonize the man.

FUN FACT: Using prayer and a vision of Our Lady, Father Baker led a procession to a natural gas well that was buried at 1,137 feet, an extreme depth. This is thought to be one of his many miracles.

There are no reports of apparitions, cold spots, or unexplained noises in the basilica. Many may argue that the Lackawanna Basilica shouldn't be considered haunted… but there is something strange happening there. Perhaps it's haunted. Maybe it's blessed. Either way, you have to visit Father Baker's beloved basilica to fully understand that there is something special—and possibly supernatural—about the Lackawanna Basilica.

EXPERIENCE:
Church

OPEN TO THE PUBLIC:
Yes

HANDICAP ACCESSIBLE:
Yes

Important Info:
Hours of Operation:
Daily:
6:00am-9:00pm
Tours:
Sundays:
1:00pm and 2:00pm
(except Christmas, Easter, Mother's Day, and Father's Day).
No appointments are necessary for the tours.
Simply meet your guide at the *Tour Begins Here* sign.

LANCASTER OPERA HOUSE

21 Central Avenue, Lancaster, New York, 14086
42.901129°, -78.669983°
www.lancopera.org

The Lancaster Opera House has become a staple among theatres in the Western New York region. It has been the home to dinner theatre productions, concerts, musicals, and plays. Whatever they decide to perform on their stage adds to the theatre's long and colorful history in the heart of downtown Lancaster.

Built in 1897, the opera house acted as both a government building and music hall. Through the 1920s, it hosted musical acts, vaudeville performers, and recitals. By the time the Great Depression rolled into town in the 1930s, it had become a food distribution center. During World War II, it was used as a massive sewing room to make parachutes for the troops.

It wasn't until 1975 that the Lancaster Opera House began to take on a new life with a full restoration that has kept her going well into the 21st Century. But like so many old buildings, once the construction crews arrive to begin their work, they stir up some ghostly energy that hasn't seemed to leave the place over the years.

The most famous ghost in the Lancaster Opera House is that of a man named William. According to legend, William hanged himself somewhere in the building in the 1920s, and his soul has been unable to leave. Today, he acts more like a poltergeist, clearly enjoying playing pranks on people. Most famously, William threw a television across the stage. Talk about a noisy ghost…

Another spirit haunting the halls of the century-old building is a bit more subtle and tends to keep to herself. Volunteers, cast and crew, and even musicians in the "pit" have all reported seeing a woman sitting alone in the balcony, watching the performers practice in the otherwise empty building. No one knows who she is, all we seem to know is that, just like William, she died in the 1920s and has decided to stick around the opera house. Today, the staff refer to her as "Lady Lavender."

FUN FACT: Throughout American history, it was common to combine music halls with the town's main government building. These buildings were all called opera houses whether or not operas were, in fact, performed.

You can visit the opera house by auditioning for an upcoming show, attending a performance, or taking part in their summer camp. Of course, the summer camp is only for kids aged seven to 18 years old, so if you're looking to make your dreams of stardom come true, you'll have to move along.

EXPERIENCE:
Theatre

OPEN TO THE PUBLIC:
Yes

HANDICAP ACCESSIBLE:
Yes

Important Info:
Box Office Hours of Operation:
Monday-Friday
9:30am-4:00pm
And one hour prior to events.
Contact:
(716) 683-1776

LINDBERGH ELEMENTARY

People don't tend to think of schools as hot spots for a haunting, especially schools that are still in operation. But Charles Lindbergh Elementary School has left an impact on many students who continue to claim that it is haunted, despite having left the school years ago.

First opened in the 1930s to serve the east side of the bustling village of Kenmore, Lindbergh Elementary School has been teaching grades K-4 ever since. Although the 500 kids that make up the student body are under 10 years old, many of them leave the school with memories filled with the paranormal and unexplained.

Students and staff have reported hearing the sound of disembodied voices as well as feeling cold spots through the school. Strange lights illuminate from inside when the building should be empty, and desks seem to like to move on their own up on the second floor.

According to a former student named Vanessa, the school is haunted by the spirit of a custodian who died tragically in a fire in the 1990s. The story tells us that the man was stuck inside the girl's bathroom while he was trying to clean it when the fire began. Ask different people their opinions, and they'll all have their own version of the story: He was locked in by a jealous coworker. No! It wasn't a coworker! He was locked in the bathroom by some naughty students. That's not it! He locked himself inside and committed suicide! Whatever story you believe, there was indeed a fire that broke out in the elementary school on June 22, 1990 and was reported by *The Buffalo News* on June 30, 1990.

While there's no mention of a casualty in the article, students and staff have seen the spirit of the former custodian still wandering through the school.

Here's hoping he isn't spending eternity scrubbing floors and cleaning up after a bunch of messy kids.

EXPERIENCE:

School

OPEN TO THE PUBLIC:

No

MURDER CREEK

Murder Creek, Newstead, New York, 14001
43.081568°, -78.518300°

With a name that sounds like it could be a B-List horror movie, you can be darn sure that Murder Creek has a horrible story to match its name. It's a story that is such a part of Akron that the Erie County Parks and Recreation Department has a (very long-winded) version of it on their official website.

For those of you who don't want to track down the "official" legend, here's a TL;DR version for you:

> **FUN FACT:** The original name for Murder Creek was De-on-go-te Gah-hun-da.

In the 1820s, a man name John Dolph and his wife, Sarah, moved to Akron where they came to help a young Native American woman named Ah-weh-hah (meaning Wild Rose). Her father had been murdered by a white man named Sanders, who hoped to marry Ah-weh-hah. The Dolphs hid her and kept her safe from Sanders until she could reunite with her fiancé, Tah-yoh-ne (Gray Wolf). When the young couple met, they journeyed together to Ah-weh-hah's father's grave where they held a funeral for the man. While engrossed in the ceremony, Sanders attacked the pair. Tah-yoh-ne and Sanders struggled against one another, but eventually, they both fell dead on the grave of Ah-weh-hah's father. Overcome with grief, Ah-weh-hah eventually died of a broken heart (or exposure) while lying on Tah-yoh-ne's grave.

The tragic story doesn't end there, though. The legend adds that on moonlit nights if you wander along Murder Creek, you'll hear the sound of the two lovers whispering to each other. Sometimes, the ghosts of Tah-yoh-ne and Ah-weh-hah are spotted.

The legend of Ah-weh-hah is the most famous story of Murder Creek, but it isn't the only tragedy (and murder for that matter) that surrounds the innocent-looking body of water.

In 1890 (on Halloween night just to add to the creep factor), 17-year-old Sadie McMullen threw Nellie May Connors, aged eight, and Delia Brown, aged six, into Murder Creek. Why would a teenager hurl two little girls off a bridge? Why, a man, of course!

> **~~FUN~~ FACT:** Nellie May Connors is buried in St. Teresa's Roman Catholic Cemetery.

Sadie admitted to a friend in Buffalo that she was in love with Simon Brown (father to little Delia). He didn't return her feelings and was engaged to Mrs. Connors (mother to Nellie). Her unrequited love made Sadie want to commit suicide, and then she'd be able to haunt Simon Brown forever. It may sound a bit overdramatic, but the letter she wrote to her friend in Buffalo even stated, *"The man I love will know me as a frequent visitor."*

Why Sadie threw the girls into the creek without finishing the deed and jumping in herself, is unknown. But luckily, she was arrested and put on trial.

Even though Delia Brown managed to survive Sadie's murder attempt and testified against the young woman, Sadie McMullen was not sentenced to the electric chair. Instead, she was deemed insane and sent to the Buffalo State Asylum (now Hotel Henry). She was diagnosed with epilepsy and was released just a few years later.

No one knows what happened to Sadie McMullen after her release. Some reports place her in Kansas while others claim she made it as far as California.

There's no word on whether the ghost of Nellie May haunts the water along with Ah-weh-hah and Tah-yoh-ne. But her story haunts the residents of Akron and Western New York, even a century after her tragic and untimely death. It's a terrifying reminder that it's the living we should fear, and not the dead.

EXPERIENCE:

Natural Wonder

OPEN TO THE PUBLIC:

Yes

HANDICAP ACCESSIBLE:

Yes

MYSTERY GOO

Snyder, New York, 14226
42.956547°, -78.790483°

A strange goo falling from the sky may not sound like a good ghost story, and you're right: it's not. But it sure as hell is weird, earning it a "paranormal" badge.

On January 18, 2011, from 9:00am to midnight, people living between Washington Highway and Berryman Drive reported something strange. An unexplainable, smelly greenish-yellow "goo" fell from the sky and splattered houses. Remnants of the goo could be seen in green and yellow icicles. Even the sidewalks and the siding of people's homes were stained.

> **FUN FACT:** "Star jelly" comes in different colors and textures, and is found all over the world. Most can be traced back to terrestrial causes, but some think it falls from the sky and has an extraterrestrial source.

At first, residents feared it was "blue ice" (frozen human waste from planes), but the FAA quickly disproved that belief.

Several neighbors blamed the local birds that liked to eat fast food. According to this theory, the junk food would make the birds sick, and their droppings would stain the houses and cause the discoloration in the ice and snow.

As if fast food bird droppings isn't weird enough (much less frozen human droppings), many locals went one step further, blaming the goo on something not from this world.

UFO enthusiasts believe that the mysterious green goo that fell in Snyder is similar to the "Red Rain" that fell in India back in 2001. When researchers studied the red rain, they found cells that could not be traced back to Earth.

Whether it was blue ice, bird droppings, or something extraterrestrial, I think we can all agree that we hope the disgusting goo doesn't fall on Western New York again any time soon.

EXPERIENCE:

Unexplained Phenomenon/Haunted Road

OPEN TO THE PUBLIC:

Yes

HANDICAP ACCESSIBLE:

Yes

NEW ERA FIELD

1 Bills Drive, Orchard Park, New York, 14127
42.773794°, -78.786993°
www.buffalobills.com/stadium

Rich Stadium. Ralph Wilson Stadium. New Era Field. Call it what you will, there's no denying that Buffalonians are obsessed with their football team and have spent many a freezing day tailgating and sitting on cold metal bleachers to be part of the Bill's Nation.

With people cheering, music blasting, and ~~yellow water~~ Bud Light flowing, it's easy to forget that the stadium has not always been part of Buffalo. There was something else here long before the Bill's began looking for a new home. And that "something" may have led to a haunting of not just the stadium, but the surrounding land as well.

The stadium's history began in 1973, but the history of the land goes back long before the 20th Century. Before it was purchased to build Rich Stadium, it was farmland with the Joseph Sheldon family cemetery on site. The first family member was buried there in 1830, and the last was interred as recently as 1940. The stadium's original plans had the family plot at the 50-yard line. Luckily, the descendants of the Sheldon Family, along with Erie County, Ralph Wilson, and the Junior Yorkers worked together to preserve the cemetery so that it wouldn't be lost beneath AstroTurf.

TIP: Look outside Gate 7 to see the Sheldon family cemetery.

If a family cemetery isn't enough to make you think that the stadium might not be built in the best spot, before the Sheldons lived there, the land was home to the local Erie Indians. Many historians believe the stadium is built on top of their village and the construction disturbed their burial ground.

Once construction began, many families living near the soon-to-be stadium reported feeling cursed. Animals and children in their homes appeared upset by unseen forces and objects would disappear and move almost as if someone (or something) was playing a prank on them.

Because the stadium is built on sacred Native American land, many believe that the ground is cursed. Could it be the cursed land has seeped into the beloved football team as well? That damned Wide Right. Our hall of famer, OJ Simpson, imprisoned for armed robbery after his infamous double murder trial. No league championships since moving into the stadium in 1973. Many think that the Bill's dry spell over the years is the result of this curse.

If curses surrounding football teams aren't your thing, how about urban legends? Old Buffalo stories tell of ousted members of the mafia and how their bodies were buried in the concrete of the stadium.

Whether you believe in curses and urban legends or not, there's no denying that New Era Field is synonymous with the city of Buffalo and Western New York as a whole. If you're a sports fan or a music junkie (some great acts have performed at the stadium including The Rolling Stones, The Who, Elton John, and Fleetwood Mac), everyone should visit New Era Field at least once. You'll be able to be a part of Buffalo's living history and a culture that is purely Buffalo. But you could still find a better beer to drink at your tailgating event (just saying).

EXPERIENCE:

Cemetery/Burial Ground/Stadium

OPEN TO THE PUBLIC:

Yes

HANDICAP ACCESSIBLE:

Yes

Admission:

Tickets to football games start at around $20 and can reach over $200 for a single game.

Season tickets start for as low as $350.

OLD MAIN CEMETERY

745 Main Street, West Seneca, New York, 14224
42.833668°, -78.747481°

Sometimes also known as the Lower Ebenezer Cemetery, this burial ground was used by members of the Ebenezer Society from 1845-1867. The Ebenezers were a small sect of German Lutherans from the Christian group called the Community of True Inspiration. Even though they started leaving West Seneca in 1855, you can still see the name Ebenezer all over the town.

Before the Ebenezers claimed that the Seneca sold them part of the Buffalo Creek Reservation in 1838 (in what some historians think was a fraudulent claim), the land was home to the local tribe. It was also the home of a woman name Kauquatau.

According to legend, Kauquatau was a medicine woman for her tribe, but when she failed to heal someone, she was accused of witchcraft. Murdered on the bank of the nearby Cazenovia Creek, her body was supposedly buried beneath her cabin.

It wasn't until the Ebenezers arrived in the 1840s, that Kauquatau's restless spirit made herself known. While they inhabited the medicine woman's cabin, they reported seeing the apparition of a native woman in chains. Eventually, they left the cabin, burnt it, and blessed the land.

> **~~FUN~~ FACT:** Chief Soonongise (Tommy Jemmy to white settlers) was not punished for Kauquatau's murder. He wasn't seen as her killer, but her executioner.

Today, the spot where the cabin once stood is a vacant plot in the cemetery and many believe that Kauquatau's body is still buried there.

Those who live near the Old Main Cemetery have reported hearing strange noises. Investigators have captured EVPs on their digital recorders as well as EMF readings. One local man recalls a time when his fishing rod snapped in half at just the mention of the medicine woman's name. The haunting doesn't seem too malicious given its origin, but it still might be safe to leave your fishing rods at home. You know, just to be on the safe side.

EXPERIENCE:

Cemetery

OPEN TO THE PUBLIC:

Yes

HANDICAP ACCESSIBLE:

Yes

PIGMAN ROAD

886 Holland Road, Angola, New York, 14006
42.622436°, -79.048335°

Pigman Road is half history, half urban legend.

> **FUN FACT:** The train's last stop to let passengers off was in Dunkirk.

The actual name of the haunted mile is Holland Road, and it was the site of the Angola Horror. On December 18, 1867, one of the worst accidents in Western New York occurred when the last car on the Buffalo-bound Lake Shore Railway derailed at a bridge and plummeted into the gorge before catching on fire. The train accident killed almost 50 people and led to reforms in railway safety. According to claims, John D. Rockefeller was supposed to be on that train but luckily missed it in Cleveland. People are drawn to the site of the wreck, hoping to see the restless spirits of the victims.

But this haunted road is far more famous among paranormal investigators and daredevils for the legend of the Pigman of the 1950s.

There is no proof that the Pigman exists, but that doesn't stop people from visiting Holland Road in the middle of the night to test their luck.

According to different stories the Pigman was (and possibly still is) a butcher and serial killer that lived in the woods around Pigman Road. His famous trademark was marking his territory with pig

heads mounted on stakes. Some stories say he shot a man and hung him from a meat hook on his front porch. Supposedly, he was responsible for the death of a group of young boys before beheading them and placing their heads on stakes.

Of course, there are other stories surrounding the Pigman that have less to do with butchers and serial killers and more to do with how truly awful humans can be to one another. There are claims that the Pigman was anything but a rogue butcher. To some, they believe he was a kind, sweet man with a facial deformity that frightened those in Angola. Over time, rumors spread and became urban legends. Today, kids tell stories of the wicked Pigman, but paranormal investigators have visited the site of his former cabin. What is it they hear from the infamous Pigman more than anything else? Crying.

Most people try to brave Pigman Road at night. If you're brave enough (or crazy enough) to visit the Angola Horror site and the Pigman's stomping grounds in the dark, be careful since it is still a road that is sometimes used by locals.

EXPERIENCE:
Haunted Road

OPEN TO THE PUBLIC:
Yes

HANDICAP ACCESSIBLE:
Yes

ROYCROFT INN & CAMPUS

40 South Grove Street, East Aurora, New York, 14052
42.766922°, -78.617467°
www.roycroftinn.com

The Roycroft Inn is unique from other haunted locations in Western New York. It is the site of a former utopian society, making it both haunting and extremely spiritual at the same time. It might be the most peaceful haunting in all of Western New York.

The Roycroft Campus was established by Elbert Hubbard (not to be confused with L. Ron Hubbard of Scientology infamy) in 1895 and acted as a haven for members of the Arts and Crafts Movement. The Roycrofters turned their backs on the Industrial Revolution and focused on quality, handmade goods. Over the next 20 years, the Roycroft Campus grew to employ nearly 500 people. It thrived through the turn of the 20th Century. But its success came to a screeching halt when Elbert and Alice Hubbard died tragically when the Lusitania sank off the coast of Ireland (a tragedy that Hubbard supposedly predicted decades before).

The Roycroft was home to artisans, free thinkers, radicals, reformers, and suffragists in a sort of utopian community. Some historians wonder if the Roycroft was also home to something a bit darker. A religion follows a set of ideas, while

FUN FACT: There are 14 buildings encompassed in the Roycroft Campus including the Roycroft Inn, the chapel, the print shop, and the copper shop.

a cult follows a specific person. Strangely enough, both are found at the Roycroft.

The mysticism of the Roycroft Inn and Campus doesn't end there. Many paranormal enthusiasts historians and, alike, suspect that Hubbard was part of a secret society, most likely Rosicrucianism (or the Order of the Rosy Cross). In his writings, Hubbard referred to himself as Fra, which is a traditional Masonic title, only fueling the suspicion that he was involved in a secret society. And the Ruskin Room is said to be where Hubbard conducted his rituals.

Unfortunately, guests cannot visit the Ruskin Room today, unless they're on a tour. However, it is still considered the most active room in the entire Inn and Campus. People have reported feeling light-headed and nauseous, hearing strange noises, and even seeing visions while in the room. It is believed that Hubbard worked with a Seneca shaman and used dowsing rods to find the perfect place to build the tower where the Ruskin Room now sits in.

The Roycroft transformed into a boutique hotel and restaurant in 1995 and has been offering guests a unique dining experience that still has an artisanal feel that would make Hubbard proud. Choose to sit in the Larkin dining room or Hubbard Hall. If the weather is beautiful, enjoy your meal on their charming peristyle. Or throw back a pint in the bar which was once Alice Hubbard's office (she was a known prohibitionist, so it's hilarious and ironic at the same time).

They have a soup of the day and salad of the day as well as a quiche of the day and crêpe of the day. The lobster bisque is to die for, and their brunch was named the Best Brunch in Buffalo by News 4 WIVB Buffalo. They're even included in the Top 100 Brunches by Open Table and Zagat Survey.

Their food and unique drink selections keep bringing customers back, and it looks as if some of them never left.

Paranormal claims have been made throughout the Roycroft. Guests leave the hotel in the middle of the night, frightened. Members of the wait staff have heard their names called out in Hubbard Hall. There are even apparitions of an older woman and a young girl in the gift shop of the Campus.

But the most extraordinary claim from the Roycroft can be found in (no surprise) the Ruskin Room. The image of a long-haired man looking out the window at the street below has been spotted through the years. No one can be sure, but it is believed that this is the ghost of Elbert Hubbard, looking down on his beloved Roycroft, even 100 years after his tragic death. No doubt, he is proud of what he sees.

TIP: Each room in the hotel has a piece of original furniture, branded with the Roycroft sigil. Look around to find yours!

EXPERIENCE:
Restaurant/Bar/Hotel

OPEN TO THE PUBLIC:
Yes

HANDICAP ACCESSIBLE:
Yes

Important Info:
Hours of Operation:
Sunday Brunch:
10:00am-2:00pm
Lunch:
Monday-Saturday:
11:30am-3:00pm
Dinner:
Sunday
4:30-9:00pm
Monday-Thursday:
5:00-9:00pm
Friday-Saturday:
5:00-10:00pm
Contact:
(716) 652-5552

SNYDER BAR & GRILL

2067 Kensington Avenue, Amherst, New York, 14226
42.950486°, -78.782293°
www.sbgbuffalo.com

Just around the corner from where Mystery Goo falls from the sky, a local bar is serving up some spooky tales of its own.

Since 2008, Snyder Bar and Grill has offered locals their very own watering hole where friends can play shuffleboard, watch a football game, and enjoy a cold beer. But hidden among their peanut butter bacon burger and famous chicken wings is something unexplained.

Staff members of the restaurant (especially the bartenders) and a few late-night customers have reported ghostly activity for several years. Strange noises echo through an otherwise empty building, doors open and close on their own, and people have claimed to see someone in the restaurant's mirrors.

Both patrons and staff have also spotted a full-body apparition. On more than one occasion, the entity has been seen making its way through the bar and even sitting at a table in the dark restaurant after hours.

No one knows why this spirit might be haunting a relatively new establishment in Western New York. Customers have left the bar after seeing the apparition, but aside from a good scare, it doesn't seem to be malicious.

EXPERIENCE:

Restaurant/Bar

OPEN TO THE PUBLIC:

Yes

HANDICAP ACCESSIBLE:

Yes

Important Info:
Restaurant Hours of Operation:
Monday-Friday:
5:00pm-12:00am
Saturday-Sunday:
12:00pm-12:00am

Bar Hours of Operation:
Monday-Friday:
3:00pm-4:00am
Saturday-Sunday:
12:00pm-4:00am

VIDLER'S

676-694 East Main Street, East Aurora, New York, 14052
42.76817°, -78.60911°
www.vidlers5and10.com

A visit to East Aurora is incomplete without stopping by one of America's last remaining five and dime shops.

Opened in 1930 by Robert S. Vidler, Sr., Vidler's is now in its third generation of owners and is bigger than ever. With the original hardwood floors, the counters are lined with everything you can imagine: from marbles and lawn ornaments to craft supplies, vintage games, and even smartphone accessories. You may not know it from the friendly customer service and old-timey popcorn machine, but according to some, Vidler's is haunted.

The family business may have started in 1930, but the building itself dates back to 1870, offering us a bit more history to play with.

According to employees, strange sounds have been heard coming from upstairs (not accessible to the general public). Some believe that these noises are caused by an electrician who died on the upper floor back in the 1930s after he electrocuted himself. There are stories of a woman singing in the basement as well as a full-body apparition of an old lady. Of

> **TIP:** Be sure to try their vintage popcorn machine! It costs only a dime (no Canadian coins, please!) and is a fun treat for the kids.

course, that's where the arts and crafts section is. Who's to say she was a ghost and not just another customer coming to get her scrapbooking supplies from East Aurora's favorite (and only) five and dime?

Situated right on Main Street (and directly across from the equally haunted Globe Restaurant), Vidler's is impossible to miss with its red and white awning, and, of course, it's "Vidler on the Roof."

EXPERIENCE:
Store

OPEN TO THE PUBLIC:
Yes

HANDICAP ACCESSIBLE:
Yes

Important Info:
Hours of Operation:
Sunday:
11:00am-5:00pm
Monday-Thursday:
9:00am-6:00pm
Friday:
9:00am-9:00pm
Saturday:
9:00am-6:00pm

WESTERN HOUSE

210 West Main Street, Springville, New York, 14141
42.508738°, -78.675130°

With a name like the Western House, you'd think it was a Wild West saloon complete with cowboys and rowdy shootouts. Well, prepare to be disappointed.

> **FUN FACT:** Saloon is just a fun name for a bar. America's oldest bar is the White Horse Tavern in Newport, Rhode Island. It opened in 1673.

The Western House was constructed in the late 1800s, acting as both a hotel and a saloon when it first opened its doors on West Main Street. Since then, the structure has gone through several transformations, sometimes sitting vacant and other times serving as a restaurant and an apartment building.

Residents who have lived in the apartments report hearing disembodied voices, footsteps, and laughter. Doors also slam shut, and electronics like to turn on and off on their own. Many have also witnessed the apparition of a female wandering through the house.

Different stories surround the mystery woman. Some accounts say that she owned the building until her death in 1939, while others insist that she is the daughter of the original owner. Whichever story is true, everyone tends to agree that the woman's name is Christine.

Last I checked, the Western House was an apartment building, making it difficult to see just what's happening inside. But who knows? Maybe it'll live up to its name again someday and open its doors as a restaurant or saloon. But only if we can kick open the saloon doors with our cowboy boots before sauntering up to the bar (chaps and stirrups optional).

EXPERIENCE:

Private Residence

OPEN TO THE PUBLIC:

No

WHITEHAVEN CEMETERY

East River Road, Grand Island, New York, 14072
43.025902°, -78.896819°

Supposedly, Whitehaven Cemetery has a ghostly connection to the former Holiday Inn of Grand Island. But whether it's somehow involved with the little ghost of Tanya or not, Whitehaven has some spooky ghost stories of its own.

Established in 1865, Whitehaven is still an active cemetery today. It's most famous residents are the Nice family who helped build a logging community on Grand Island in the mid-19th Century. Whether or not one of the Nice's daughters haunts the local hotel on the island doesn't seem to affect the restless spirits in this cemetery.

People who venture into Whitehaven Cemetery report all sorts of paranormal activity. From the sound of footsteps when no one else is around to cold spots (which isn't too bizarre in Western New York), and even glowing tombstones! The hallowed ground is also said to be the home of three apparitions: a little girl, a mother, and a soldier from the Gulf War.

> **TIP:** The Nice family monument is to your right as you enter.

Don't confuse Whitehaven Cemetery with Assumption Cemetery. Whitehaven is located just down the road from the equally haunted former Holiday Inn on East River Road near Whitehaven Road.

EXPERIENCE:

Cemetery

OPEN TO THE PUBLIC:

Yes

HANDICAP ACCESSIBLE:

Yes

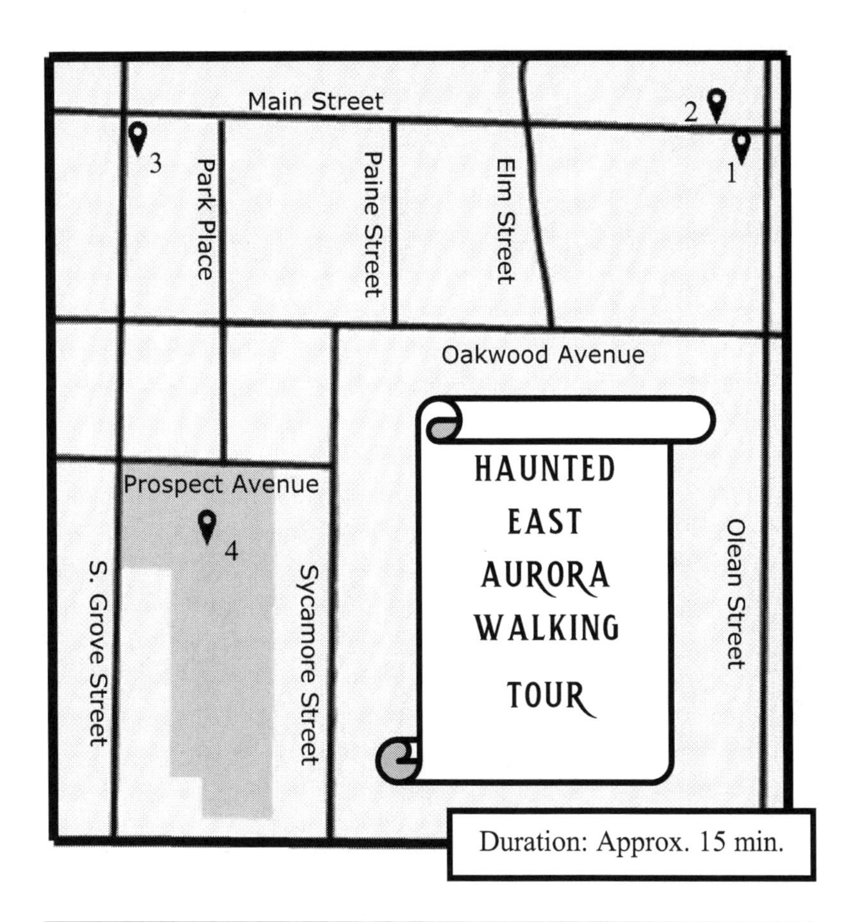

Begin on the corner of Olean Street and East Main Street where the **Globe Restaurant (1)** has sat for nearly 200 years. Just across the street is the iconic Vidler on the Roof and the kitschy and fun **Vidler's (2)**. Put a dime in their popcorn machine for a snack as you head west down Main Street. Walk 10 minutes and you'll find the **Roycroft Inn & Campus (3)** on the corner of Main Street and South Grove Street. Cross South Grove Street to spot the terracotta face on the side of the chapel (the north side wall facing East Aurora Middle School). Wander down South Grove Street and explore the Campus or dine at the Inn. Continue down South Grove Street another five minutes before arriving at Hamlin Park, home to the **Aurora Players Pavilion (4).**

ORLEANS
COUNTY

ORLEANS COUNTY

Situated on the southern banks of Lake Ontario lies Orleans County. Founded in 1824, there is some debate over where the name of Orleans originated. Some theories suggest it was to honor the Royal House of Orleans. A more likely theory is that it was meant to honor Andrew Jackson's victory in New Orleans. But no matter the origins of its name, Orleans County was built by waterways (the Erie Canal) and railways (New York Central Railroad). It was also home to Frances Folsom (America's youngest first lady) and Henry Lyon Porter (animator on *Snow White and the Seven Dwarfs*).

1. Beechwood Cemetery
2. Cobblestone Inn
3. County House Road
4. Ford Street Beast
5. Fuller Road
6. Hart House Hotel
7. Pillars Estate
8. Tillman's Historic Village Inn

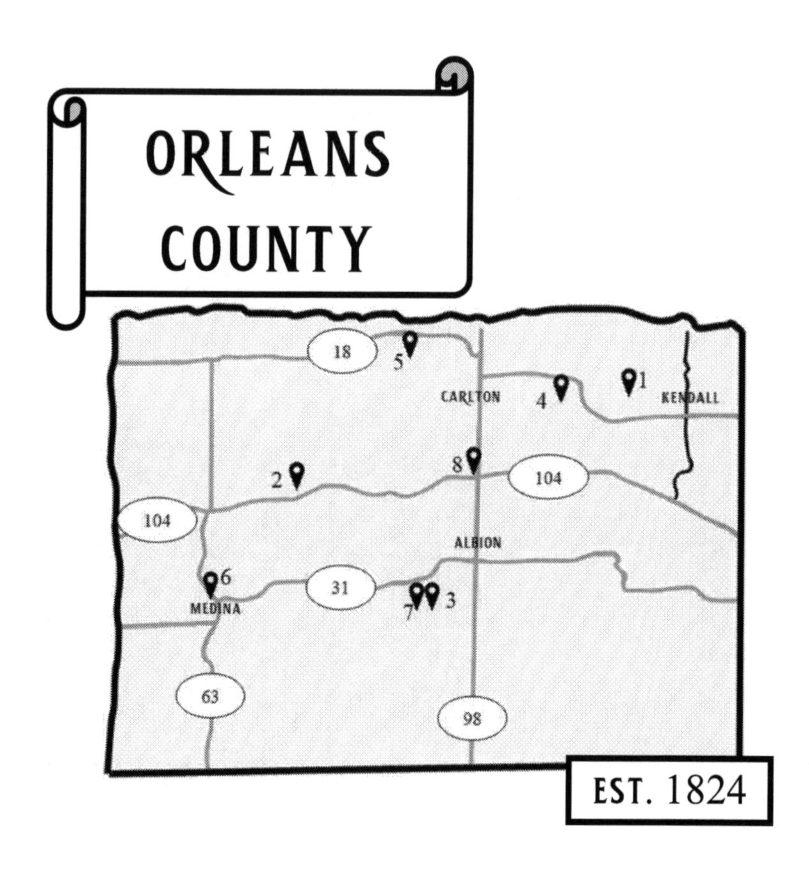
ORLEANS
COUNTY
18
5
CARLTON
4
1
KENDALL
2
8
104
104
ALBION
6
31
7
3
MEDINA
63
98
EST. 1824

BEECHWOOD CEMETERY

1523 West Kendall Road, Kendall, New York, 14476
43.344396°, -78.075703°

If you find yourself driving along Woodchuck Alley in Kendall, then you'll end up in the town's small cemetery, shrouded by a canopy of protective oak trees.

First established in 1828, Beechwood Cemetery is still an active cemetery, but that hasn't stopped the vandals from destroying headstones and even the sandstone chapel which was built in 1898. Sadly, in recent years, the windows have been shattered, and the doors were removed. Inside is nothing but graffiti and garbage, leading many people to think that the trespassers have stirred up several angry spirits in the historic cemetery.

Those who visit the cemetery will find that it is removed from much of the town and not too many cars pass by. The silence can be unnerving to some, but the only thing more disturbing than the silence is the sound of voices coming from behind the nearby trees.

The best time to visit Beechwood Cemetery is in the fall when all of the leaves on the trees have begun to change colors, turning the otherwise sad-looking cemetery into something quite beautiful.

EXPERIENCE:

Cemetery

OPEN TO THE PUBLIC:

Yes

HANDICAP ACCESSIBLE:

Yes

COBBLESTONE INN

12225 Ridge Road, Medina, New York, 14103
43.274453°, -78.332949°

Nestled on the corner of Route 104 and Orleans County Road 53 lies one of the most impressive houses in not just Orleans County, but all of Western New York.

FUN FACT: New York State has the highest concentration of surviving cobblestone buildings in the country.

The Cobblestone Inn was built in the early 19th Century by Zachariah Spencer and served the Medina area as an inn and stagecoach stop. At the time, it was an impressive structure. Today, the Cobblestone Inn is the largest cobblestone building in the state and one of the largest in the entire country.

The land surrounding the Cobblestone Inn was wrought with tragedy. Spencer's son, Henry, shot himself on the property shortly after his father had given him the inn to run. In 1889, one of the area's most horrific murders occurred: the killing of a 13-year-old girl named Cora at the hands of the man who loved her, Eugene Emry (who was definitely not 13).

But these traumatic events didn't put a damper on business at the inn. When stagecoach traffic died due to the construction of the Erie Canal, it transformed into a restaurant. The Cobblestone Inn continued to serve Medina and Western New York until the mid-20th Century when it finally closed its doors and became a private residence.

In recent years, it was placed on the National Register of Historic Places and ghostly activity was reported by those living inside the cobblestone house.

According to reports, footsteps and screams echo through the home. People report seeing objects moving on their own, shadow figures, and full-body apparitions, including a woman in a white dress. Doors slam, people say they are being touched, and some think that there is a vortex in one of the bedroom closets.

The house has changed hands over the years. However, there are no plans to open the Cobblestone Inn to the public anytime soon. Luckily, it's still an impressive sight, even from Route 104.

> As seen on *Dead Files* season 7, episode 13.

EXPERIENCE:

Landmark/Private Residence

OPEN TO THE PUBLIC:

No

COUNTY HOUSE ROAD

County House Road, Albion, New York, 14411
43.223998°, -78.149400°

This nine-mile stretch of road runs from Millville to just south of Albion. It's a scenic drive through farm country, past some other haunted locations such as the Pillars Estate (seen on your right when traveling from Millville). But don't let the stories of the Pillars mansion take away from the road's own eerie activity. It's just as impressive and might be even more unnerving if you find yourself driving along County House Road as the sun sets.

Most stories come from the area between Riches Corner Road and Lee Road, where County House Road comes to a dead end. People who visit at night report hearing screams and even gunshots with no apparent source. There are also stories of shadows moving around people who walk along the road.

FUN FACT: Haunted roads are found all over the world including Indonesia, England, South Africa, India, and Croatia.

As if stories of shadows following you along a dark country road and a haunted mansion aren't enough, there used to be a sanitarium (also known as a county house… what's the name of this street again?) along this stretch of highway.

When visiting, try to avoid wandering into the road at night. A). It's not safe. B). Someone might mistake you for a phantom hitchhiker.

EXPERIENCE:

Haunted Road

OPEN TO THE PUBLIC:

Yes

HANDICAP ACCESSIBLE:

Yes

FORD STREET BEAST

Ford Street, Kent, New York, 14477
43.327899°, -78.132819°

No, I'm not talking about the 1934 car (though it is a sweet ride). I'm talking about an actual beast lurking on Ford Street in Orleans County.

For a stretch of road that is less than a football field in length, it manages to be pretty terrifying. And people from all different walks of life have experienced the Ford Street Beast.

Those who have seen the creature share similar details of the monster: it stands between six and seven feet tall, dark fur covers its entire body, it has a dog-like face that sits right on its shoulders, and it runs on all fours, but it will stand on its hind legs when it feels threatened.

Sounds an awful lot like a werewolf.

These stories go even further into the werewolf lore. People have only encountered this creature at night, it is said to be extremely violent, and some reports claim that it disappears into a cloud of dust or vapor.

Now, this may sound a bit random, but according to werewolf folklore, this is perfectly normal. Depending on which moon they're born under, there are some species of werewolf (yes, there is apparently more than one type… you learn something new every day!) that can make themselves disappear into a swirl of dust. The logistics behind it are a bit more complicated—they can only turn

> **FUN FACT:** The word werewolf is Old English for man-wolf:
> (man=were, wolf=wulf)

into dust while they're still moving; once they stand still, their physical form manifests once more. But it's a fairly specific detail that connects the Ford Street Beast to the werewolf mythos.

When you stand in the middle of Ford Street (not necessarily recommended), you can see Kent Road and East Kent Road, making it a bit difficult to think that anything monstrous could be lurking in the surrounding trees. But if the multiple claims and reports are to be believed, it's best to stay safe in your car. We already have one werewolf running around—we don't need two!

FUN FACT: Many believe the werewolf legend stems from the rabies virus.

EXPERIENCE:

Cryptid Sighting/Haunted Road

OPEN TO THE PUBLIC:

Yes

HANDICAP ACCESSIBLE:

Yes

FULLER ROAD

Fuller Road, Carlton, New York, 14571
43.344079°, -78.258257°

If there's any street in Western New York that will make you feel isolated, it's one made up of farmland, woods, and just five houses.

People who live near Fuller Road have reported some unnerving activity as they've wandered along it at night, mainly revolving around shadow people.

One young man reported that he felt the sensation of someone following him one autumn evening as he was walking to a friend's house. Even though there were crunchy leaves on the ground at the time, he says he never heard anyone walking behind him, he just felt it. Ignoring his gut feeling, the anonymous man refused to look back until he reached the end of the road. When he did turn around, a shadowy figure was standing about halfway up the road, watching him from the exact location he first felt uneasy.

> **FUN FACT**: There are urban legends surrounding phantom cars as well as trains, boats, and planes.

Another story comes from a young woman on a bicycle ride. She claims that an old pickup truck appeared virtually out of nowhere and sped up behind her. Just when she feared it would hit her, the truck slammed on its breaks and vanished.

Of course, phantom stalkers and wannabe *Christine*s aren't enough for Fuller Road. According to local legend, on moonlit nights, silhouetted figures are seen standing on people's front lawns as well as in the street and up in the trees.

Most stories come from people who choose to travel down Fuller Road out in the open such as walkers, joggers, or bicyclists. To avoid being run over by a runaway beater truck (or real-life cars for that matter), it's best to visit Fuller Road in the safety of your vehicle.

EXPERIENCE:

Haunted Road

OPEN TO THE PUBLIC:

Yes

HANDICAP ACCESSIBLE:

Yes

HART HOUSE HOTEL

113 West Center Street, Medina, New York, 14103
43.220181°, -78.387697°
www.harthousehotel.com

In our nation's centennial year, Medina's finest inn welcomed her first guests. Opening in 1876, the Hart House Hotel had all of the comforts you'd expect from a 19th Century inn—30 rooms, a restaurant and bar, and even a billiards room. At the time of the Hart House Hotel's opening, Medina was a bustling and prosperous port town along the Erie Canal. But, sadly, after the turn of the 20th Century, there wasn't nearly as much of a need for high-end inns, and in 1918, the Hart House Hotel closed her doors to guests.

For the next 85 years, the three-story brick building became the famous Newell Shirt Factory, with patrons such as Bob Hope, Winston Churchill, and Warren G. Harding. In 2005, work began on the building to transform it back into a boutique hotel. Today, it continues to serve both locals and visitors.

With the Hart House Hotel's popularity in the late 19th and early 20th Centuries, it is the most visited site in the small town of Medina. And with multitudes of visitors come imprints and souls.

Even at the time of the shirt factory, employees reported some unusual activity. Factory workers claimed to hear the sound of footsteps in an otherwise empty building, and they even spotted women dressed in white on several occasions.

After over 140 years standing in the heart of Medina, the Hart House Hotel is still seemingly alive with paranormal activity.

Guests checking in for the night report hearing their names called out. A woman in a flowing dress with shoulder-length brown hair can also be spotted at the top of the stairs as if she is greeting patrons upon their arrival.

115 West Center Street is home to the historic Hart House Hotel as well as 810 Meadworks and the aptly named Shirt Factory Café, making it an all-inclusive place to visit. Grab a bite to eat at the café (they have a beef on weck grilled cheese and even a sandwich named after Bob Hope). Toast the spirit of the mystery woman at the meadery with over 20 meads to choose from. Then tuck yourself into bed in a haunted room for the night (prices start at $109 per night).

TIP: Each room has a different theme and some are named after patrons of the shirt factory such as the Churchill and Astor rooms.

EXPERIENCE:

Restaurant/Bar/Hotel

OPEN TO THE PUBLIC:

Yes

HANDICAP ACCESSIBLE:

No

PILLARS ESTATE

13800 West County House Road, Albion, New York, 14411
43.218156°, -78.230080°

Pillars Estate has gone through quite the transformation over the last few years. But, today, it looks like it has entered the same dark ages that plague many Western New York haunted houses.

Built after the Civil War in 1878, the Pillars Estate has been a private residence, an apartment building, a hotel, and an event venue. Recently, it was a restaurant and hotel, complete with *Titanic* reenactments every April. The house went through some significant renovations, including the addition of an incredible ballroom in 2011. Despite all the updates and years as a restaurant and wedding venue, in 2018, the owner closed its doors and put an asking price of $500,000 on the mansion.

While it was a hotel, guests needed to sign a waiver, promising not to hold any séances or try to communicate with the spirits haunting the establishment. However, they did offer ghost tours.

People visiting both the restaurant and staying in the hotel reported hearing unexplained noises as well as a piano playing. The spirits of young children were seen as well as the ghost of Patricia Carr, who lived in the house in the mid-20th Century.

> As seen on *Ghost Hunters* season 12, episode 2.

At the time of publication, the Pillars Estate was closed to the public. But if anyone has half a million dollars lying around, then maybe the Pillars Estate will finally be restored to its 19th Century grandeur for the public to enjoy once more.

EXPERIENCE:

Landmark/Former Restaurant/Hotel

OPEN TO THE PUBLIC:

No

TILLMAN'S HISTORIC VILLAGE INN

14369 Ridge Road West, Albion, New York, 14411
43.287038°, -78.192218°
www.tillmansvillageinn.com

One of Orleans County's most historic buildings also happens to be one of its most haunted.

Opened in 1824 (the same year the county was formed), Tillman's was a place for people to rest as they traveled between the Niagara and Genesee Rivers. Acting as a stagecoach stop, the tavern and inn thrived over the years. Today, Tillman's Historic Village Inn and the Fair Haven Inn offer visitors a chance to eat in a haunted restaurant and sleep in a haunted hotel.

The Village Inn is an award-winning restaurant best known for its prime rib and seafood as well as one of the best Sunday brunches in Western New York. With their comfort food, seafood feast, BBQ from their in-house smoke pit, and over a dozen dry rubs, sauces, and marinades, there is something for everyone at the historic Village Inn… including the wannabe ghost hunter in your life.

In both the restaurant and the Fair Haven Inn, doors slam shut on their own, and people have reported feeling uneasy as if there is something else in the room with them.

> **TIP:** At the restaurant, request booth A1. In the hotel, request room 3. Both are said to be active.

Several apparitions have also been spotted by guests over the years, including two little girls in white dresses from the 1800s and a cowboy sitting at the bar (someone should tell him the Western House is in Springville, not Albion).

EXPERIENCE:

Restaurant/Bar/Hotel

OPEN TO THE PUBLIC:

Yes

HANDICAP ACCESSIBLE:

Yes

Important Info:
Hours of Operation:
Sunday:
10:00am-8:00pm
Monday-Thursday:
11:30am-8:00pm*
Friday-Saturday:
11:30am-9:00pm
*Closed on Mondays from
January 1st-March 21st
Contact:
(585) 589-9151

WYOMING COUNTY

WYOMING COUNTY

Officially becoming a county of Western New York in only 1841, Wyoming County was home to Mary Jemison, the White Woman of the Genesee, and welcomed visitors such as Theodore Roosevelt and Susan B. Anthony to its famed Hillside Inn. The name "Wyoming" comes from the Lenape word meaning "broad bottom lands." Today, it is home to natural sights such as Letchworth State Park and Silver Lake as well as the Arcade and Attica Railroads… oh, and Attica Correctional Facility.

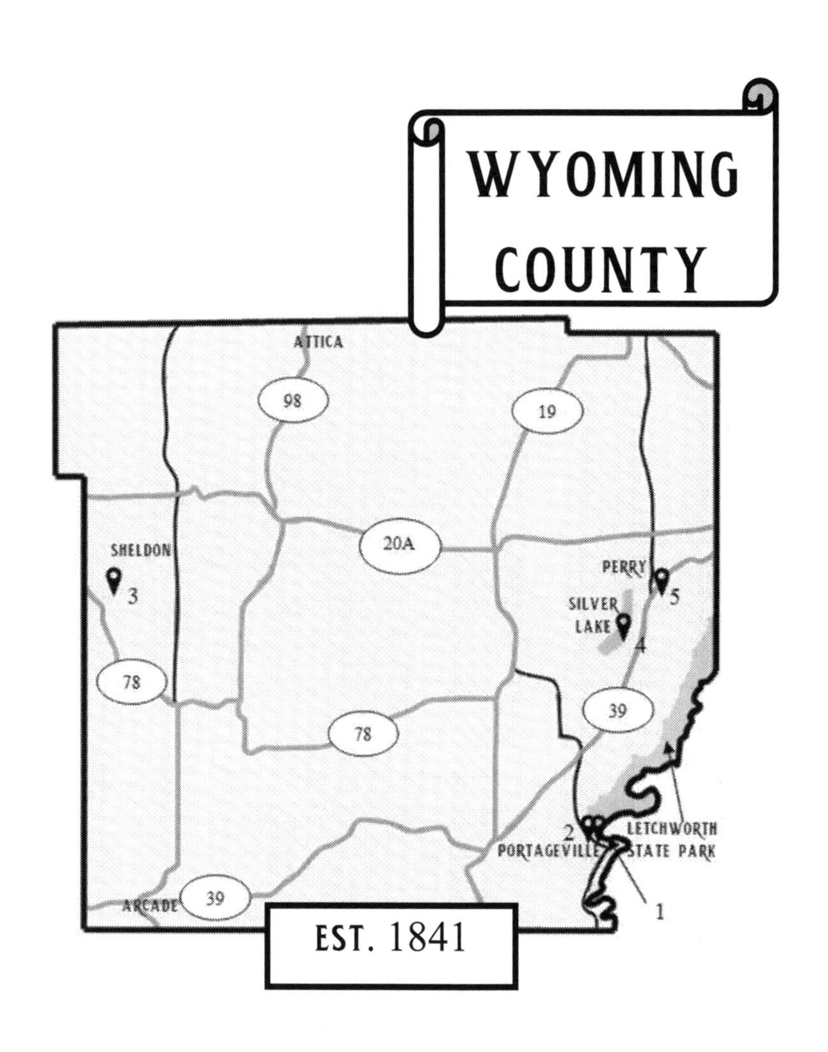
WYOMING
COUNTY
ATTICA
98
19
20A
SHELDON
3
PERRY
5
SILVER
LAKE
4
78
39
78
2
LETCHWORTH
PORTAGEVILLE
STATE PARK
ARCADE
39
1
EST. 1841

GENESEE FALLS INN

6901 Hamilton Street, Portageville, New York, 14536
42.570022°, -78.039922°
www.thegeneseefallsinn.com

The old brick Victorian along NY-436 doesn't just offer guests a quaint bed and breakfast experience. People checking in might walk away with a few ghost stories.

Built in 1870, the Genesee Falls Inn has almost always been a hotel. In previous years, it was also a restaurant with a ballroom on the third floor used for bare-knuckle fisticuff fighting!

FUN FACT: The first bare-knuckle boxing champ was crowned in 1719.

Today, the B&B offers about a dozen newly renovated rooms starting at $89 per night. With breakfast included and Letchworth State Park just a half mile down the road, Genesee Falls Inn is a cozy place to put up your feet and relax for a while… until the ghosts start to stir up some trouble.

Many people report feeling uneasy as soon as they step foot in the building. The old photos hanging on the walls and antique dolls don't help ease that feeling. And there's a reason why people sense something different about the Genesee Falls Inn. It was built on the site of several devastating fires, there have been multiple suicides on the land, drownings in the Genesee River, and a nearby cemetery was almost destroyed in a flood. All of these tragedies—including the death of the former caretaker of the inn—have led many to believe that the inn is haunted. And the paranormal activity certainly helps to back that up.

Guests who spend the night, report hearing the sound of someone walking up and down the hall all night long, as well as doors opening and closing on their own. The apparition of a man is sometimes seen sitting in the guest rooms. A child in period clothes has been spotted walking through the kitchen on several occasions. Oh, and a friendly word of warning: things you bring with you might go missing. But if you ask nicely, the spirits will put them back for you.

The inn offers ghost tours for groups of up to 10 people as well as paranormal investigations. Appointments are required for the tours and hunts. However, the owners welcome anyone who is in the area who wishes to stop by and simply look around.

EXPERIENCE:

Hotel/Ghost Hunt/
Ghost Tour

Contact:
(585) 493-2484

OPEN TO THE PUBLIC:

Yes

HANDICAP ACCESSIBLE:

No

HEAVEN SENT B&B

SPOOK APPROVED EATS

6440 Pike Street, Portageville, New York, 14536
42.567761°, -78.043243°

Literally around the corner from Genesee Falls Inn is yet another haunted bed and breakfast, this time in a converted church and rectory.

> **FUN FACT:** There are about 20 churches with documented hauntings in New York State.

The former church was the very first Catholic Church in Wyoming County when it opened in 1848, and it remained an active church until the Diocese of Buffalo closed it in 2008. At that time, Michael Vasile took over (having been a member of the church most of his life), and began renovating the plumbing and electric before opening it up as a B&B and event venue.

Like so many historic buildings, the renovations seemed to churn up the activity that has continued to this day.

Guests have left after just one night in the bed and breakfast (even leaving without their breakfast!). They've reported being touched and woken up in the middle of the night. Lights turn off and on. Footsteps are heard in the halls as well as whispering in an otherwise empty room. There have also been reports of children playing in the bedrooms and even the ghost of Father Maurice, a priest who died of pneumonia in the rectory.

Despite the haunting, there is nothing negative surrounding it. Feeling someone rub your back in the middle of the night when your partner is fast asleep may be a bit unnerving, but not terrifying. Who can say no to a good back rub, after all?

At first, Vasile tried to downplay the haunting, but as more people learned about it, the more popular the inn has become.

With only four rooms available (and only one with a private bath), it may be a bit difficult to snag a night in this haunted B&B. However, Heaven Sent is open to the public for holiday brunches such as Easter and Mother's Day, as well as Friday Fish Fries during Lent. Only in Western New York would people love their fish fry enough to sit in an old converted church and eat their fried haddock in the presence of a phantom priest.

EXPERIENCE:

Hotel/Event Venue/
Ghost Tour

Contact:
(585) 468-5968

OPEN TO THE PUBLIC:

Yes

HANDICAP ACCESSIBLE:

Yes

ST. JOHN'S CEMETERY

Goose Hill Road, Sheldon, New York, 14145
42.737315°, -78.447612°

Its full name is St. John's Dutch Hollow Cemetery. Sometimes it is known among investigators as Goose Hill Cemetery because of its location on Goose Hill Road. No matter what name you call it, this cemetery is extremely haunted.

> **TIP:** Don't be confused if you find yourself on Centerline Road instead of Goose Hill. They're the same.

Although it was only founded in the mid-1800s and has several dozen graves on site, St. John's Cemetery is overwhelming when it comes to its paranormal stories. These tales come from people who have sought out the location based on its hauntings as well as unsuspecting neighbors whose land ends where the cemetery begins.

There are disembodied voices, screams, and even someone crying out, "Momma!" (many children are buried here). Visitors report seeing apparitions and shadow figures. Neighbors have complained of things being thrown at them, and some people have even been pushed and attacked by an unseen entity.

St. John's Cemetery is associated with St. John's Evangelical and Reformed Church just down the road which opened its doors to the local German immigrants around 1840. Also at this time, a local farmer donated some of his land to act as the church's cemetery with the first burial dating to

November 1841. Many of the graves are difficult to read—some are in German, while others have been weathered down over the years. However, it's a fantastic example of Victorian grave art including clasped hands (holy matrimony), wreaths (sometimes meaning redemption), weeping willows (mourning), upward-pointing hands (ascension into heaven), scales (balance), and lambs (the death of a child).

St. John's Cemetery is located along Goose Hill Road. There is a small driveway to the right of the cemetery for you to pull off the road and explore. Please be respectful of the surrounding houses if you visit early in the morning or late at night.

EXPERIENCE:
Cemetery

OPEN TO THE PUBLIC:
Yes

HANDICAP ACCESSIBLE:
Yes

SILVER LAKE SERPENT

Silver Lake, Castille, New York, 14549
42.694044°, -78.029022°

New York has her fair share of lakes from the Great Lakes and the Finger Lakes in the West to Lake George and Lake Champlain in the east. It seems that with every lake, there comes a lake monster. Less than 10 miles northwest of Letchworth State Park is Silver Lake in Perry. According to tales, it has its own sea monster (sans the sea, of course) which put the little town of Perry on the map in the 1800s.

On July 13, 1855, five men and two boys were out in the middle of the lake fishing in the twilight. Each of them reported seeing something unnerving in the water near their boat. What they first thought was just a log, began to move and eventually, they spotted what would be dubbed the Silver Lake Serpent. According to the reports of the men, the creature ran about 60 feet long and had glowing red eyes. This may sound a bit dramatic (especially the red eyes bit), but over a hundred other people claimed to see the monster through the summer.

Bounty hunters, fishermen, and those merely curious about the beast made their way to Perry, and the local hotels "struck a bonanza." Of course, the hype didn't last forever, and in 1857, firefighters found the remains of what could very well be the hoax that brought the Silver Lake Serpent to life.

The Walker Hotel, owned by Artemus B. Walker, burned down two years after the 1855 sighting, and firefighters found wire and canvas—what many people believe was the Silver Lake Serpent. Walker confessed to fabricating the serpent in the hopes of building up business for the local hotels (we can't fault him: it did work). After this revelation, the serpent craze seemingly died out, but some still insist that the Silver Lake Serpent is real.

Sightings were reported some 30 years before the 1855 incident, and before that, local Native American tribes told stories of a monster living in Silver Lake. Advocates for the serpent point to these legends as proof that there has always been something lurking beneath the water of Silver Lake.

Of course, the 7.4-mile long lake isn't quite that big. While it is home to walleye, largemouth bass, northern pike, and other fish, its depth only runs 37 feet at its deepest. It'd be a bit difficult for a 60-foot-long creature to hide so well for so long. If we use the Silver Lake Serpent's famous cousin, Nessie, you'll see that Loch Ness runs over 700 feet deep and its monster is only 25 feet long. If the Silver Lake Serpent did exist in the shallow lake, we should have found her by now.

> **TIP:** You can spot a replica of the serpent outside the country club near the first hole of the golf course.

Nevertheless, the people of Perry have embraced their cryptid. In years past, Perry has held its own Silver Lake Serpent Festival. If you visit today, you'll find the creature on signs and souvenirs. And maybe while you're visiting Silver Lake State Park, you'll even find a pair of glowing red eyes watching you from the waves.

EXPERIENCE:

Cryptid Sighting

WATER STREET

Water Street, Perry, New York, 14530
42.719508°, -78.000035°

Established in 1814, Perry has had a relatively quiet history (aside from its lake monster). Of course, Chester A. Arthur, vice president to James Garfield, and eventually, President of the United States, spent some of his childhood in Perry. But there really isn't much reason for this little town to be haunted. Yet, it is.

People who live along Water Street have reported some unusual activity. There are stories of a young girl about 16 years old who wanders along the road and through people's backyards. It doesn't seem like she's trying to get anyone's attention—no one experiences her presence inside their homes. But people claim to see her on a fairly regular basis. No one knows who the phantom girl is or why she wanders along this stretch of road. Nevertheless, she persists.

> **FUN FACT:** Paranormal researchers believe areas near running water, limestone, and railroads experience higher levels of activity.

EXPERIENCE:

Haunted Road

OPEN TO THE PUBLIC:

Yes

HANDICAP ACCESSIBLE:

Yes

DRIVING TOURS

If you want to venture beyond the stories in these pages and experience the paranormal for yourself, here are some driving tours for you to explore. As always, please respect posted signs, fences, private property, and schools. It is up to you to acquire the proper permission before visiting a location.

Due to the length of many of these haunted driving tours, it might be best to split them up by county.

In each chapter, I've included approximate addresses and coordinates to help you locate the various haunted cemeteries, roads, and landmarks throughout Western New York. Some may be off the beaten path and others have been lost to history or time. Please research each place you intend on visiting before you set out. The directions provided here are minimal (at best) so it's best to use GPS to assure safer travels.

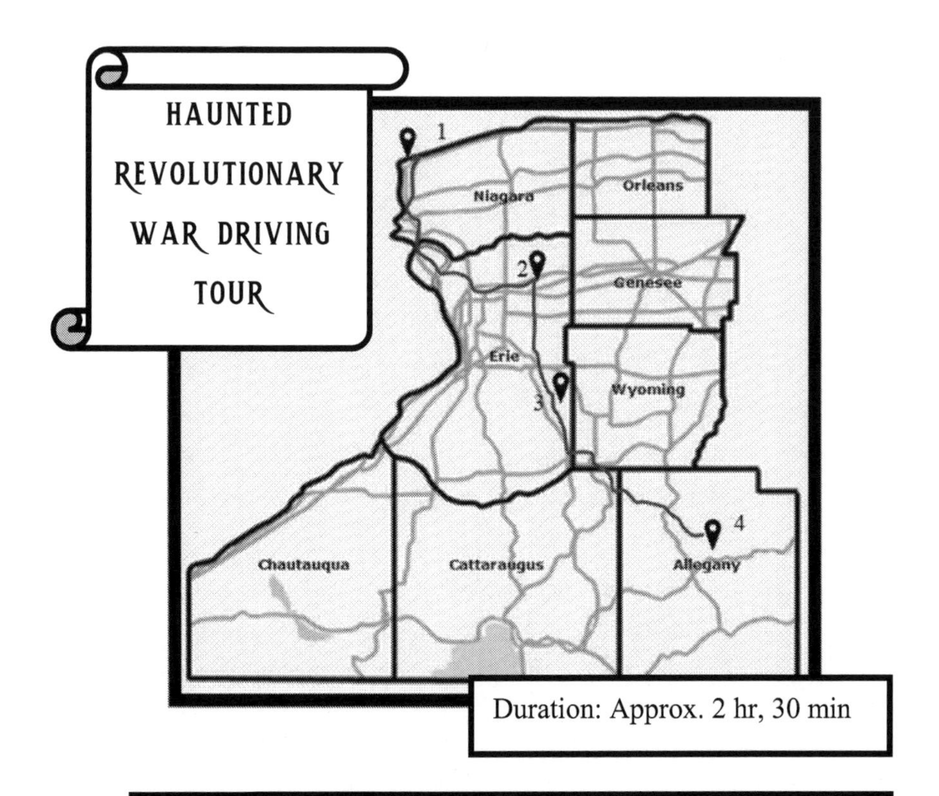

Many Loyalists settled along the Niagara River and in parts of Western New York during the American Revolution. While not much remains of the war, take this driving tour to get a glimpse of our role in the fight for America's independence.

Start your journey at **Old Fort Niagara (1)** which was the hub for the British and Loyalists during the war, until it was ceded to the Americans in 1783. Travel along I-190S to the town of Lancaster and the **Hull Family Home (2)**. While the house wasn't built until 1810, Warren Hull was a veteran of the war. Continue south through winding country roads until you reach **Goodleburg Cemetery (3)**, eternal resting place of Absalom Blair, a veteran of the war. The final stretch of the journey is an hour south on NY-98S, NY-243E, and NY-19S to Angelica. Named for Angelica Schuyler (sister-in-law to founding father Alexander Hamilton), it is the home of the **Angelica Inn (4)**.

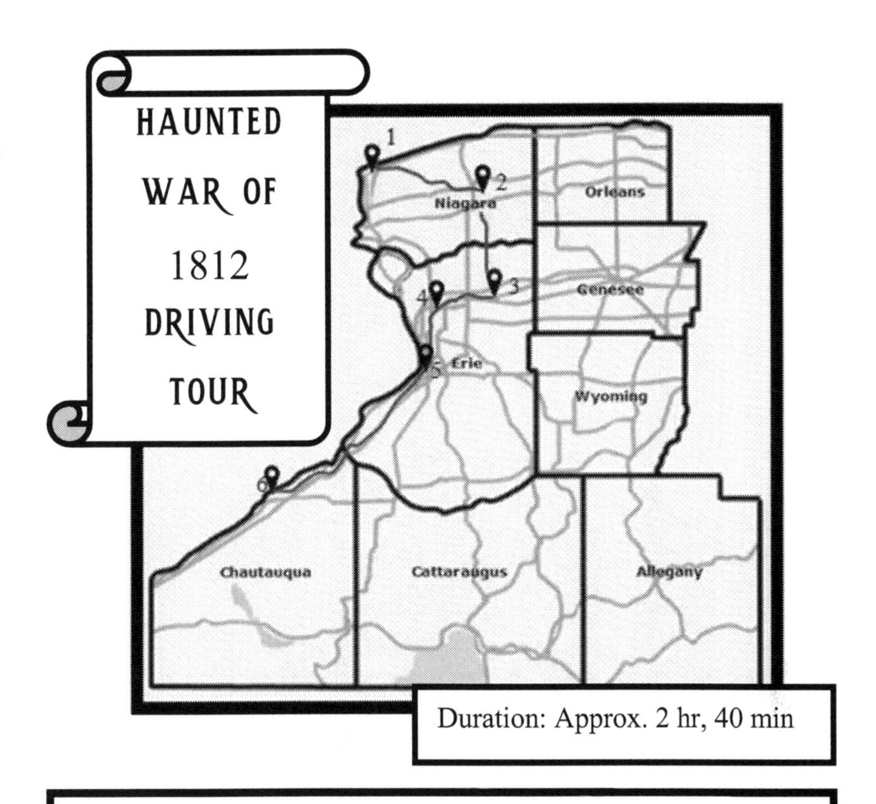

Duration: Approx. 2 hr, 40 min

Western New York was in the middle of the action during the War of 1812, and there are buildings, cemeteries, and hidden pieces of its history scattered all throughout the region.

Begin at **Old Fort Niagara (1)** which was recaptured by the British in 1813. Take NY-93E to **Cold Springs Cemetery (2)** where a group of soldiers mysteriously died on their way to the Niagara Frontier. Continue directly south to the town of Lancaster and the **Hull Family Home (3)**. The house was a witness to the war and today acts as a museum. Take NY-33W into Downtown Buffalo. Over 300 soldiers are buried under the Delaware Park Golf Course in an area known as **Flint Hill (4)**. See if you can find the boulder marking their sacrifice near the fourth hole! Back track to NY-33W and get on NY-5W. You'll pass **Dos on the Lake (5)** which was once the Dock at the Bay. During the War of 1812, it was the Willink Hotel, and a man named James Byrd still haunts the restaurant. Hop over to I-90W until you reach Dunkirk. They say the first shot of the War of 1812 was fired near where the **Dunkirk Lighthouse (6)** now stands!

HAUNTED CIVIL WAR DRIVING TOUR

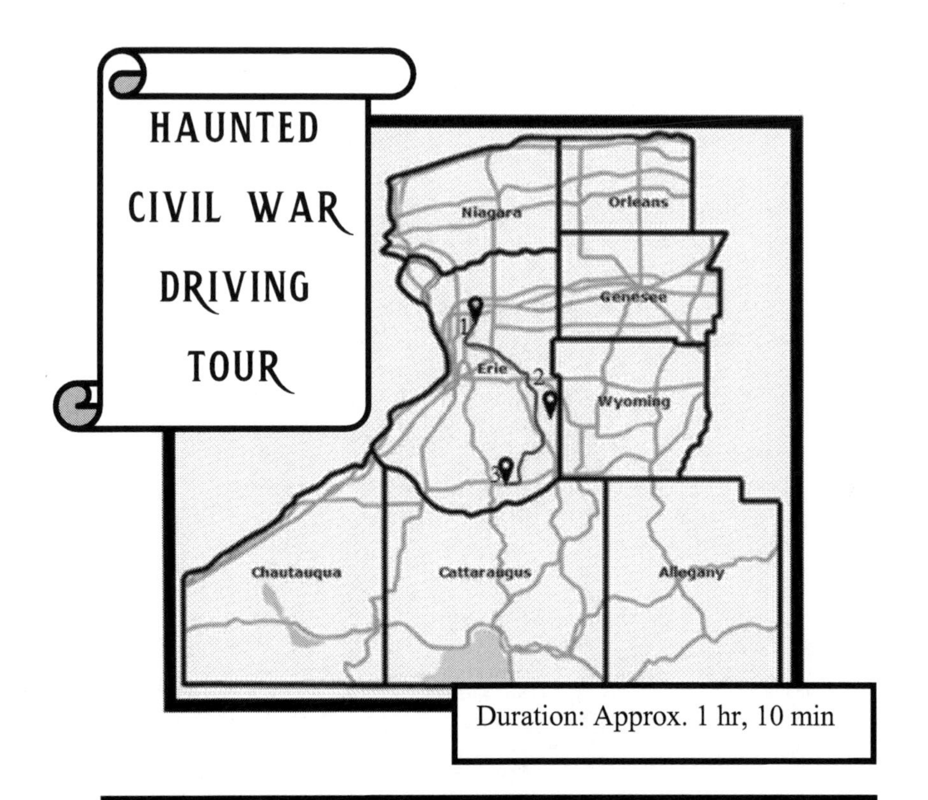

Duration: Approx. 1 hr, 10 min

New York was the most populous state during the Civil War. It also supplied more soldiers for the Union Army than any other state at the time. However, aside from the Draft Riots in Manhattan, there were no battles in New York. That being said, there are still some great locations for the history buff in your life.

You'll want to start at **Buffalo's largest cemetery (1)**. On occasion, they offer a Civil War Trolley tour, but it's fun to just walk around on your own, too (you might end up spending the entire day here). Take NY-33E to I-90W and NY-400S past East Aurora to **Goodleburg Cemetery (2)**. There is a Civil War soldier buried there. After paying your respects (and possibly holding an EVP session), continue south to Springville. You'll end your tour at the **Gardenier House (3)** at 105 East Main Street. The apartment complex was originally home to JP Myers. Myers fought in the Battle of Gettysburg and survived imprisonment in Andersonville, only to disappear without a trace.

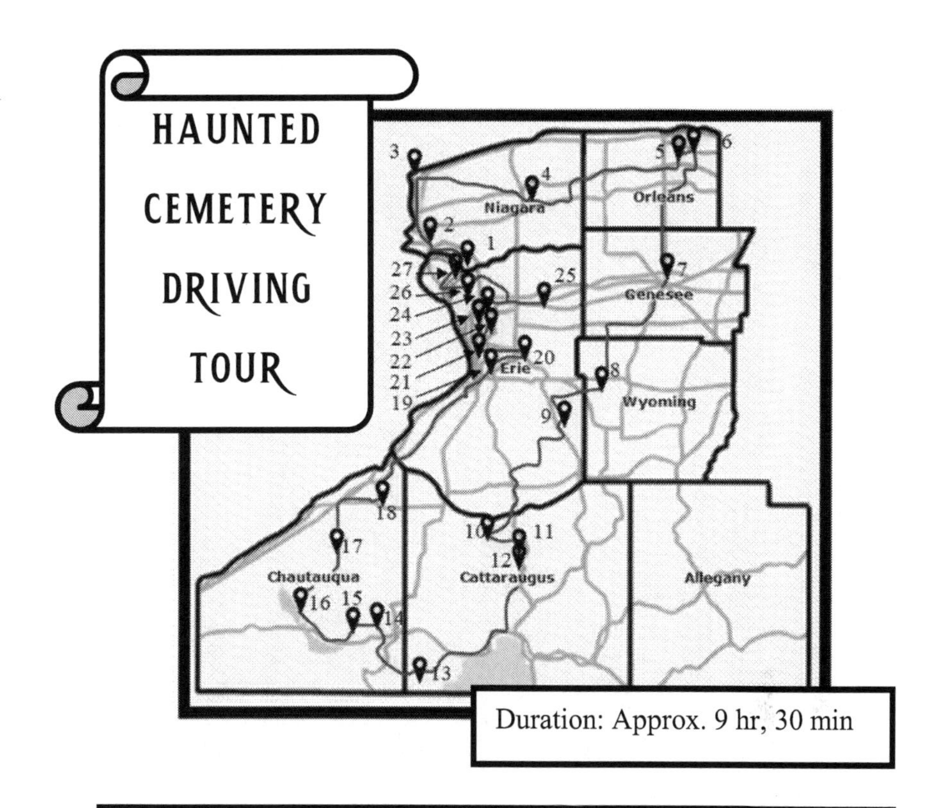

This driving tour includes cemeteries with paranormal claims as well as cemeteries located near haunted houses and roads. Please keep in mind that respect should be shown at all cemeteries, both active and inactive.

Begin your taphophile journey in **Niagara County** at the grave of Aunt Hannah in **Sweeney Cemetery (1)** (not actually located on Sweeney Street, but rather, Payne Avenue). Take River Road and the LeSalle Expressway to **Oakwood Cemetery (2)** in the heart of Niagara Falls. Continue north on the Niagara Scenic Parkway to **Old Fort Niagara (3)** and one of the region's oldest cemeteries. Take NY-93E to Lockport and **Cold Springs Cemetery (4)**.

Enter **Orleans County** along NY-104E and stop on **Ford Street (5)**. There is a small cemetery to go with the werewolf legends along this road. Less than 10 minutes north is **Beechwood Cemetery (6)**.

Head south on NY-98S towards Batavia in **Genesee County**. While there is nothing left of the **Old West Main Street Cemetery (7)**, Batavia Cemetery has some interesting eternal residents.

Take NY-98S and NY-77S to Wyoming County where you'll find **St. John's Cemetery (8)** on Goose Hill Road.

Sneak a peek at **Erie County**'s cemeteries by stopping at the infamous **Goodleburg Cemetery (9)**, just 15 minutes away from Goose Hill Road.

Follow the winding country roads into **Cattaraugus County** until you hit NY-219S and East Otto. You'll find **East Otto Cemetery (10)** on Mill Street just off of Main Street. Back track to Main Street and follow East Flat/East Otto Road (it will bear right and turn into Mill Valley Road). Turn left onto Rohr Hill. You'll find the **grave of the Ashford Hollow Witch (11)** on your left. Head south towards Hencoop Hollow Road in Ellicottville. There is no evidence of **Hencoop Hollow Cemetery (12)**, but keep an eye out for childlike spirits either way. Take the scenic route past Holiday Valley and Allegany State Park along NY-242W, NY-353S, I-86W, and West Bank Perimeter Road to **Gurnsey Hollow Cemetery (13).**

Head northwest to **Chautauqua County**, Jamestown, and **Lake View Cemetery (14)** to find the grave of Lucille Ball and the Lady in Glass. Just three miles beyond that is **Hollenbeck Cemetery (15)**, home to our very own headless horseman. Follow NY-430W along the picturesque Chautauqua Lake to **Dewittville Cemetery (16)** before venturing up County Touring Route 58 to **Lily Dale** to see one of **America's oldest pet cemeteries (17)**. Finish off your time in Chautauqua by following NY-60N and NY-39E to Forestville to check out **Pioneer Cemetery (18)** next to the Bennett House.

Return to **Erie County** by entering Bill's Country and stopping at the **Sheldon Family Cemetery (19)** at New Era Field. Head north on Highway 20 and NY-277 to the **Old Main Street Cemetery (20)** in West Seneca, before continuing up NY-277. Turn onto Indian Church Road where you'll find the **Buffum Street Cemetery (21)**. Head downtown on I-190N to **North Street (22)** and see what we've done to two forgotten cemeteries (hint: we built on top of them). Move north on Delaware Avenue to **Buffalo's largest cemetery (23)** and **Flint Hill in Delaware Park (24)**.

Leave Downtown Buffalo behind you as you hop on the Scajaquada Expressway and NY-33E. Stop at the **Hull Family Home (25)** and take a look around their family cemetery located near the house. Get on I-90W from NY-33W and follow it as it becomes I-290W until you reach **Elmlawn Cemetery (26)** on Delaware Avenue. Return to the highway and cross the Grand Island Bridge. You'll find **Whitehaven Cemetery (27)** next to the former Holiday Inn on Grand Island. If you've timed this right, head back to the Holiday Inn (currently a Radisson) and enjoy their happy hour… you've earned it!

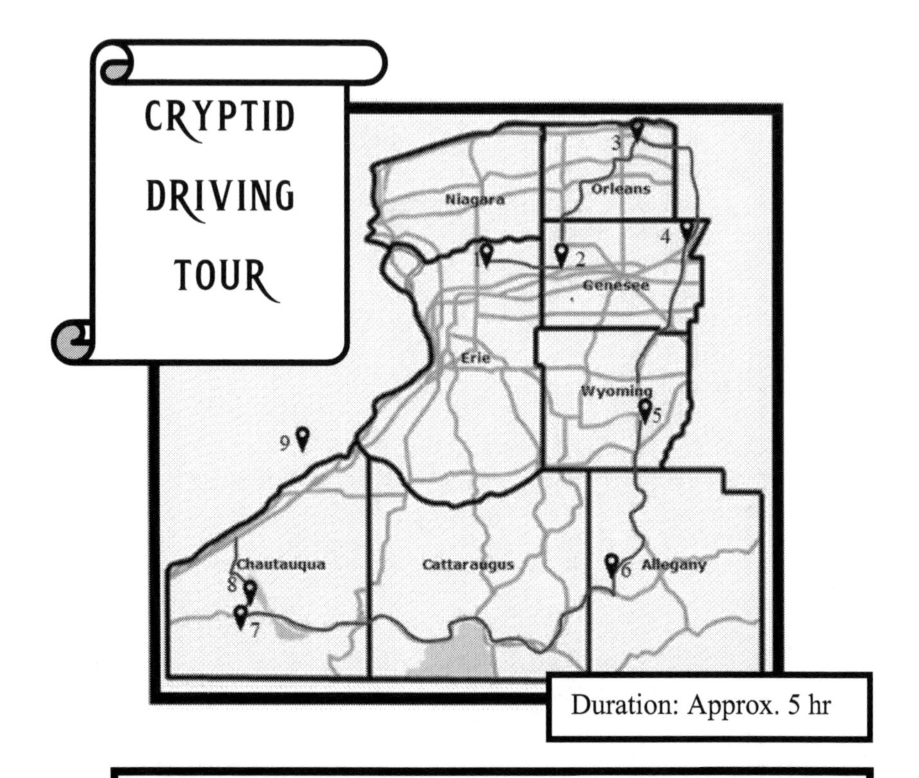

Duration: Approx. 5 hr

Maybe cryptids are more your paranormal cup of tea. Take this wild driving tour to see some of the stranger sights in Western New York.

You'll begin on **Delaware Road (1)** in Clarence Center. Along this stretch are reports of a creature that looks half-horse/half-dog. Head east towards **Sandhill Road (2)** where changelings and little people of Native American lore are spotted. When you arrive in Kent, **Ford Street (3)** will be to the right. Keep an eye out for its resident werewolf. Backtrack to NY-104E and head to Bergen where you'll find the **Bergen House (4)**. Around here, there are reports of fairies and Bigfoot. Continue south to **Silver Lake (5)** to see if you can catch a glimpse of the elusive Silver Lake Serpent. Follow NY-19S to **Spring Valley Road (6)** where there have been reports of an albino Bigfoot since the 1970s. Up next is the long drive west to **Sherman (7)**, home of the Sherman Beast (keep an eye out for giant sloths). You're also in Bigfoot territory now between **Chautauqua (8)** and Findley Lakes. Finish the tour by driving home along **Lake Erie (9)** and keep a weather eye for Bessie (though you're more likely to find her down near Ohio).

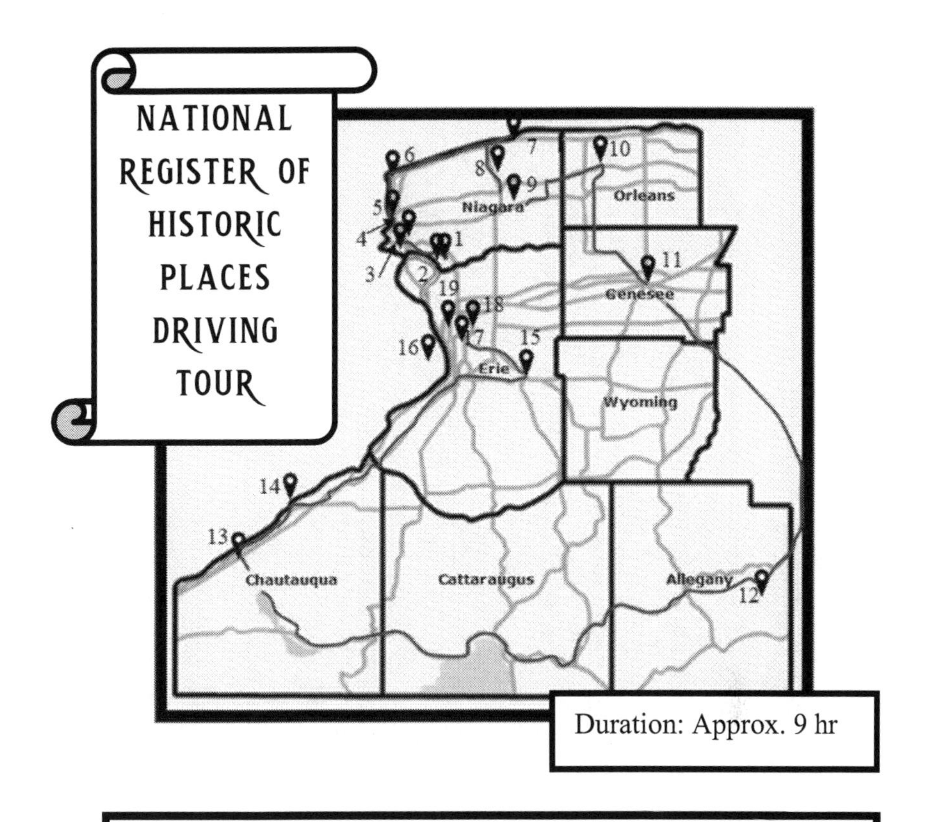

If you're not a believer in the paranormal, why not take this driving tour that brings you to some of our National Historic Landmarks?

Begin in North Tonawanda at the **Riviera Theatre (1)** and **Dick Block (2)**. Head to Niagara Falls where you'll find the **Historic Holy Trinity Church (3)** and **Oakwood Cemetery (4)**. Continue north to the **Frontier House (5)** in Lewiston and **Old Fort Niagara (6)** in Youngstown. Follow NY-18E to **Thirty Mile Point Lighthouse (7)** and the nearby **Van Horn Mansion (8)**. Head south on NY-78 to **Cold Springs Cemetery (9)** before hopping on NY-104 to the **Cobblestone Inn (10)**. Journey south to Batavia where you'll find the **Seymour Place (11)**. You'll continue south into Allegany County to Alfred University and the **Steinheim Castle (12)**. Take I-86W past Allegany State Park and Chautauqua Lake to the **McClurg Mansion (13)**. Drive along Lake Erie to the **Dunkirk Lighthouse (14)** before heading back north to Erie County. Hop on I-90E to East Aurora and the **Roycroft Inn & Campus (15)** before heading downtown. There, you'll find the **Buffalo Naval Park (16)**, **Shea's Performing Arts Center (17)**, **Buffalo's largest cemetery (18)**, and **Hotel Henry (19)**.

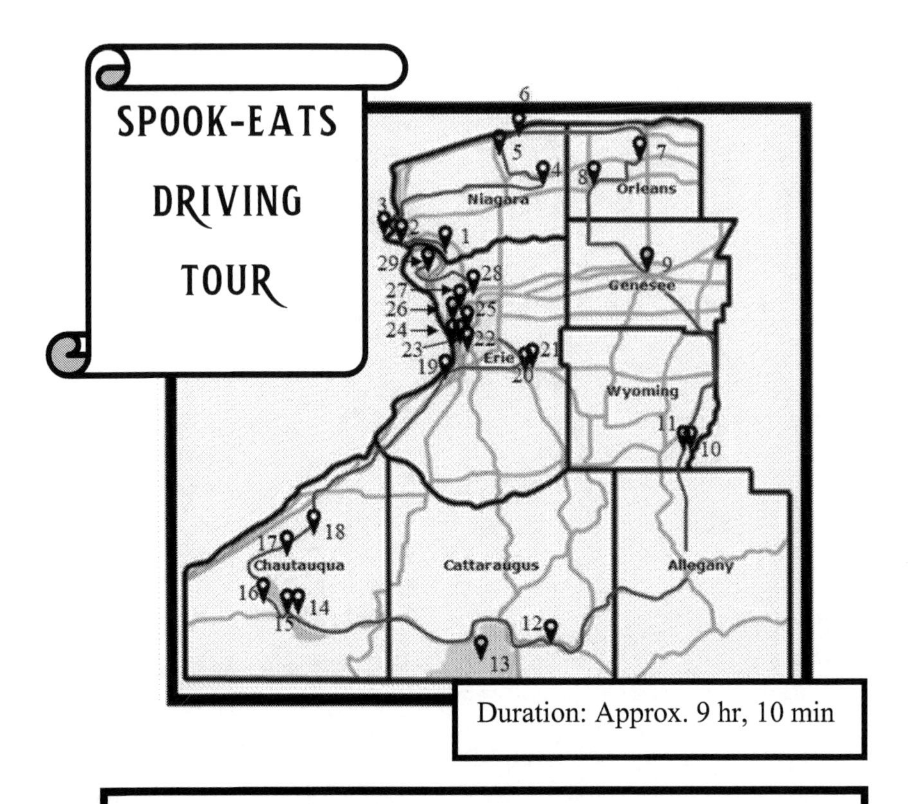

At Spook-Eats, we believe that everyone should be able to experience the paranormal… not just professional investigators. Spook-Eats is all about food, travel, and the supernatural! Check out these restaurants, bars, and hotels for a deliciously spooky time. At these locations, you'll come into contact with some of the most haunted locations in Western New York, and it will only cost you the price of a pint or an appetizer.

Your first stop is the **Dick Block (1)** at Canal Club 62. Head north on River Road to Niagara Falls and the **Red Coach Inn (2)** and **Legends (3)**. Take NY-104E to **Graestone Manor (4)** before heading north. On the shores of Lake Ontario you'll find the **Winery at Marjim Manor (5)** and **Thirty Mile Point Lighthouse (6)** where you can book a night.

Continue down NY-18E to **Tillman's Historic Village Inn (7)** or head further south to Medina and the **Hart House Hotel (8)**.

In Batavia, you'll find the **Seymour Place (9)** and down near Letchworth State Park is the **Genesee Falls Inn (10)** and **Heaven Sent B&B (11)**.

Take I-86W to **Randy's Up the River Bar & Grill (12)** or go camping at **Allegany State Park (13)**.

Continue along I-86 to Chautauqua Lake, home to **Hotel Lenhart (14)**, **Bemus Point Village Casino (15)**, and the **Athenaeum Hotel (16)**. Head northeast to the **Stockton Hotel (17)** and **Lily Dale/Maplewood Hotel (18)**.

Hop on I-90E to **Dos on the Lake (19)** before taking Highway 20A to East Aurora and the **Roycroft Inn (20)** and the **Globe Restaurant (21)**. Follow NY-400N to Downtown Buffalo to visit the **Swannie House (22)**, **Statler City (23)**, **Shea's Performing Arts Center (24)**, the **Mansion on Delaware (25)**, the **Gypsy Parlor (26)**, and **Hotel Henry (27)**. Take NY-33E to **Snyder Bar & Grill (28)** before ending at the **Former Holiday Inn (29)**.

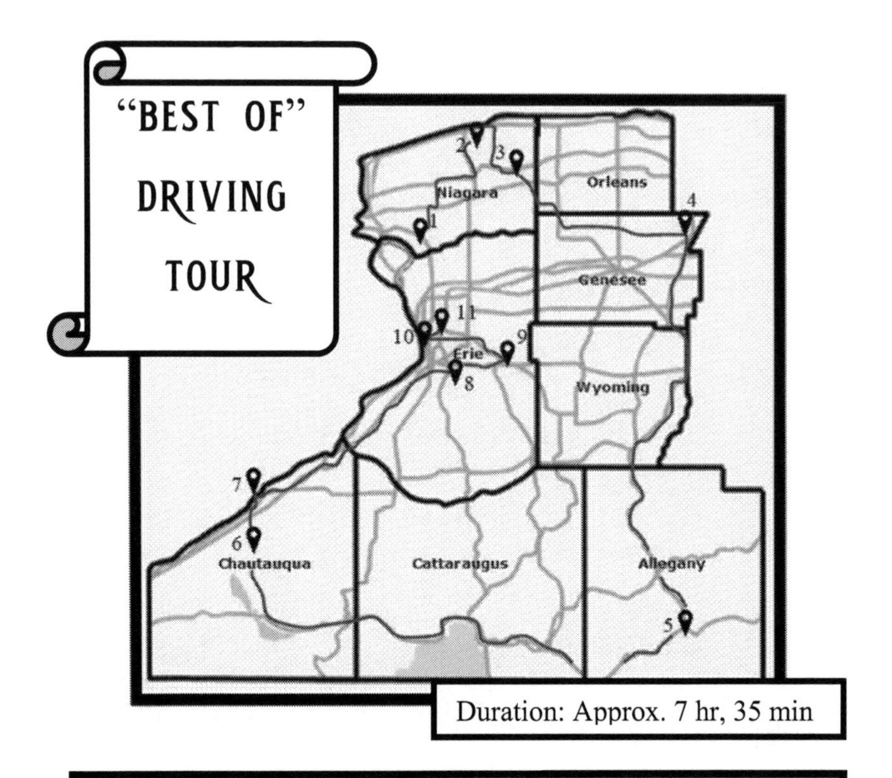

On this "Best of" tour, I'll take you to my favorite haunts. Many of these places I consider to be friends of Spook-Eats and highly recommend you check them out!

The **Ghostlight Theatre (1)** is the first stop on this list where ghosts are captured in photos both on stage and off! Head as far north as you can go (before getting wet) to the **Winery at Marjim Manor (2)** and sample their wines inspired by their ghost stories. Dare to spend the night at **Graestone Manor (3)**, Western New York's most haunted B&B. Journey east to Bergen to check out the incredibly haunted **Bergen House (4)**, then it's the long drive south to the **Pink House (5)** [This is out of the way, but worth it! If you want to cut this from your tour, I'll try not to be too upset.] Take I-86W to the **Stockton Hotel (6)**. Be sure to try their variety of wing sauces! Then it's up to the **Dunkirk Lighthouse (7)** on the shores of Lake Erie. Enjoy the scenic drive along NY-5E to **Eternal Flame Falls (8)**. By now I'm sure you've worked up an appetite, so head to the **Roycroft Inn (9)**. If you're looking for cheaper eats, head up to Buffalo and dine at the **Swannie House (10)**. End your tour at **Iron Island Museum (11)**, one of Buffalo's most haunted locations as seen on *Ghost Hunters*!

SPOOKY BUCKET LIST

___ Allendale Theatre
___ Buffalo Central Terminal
___ Buffalo Museum of Science
___ Buffalo Naval Park
___ Buffalo Public School #61
___ Buffum Street Cemetery
___ Canisius College
___ Coatsworth Mansion
___ Episcopal Church of Ascension
___ Flint Hill
___ German Roman Catholic
___ Orphanage Asylum
___ Gypsy Parlor
___ Iron Island Museum
___ Koessler Admin Building
___ The Mansion on Delaware Ave
___ Maytham Mansions
___ Medaille College
___ North Street
___ St. Mary's School for the Deaf
___ Shea's Performing Arts Center
___ Statler City Hotel
___ The Swannie House
___ Town Ballroom
___ Bergen House
___ Big Falls
___ Darien Lake
___ Old West Main St. Cemetery
___ Sandhill Road
___ Seymour Place
___ Alfred State
___ Alfred University
___ Allegany County Poorhouse
___ Angelica Inn
___ The Pink House
___ Spring Valley Road
___ Allegany State Park
___ Ashford Hollow Witch
___ Dudley Hotel
___ East Otto Cemetery
___ Henrietta Road
___ Hinsdale House
___ J.N. Adam Hospital
___ Randy's Up the River
___ St. Bonaventure
___ Salamanca Historical Society
___ Wildwood Sanitarium
___ Wing Hollow
___ Zoar Valley
___ Assembly Hall
___ Athenaeum Hotel
___ Bemus Point Village Casino
___ The Bennett House
___ Bigfoot Sightings
___ Dewittville Cemetery
___ Dunkirk Lighthouse
___ Gurnsey Hollow Cemetery
___ Hencoop School & Cemetery
___ Hollenbeck Cemetery
___ Holy Cross Seminary Site
___ Hotel Lenhart
___ House of Seven Secrets
___ Igoe Hall
___ Inspiration Stump
___ Jacquins Pond
___ Jefferson Middle School
___ The Lady in Glass
___ Lucille Ball Little Theatre
___ Maplewood Hotel
___ Reg Lenna Civic Center
___ Sherman Beast
___ Stockton Hotel
___ White Inn
___ Aunt Hannah's Grave

___ Black Nose Spring Road
___ Clet Hall
___ Cold Springs Cemetery
___ Cold Springs Road
___ Devil's Hole State Park
___ Dick Block
___ Echo Club
___ Frontier House
___ Ghostlight Theatre
___ Graestone Manor
___ Hall's Apple Farm
___ Historic Holy Trinity Church
___ Kenan House & Center
___ Legends Bar & Grill
___ Lewiston Public Library
___ Lockport Cave
___ Marjim Manor
___ Oakwood Cemetery
___ Old Fort Niagara
___ Rapids Theatre
___ Red Coach Inn
___ Riviera Theatre
___ Thirty Mile Point Lighthouse
___ Tonawanda Island Giants
___ Van Horn Mansion
___ Aurora Players Pavilion
___ Bessie
___ Curtis Hall
___ Delaware Road
___ Dos on the Lake
___ Elmlawn Cemetery
___ Erie County Home
___ Eternal Flame Falls
___ Former Amherst Synagogue
___ Former Holiday Inn
___ Gardenier House
___ Hull Family House
___ The Globe Restaurant
___ Goodleburg Cemetery
___ Lackawanna Basilica
___ Lancaster Opera House
___ Lindbergh Elementary School
___ Murder Creek
___ Mystery Goo
___ New Era Field
___ Old Main Cemetery
___ Pigman Road
___ Roycroft Inn & Campus
___ Snyder Bar & Grill
___ Vidler's
___ Western House
___ Whitehaven Cemetery
___ Beechwood Cemetery
___ Cobblestone Inn
___ County House Road
___ Ford Street Beast
___ Fuller Road
___ Hart House Hotel
___ Pillars Estate
___ Tillman's Historic Village Inn
___ Genesee Falls Inn
___ Heaven Sent Bed & Breakfast
___ St. John's Cemetery
___ Silver Lake Serpent
___ Water Street

APPRECIATION

A book of this size filled with history and mysteries is only possible with the help of countless people and locations who took the time to edit, fact-check, and share their stories with me. This book would be impossible without the help of:

Alfred University Paranormal Investigator's Club

Allegany County Historical Society

The Bergen House

Buffalo Olmsted Parks Conservancy

Cassandra Krysztof

Cathy Heglund (and Walt)

Chautauqua Lake Bigfoot Expo

The Dunkirk Lighthouse

Ellicotville Historical Society

The Ghostlight Theatre

The Globe Restaurant

Grace Pyszczek

Graestone Manor

Heather Rease Mattison

Iron Island Museum

L. Don Swartz

Linda Hastreiter (and Marge)

Liz Staley

Margo Sue Bittner

Marjim Manor

Molly Flynn

North Tonawanda Historical Society

Pete Herr

Peter Wiemer

Roycroft Inn & Campus

Salamanca Historical Society

Soul's Gate Paranormal

Starry Night Theatre, Inc.

Stockton Hotel

Tim Wiles

The Swannie House

The Toy Family

And of course, my family, particularly, my mother and my husband. I dragged them to so many haunted houses, abandoned cemeteries, and creepy roads. But I think they enjoyed it most of the time.

INDEX

RESEARCH

When working in the realm of the paranormal, folklore, and hearsay, it's difficult to cite sources for all the legends and lore.

ALLENDALE THEATRE

Ingersoll, A. (2016, October 26). Allendale employees share tales from inside reportedly haunted theater. Retrieved from https://www.wivb.com/news/allendale-employees-share-tales-from-inside-reportedly-haunted-theater/

(n.d.). Retrieved from http://www.theatreofyouth.org/about-allendale-theatre

Winfield, M. (2008). *Haunted Places of Western New York*(Third ed.). Buffalo, NY: Western New York Wares.

BUFFALO CENTRAL TERMINAL

Buffalo Central Terminal. (n.d.). Retrieved from http://buffalocentralterminal.org/

Speaking with the Dead [Television series episode]. (2008, September 24). In *Ghost Hunters*. Buffalo, NY: SyFy.

Top 10 Most Haunted Places in Buffalo, NY (Updated 2019). (n.d.). Retrieved from https://www.hauntedrooms.com/10-haunted-places-buffalo-ny

Winfield, M. (2008). *Haunted Places of Western New York*(Third ed.). Buffalo, NY: Western New York Wares.

BUFFALO MUSEUM OF SCIENCE

Reilley, C. (n.d.). Find Why. Retrieved from https://www.sciencebuff.org/

Winfield, M. (2008). *Haunted Places of Western New York*(Third ed.). Buffalo, NY: Western New York Wares.

BUFFALO NAVAL PARK

Buffalo and Erie County Naval & Military Park: Family Museum. (n.d.). Retrieved from https://buffalonavalpark.org/

Phantom Fleet [Television series episode]. (2014, January 29). In *Ghost Hunters*. Buffalo, NY: SyFy.

Top 10 Most Haunted Places in Buffalo, NY (Updated 2019). (n.d.). Retrieved from https://www.hauntedrooms.com/10-haunted-places-buffalo-ny

BUFFALO PUBLIC SCHOOL #61

Haunted New York. (n.d.). Retrieved from http://www.ghostquest.net/haunted-new-york.html

BUFFUM STREET CEMETERY

Winfield, M. (2008). *Haunted Places of Western New York*(Third ed.). Buffalo, NY: Western New York Wares.

CANISIUS COLLEGE

Canisius College. (2019, July 29). Retrieved from https://www.canisius.edu/

Rooney, M., & Brandel, R. (2016, October 28). Ghosts of Canisius. *The Griffin*. Retrieved from https://canisiusgriffin.wordpress.com/2016/10/28/ghosts-of-canisius/

Top 10 Most Haunted Places in Buffalo, NY (Updated 2019). (n.d.). Retrieved from https://www.hauntedrooms.com/10-haunted-places-buffalo-ny

COATSWORTH MANSION

LaChiusa, C. (n.d.). Thomas Coatsworth House - Exterior Photos and History. Retrieved from https://www.buffaloah.com/a/cott/49/1/index.html

Nussbaumer, N. (2017, September 28). Sutton Restores Order @ The Coatsworth. Retrieved from https://www.buffalorising.com/2017/09/the-coatsworth/

Winfield, M. (2008). *Haunted Places of Western New York*(Third ed.). Buffalo, NY: Western New York Wares.

EPISCOPAL CHURCH OF ASCENSION

Winfield, M. (2008). *Haunted Places of Western New York*(Third ed.). Buffalo, NY: Western New York Wares.

FLINT HILL

Cichon, S. (2016, November 21). The Mound in the Meadow: Buffalo's Tomb of the Unknowns at Delaware Park [Web log post]. Retrieved from http://blog.buffalostories.com/the-mound-in-the-meadow-buffalos-tomb-of-the-unknowns-at-delaware-park/

Moran, J. (2012, May 25). Monument honors Buffalo's War of 1812 veterans. Retrieved from https://news.wbfo.org/post/monument-honors-buffalos-war-1812-veterans

Schobert, C. (2012, June). 300 bodies in Delaware Park: The War of 1812. *Buffalo Spree.*

Winfield, M. (2008). *Haunted Places of Western New York*(Third ed.). Buffalo, NY: Western New York Wares.

GERMAN ROMAN CATHOLIC ORPHANAGE ASYLUM

German Roman Catholic Orphan Asylum. (n.d.). Retrieved from https://www.hauntedplaces.org/item/german-roman-catholic-orphan-asylum/

Josker, K. R. (n.d.). The German Roman Catholic Orphan Asylum by Karl R. Josker. Retrieved from https://pbase.com/kjosker/germanorphanasylum&page=all

Kirst, S. (2018, March 19). Together as Buffalo orphans, together again a lifetime later. *Buffalo News*. Retrieved from https://buffalonews.com/2018/03/19/sean-kirst-together-as-buffalo-orphans-together-again-a-lifetime-later/

LaChiusa, C. (n.d.). German RC Orphan Home. Retrieved from https://buffaloah.com/a/dodge/564/index.html

Top 10 Most Haunted Places in Buffalo, NY (Updated 2019). (n.d.). Retrieved from https://www.hauntedrooms.com/10-haunted-places-buffalo-ny

GYPSY PARLOR

Gypsy Parlor - Home. (n.d.). Retrieved from http://www.thegypsyparlor.com/

IRON ISLAND MUSEUM

Hastreiter, L. (n.d.). Iron Island Museum Home. Retrieved from https://www.ironislandmuseum.com/

Iron Island [Television series episode]. (2008, September 3). In *Ghost Hunters*. Buffalo, NY: SyFy.

Phillips, M. (Producer). (2011, April 9). A Haunted House [Television series episode]. In *My Ghost Story*. Buffalo, NY: Biography.

The Innocent [Television series episode]. (2010, December 18). In *Ghost Lab*. Buffalo, NY: Discovery.

Top 10 Most Haunted Places in Buffalo, NY (Updated 2019). (n.d.). Retrieved from https://www.hauntedrooms.com/10-haunted-places-buffalo-ny

KOESSLER ADMIN BUILDING

C. (2011, October 17). The Koessler Administration Building (KAB) Gives Me the Creeps. Retrieved from http://voices.dyouville.edu/students/2011/10/17/the-koessler-administration-building-kab-gives-me-the-creeps/

D'Youville: Buffalo New York: D'Youville. (n.d.). Retrieved from http://www.dyc.edu/

THE MANSION ON DELAWARE AVENUE

Buffalo's Luxury Hotel & Wedding Venue - The Mansion on Delaware Ave. (n.d.). Retrieved from https://www.mansionondelaware.com/en-us

LaChiusa, C. (n.d.). Charles F. Sternberg House / The Mansion on Delaware Avenue. Retrieved from https://www.buffaloah.com/a/del/414/ext414/index.html

Winfield, M. (2008). *Haunted Places of Western New York*(Third ed.). Buffalo, NY: Western New York Wares.

MAYTHAM MANSIONS

Claud, D., & OConnor, C. (2009). *Haunted Buffalo: Ghosts of the Queen City*. Charleston, SC: History Press.

LaChiusa, C. (n.d.). The Maytham Houses (Also known as the Millonzi House). Retrieved from https://buffaloah.com/a/sym/71/index.html

Winfield, M. (2008). *Haunted Places of Western New York*(Third ed.). Buffalo, NY: Western New York Wares.

MEDAILLE COLLEGE

Haunted Buffalo: The Hanged Boy of Medaille College. (2019, June 17). Retrieved from https://backpackerverse.com/haunted-buffalo-the-hanged-boy-of-medaille-college/

Higher Ed That Prepares for Your Career. (n.d.). Retrieved from https://www.medaille.edu

NORTH STREET

Hodge, W. (1879, February 4). Excerpts from "Buffalo Cemeteries". Retrieved from https://buffaloah.com/h/cemet/hodge.html

Kunz Goldman, M. (2016, October 30). Could these WNY houses truly be haunted? *Gusto*. Retrieved from https://buffalonews.com/2016/10/30/wny-houses-truly-haunted/

Winfield, M. (2008). *Haunted Places of Western New York*(Third ed.). Buffalo, NY: Western New York Wares.

ST. MARY'S SCHOOL FOR THE DEAF

Haunted New York. (n.d.). Retrieved from http://www.ghostquest.net/haunted-new-york.html

School Information / History. (n.d.). Retrieved from https://www.smsdk12.org/domain/21

Top 10 Most Haunted Places in Buffalo, NY (Updated 2019). (n.d.). Retrieved from https://www.hauntedrooms.com/10-haunted-places-buffalo-ny

SHEA'S PERFORMING ARTS CENTER

Homepage. (n.d.). Retrieved from https://www.sheas.org/

Top 10 Most Haunted Places in Buffalo, NY (Updated 2019). (n.d.). Retrieved from https://www.hauntedrooms.com/10-haunted-places-buffalo-ny

Winfield, M. (2008). *Haunted Places of Western New York* (Third ed.). Buffalo, NY: Western New York Wares.

STATLER CITY HOTEL

Randall, M. (2016, February 8). Hunting for ghosts at Statler City. Retrieved from https://www.wkbw.com/news/hunting-for-ghosts-at-statler-city

Statler City. (n.d.). Retrieved from https://www.statlercity.com/

Statler City Hotel [Television series episode]. (2017, January 27). In *Paranormal Lockdown*. Buffalo, NY: Destination America.

Statler Ghost Tours. (n.d.). Retrieved from https://statlerghosttours.com/

THE SWANNIE HOUSE

LaChiusa, C. (n.d.). Swannie House. Retrieved from https://buffaloah.com/a/wat/swan.html

TOWN BALLROOM

Top 10 Most Haunted Places in Buffalo, NY (Updated 2019). (n.d.). Retrieved from https://www.hauntedrooms.com/10-haunted-places-buffalo-ny

Town Ballroom. (n.d.). Retrieved from https://www.townballroom.com/

Winfield, M. (2008). *Haunted Places of Western New York* (Third ed.). Buffalo, NY: Western New York Wares.

BERGEN HOUSE

Book Query [E-mail to C. Heglund]. (2019, June 30).

De France, S. (Producer). (2017, May 31). Multiple Spirit Disorder [Television series episode]. In *Paranormal Survivor*. Bergen, NY: Travel.

BIG FALLS

Big Falls at Indian Falls. (2015, December 4). Retrieved from https://www.newyorkhauntedhouses.com/real-haunt/big-falls-at-indian-falls.html

DARIEN LAKE

A. (1988, June 14). 86 Deaths by Lightning in '87, Highest Toll of This Decade. *New York Times*. Retrieved from https://www.nytimes.com/1988/06/14/us/86-deaths-by-lightning-in-87-highest-toll-of-this-decade.html

Katrandjian, O. (2011, July 9). Double Amputee and Iraq War Veteran Dies After Being Ejected From a Roller Coaster in NY. *ABC News*. Retrieved from https://abcnews.go.com/US/double-amputee-iraq-war-veteran-dies-ejected-roller/story?id=14036837

Missing man's body pulled from water at Darien Lake. (2009, September 6). *Buffalo News*. Retrieved from https://web.archive.org/web/20090908011458/http://www.buffalonews.com/258/story/786889.html

Winfield, M. (2008). *Haunted Places of Western New York* (Third ed.). Buffalo, NY: Western New York Wares.

OLD WEST MAIN STREET CEMETERY

West Main Street Cemetery. (2015, August 15). Retrieved from https://www.newyorkhauntedhouses.com/real-haunt/west-main-street-cemetery.html

Winfield, M. (2008). *Haunted Places of Western New York* (Third ed.). Buffalo, NY: Western New York Wares.

SANDHILL ROAD

Furtman, M. (2000). *Magic on the rocks: Canoe country pictographs*. Duluth, MN: Birch Portage Press.

Winfield, M. (2008). *Haunted Places of Western New York* (Third ed.). Buffalo, NY: Western New York Wares.

SEYMOUR PLACE

Home. (n.d.). Retrieved from https://www.goart.org/

Tavern 2.o.1. (n.d.). Retrieved from https://www.goart.org/tavern-2o1

ALFRED STATE MACKENZIE COMPLEX

MacKenzie Complex. (n.d.). Retrieved from http://www.alfredstate.edu/student-life/housing/mackenzie-complex

Ross, K. (2015, October 15). LIST: Haunted places in Allegany, Cattaraugus and Steuben counties. *The Evening Tribune*. Retrieved from https://www.eveningtribune.com/article/20151015/NEWS/151019838

ALFRED UNIVERSITY

HauntedPlaces.org. (n.d.). Alfred University. Retrieved from https://www.hauntedplaces.org/item/alfred-university/

Outside of Ordinary: Alfred University. (n.d.). Retrieved from https://www.alfred.edu/

Paranormal Investigators of Alfred University. (n.d.). Retrieved from https://alfred.campuslabs.com/engage/organization/ghosts

Ross, K. (2015, October 15). LIST: Haunted places in Allegany, Cattaraugus and Steuben counties. *The Evening Tribune*. Retrieved from https://www.eveningtribune.com/article/20151015/NEWS/151019838

ALLEGANY COUNTY POORHOUSE

Cahal, S. (2018, September 25). Allegany County Poorhouse. Retrieved from http://abandonedonline.net/location/allegany-county-poorhouse/

Wagner, C. (2018, January 8). Allegany County poorhouse 'old, rotten and filthy'. *Orlean Times Herald*. Retrieved from http://www.oleantimesherald.com/news/allegany-county-poorhouse-old-rotten-and-filthy/article_e15a3862-f423-11e7-a2d0-6339213dd122.html

Wheeler, A. (2018, July 13). Smouldering Embers : Abandoned Allegany County Home. Retrieved from https://www.theexplorographer.com/2013/12/smouldering-embers-allegany-county-home-2/

ANGELICA INN

Donohue, D. M. (2015, April 11). Angelica Inn on auction block for fifth time. *Olean Times Herald*. Retrieved from http://www.oleantimesherald.com/news/angelica-inn-on-auction-block-for-fifth-time/article_79326e5c-e00e-11e4-9744-63db3051fb0a.html

Ross, K. (2012, April 20). Angelica Inn's history at an end Saturday with auction. *Wellsville Daily Reporter*. Retrieved from https://www.wellsvilledaily.com/article/20120420/NEWS/304209984

Winfield, M. (2008). *Haunted Places of Western New York* (Third ed.). Buffalo, NY: Western New York Wares.

THE PINK HOUSE

Doyle, K. (2008, October 30). Pink paint, ghost tales won't fade in Wellsville. *Orlean Times Herald*. Retrieved from http://www.oleantimesherald.com/news/pink-paint-ghost-tales-won-t-fade-in-wellsville/article_e103df24-97c9-5232-8c53-2065965015dc.html

Potter, C. (2018, December 28). Pink House still fascinates after 150 years. *Wellsville Daily Reporter*. Retrieved from https://www.wellsvilledaily.com/news/20181228/pink-house-still-fascinates-after-150-years

Winfield, M. (2008). *Haunted Places of Western New York* (Third ed.). Buffalo, NY: Western New York Wares.

SPRING VALLEY ROAD

Report # 11726 (Class A). (2005, May 16). Retrieved from http://bfro.net/GDB/show_report.asp?id=11726

Winfield, M. (2008). *Haunted Places of Western New York* (Third ed.). Buffalo, NY: Western New York Wares.

Witness has two encounters with an animal near Genesee River. (1998, February). Retrieved from http://squatchable.com/report.asp?id=2597&title=Witness has two encounters with an animal near Genesee River

ALLEGANY STATE PARK

Everts, D. (2015, October 31). Hauntings at Allegany State Park recalled. *Salamanca Press*. Retrieved from http://www.salamancapress.com/news/hauntings-at-allegany-state-park-recalled/article_b9aa67d4-7da5-11e5-8275-f3f51d303d4f.html

Winfield, M. (2008). *Haunted Places of Western New York* (Third ed.). Buffalo, NY: Western New York Wares.

ASHFORD HOLLOW WITCH

Clemens, C. (2017, November 12). Grave of the Ashford Hollow Witch |. Retrieved from https://exploringupstate.com/grave-ashford-hollow-witch/

DUDLEY HOTEL

Event. (n.d.). Retrieved from https://www.brownpapertickets.com/event/2601119

Place, R. (2014, August 8). Potential buyer eyeing Dudley Hotel. *Salamanca Press*. Retrieved from http://www.salamancapress.com/news/potential-buyer-eyeing-dudley-hotel/article_2ba8e368-1f17-11e4-a59b-0019bb2963f4.html

Quigley, K. (2015, April 28). Theories of a haunted hotel again tested at the Dudley. *Salamanca Press*. Retrieved from http://www.salamancapress.com/news/theories-of-a-haunted-hotel-again-tested-at-the-dudley/article_48620bec-edde-11e4-9d02-a73ad309bdb7.html

EAST OTTO CEMETERY

East Otto Cemetery. (n.d.). Retrieved from https://www.hauntedplaces.org/item/east-otto-cemetery/

GURNSEY HOLLOW CEMETERY

Gethard, C., Moran, M., & Sceurman, M. (2010). *Weird New York: Your travel guide to New Yorks local legends and best kept secrets* (Second ed.). New York: Sterling Pub.

Haunted Gurnsey Hollow Cemetery : Frewsburg, NY. (n.d.). Retrieved from https://www.trytoscare.me/legend/gurnsey-hollow-cemetery-frewsburg-ny/

Winfield, M. (2008). *Haunted Places of Western New York* (Third ed.). Buffalo, NY: Western New York Wares.

HENCOOP SCHOOL & CEMETERY

Haunted New York. (n.d.). Retrieved from http://www.ghostquest.net/haunted-new-york.html

HENRIETTA ROAD

Winfield, M. (2008). *Haunted Places of Western New York* (Third ed.). Buffalo, NY: Western New York Wares.

HINSDALE HOUSE

Alexander, K. (2018, October 31). Buffalo's Best Haunted Place: The Hinsdale House. Retrieved from https://www.wivb.com/buffalos-best/buffalos-best-haunted-place-the-hinsdale-house/

Hinsdale House [Television series episode]. (2016, April 1). In *Paranormal Lockdown*. Hinsdale, NY: Destination America.

Silverman, L. (Producer). (2006, September 21). Dark Forest [Television series episode]. In *A Haunting*. Hinsdale, NY: Discovery.

J.N. ADAM HOSPITAL

Cichon, S. (2016, November 28). Buffalo in the '20s: At JN Adam Memorial, a groundbreaking 'sun cure' for tuberculosis. *Buffalo News*. Retrieved from https://buffalonews.com/2016/11/28/buffalo-20s-sun-cure-tuberculosis/

J N Adam Facility. (n.d.). Retrieved from https://historicpath.com/article/j-n-adam-facility-192

Kuczkowski, A. (2017, October 29). No easy answers for JN Adam Center. *Observer*. Retrieved from https://www.observertoday.com/news/2017/10/no-easy-answers-for-jn-adam-center/

RANDY'S UP THE RIVER BAR & GRILL

Fish Fry, Beer. (n.d.). Retrieved from https://www.randysuptheriver.com/

Sager, K. D. (2009, October 31). Owners can't explain tavern's creepy incidents. *Olean Times Herald*. Retrieved from http://www.oleantimesherald.com/news/owners-can-t-explain-tavern-s-creepy-incidents/article_8b1c38a9-0b47-5ede-8d1a-1977725933ef.html

ST. BONAVENTURE

St. Bonaventure University. (n.d.). Retrieved from https://www.sbu.edu/

Winfield, M. (2008). *Haunted Places of Western New York* (Third ed.). Buffalo, NY: Western New York Wares.

Zaniello, J. (1988, January 22). The Curious Truth:Ghosts and haunted mysteries of St. Bonaventu. Retrieved from http://archives.sbu.edu/studentpages/ghost/paranormal_rumors_lurk_in_the_shadows_of_st__bonaventure.htm

SALAMANCA HISTORICAL SOCIETY

Book Inquiry [E-mail to N. Riggs]. (2018, December 8).

Shsm. (n.d.). Retrieved from https://www.salamancanyhistoricalmuseum.org/

WILDWOOD SANITARIUM

Welcome to Wildwood Sanitarium. (n.d.). Retrieved from http://www.wildwoodsanitarium.com/

Wildwood Sanitarium [Television series episode]. (2018, March 8). In *Paranormal Lockdown*. Salamanca, NY: Destination America.

WING HOLLOW

Hancock, P. (n.d.). Haunted Places - New York USA. Retrieved from https://www.psychic-revelation.com/reference/e_h/haunted_places/usa/new_york/usa_ny_001.html

Herbeck, D. (2017, January 14). Cold Case Files: The Ski Wing murders of 1978. *Buffalo News*. Retrieved from https://buffalonews.com/2017/01/14/ski-wing-murders-39-year-southern-tier-mystery/

Potter, E. (n.d.). Grosstal/Ski Wing/Wing Hollow: A Storied History, Races, Parties and Unsolved Murder. *Ellicottville Times*. Retrieved from http://www.ellicottvilletimes.com/2016/02/04/grosstalski-wingwing-hollow-a-storied-history-races-parties-and-unsolved-murder/

ZOAR VALLEY

Gethard, C., Moran, M., & Sceurman, M. (2010). *Weird New York: Your travel guide to New Yorks local legends and best kept secrets* (Second ed.). New York: Sterling Pub.

McShea, K. (2018, June 10). At beautiful and dangerous Zoar Valley, a cautionary tale for hikers. *Buffalo News*. Retrieved from https://buffalonews.com/2018/06/10/at-beautiful-and-dangerous-zoar-valley-a-cautionary-tale-for-hikers/

Winfield, M. (2008). *Haunted Places of Western New York* (Third ed.). Buffalo, NY: Western New York Wares.

ASSEMBLY HALL

Assembly Hall. (n.d.). Retrieved from https://lilydaleassembly.org/venue/lakeside-assembly-hall/

Gethard, C., Moran, M., & Sceurman, M. (2010). *Weird New York: Your travel guide to New Yorks local legends and best kept secrets* (Second ed.). New York: Sterling Pub.

ATHENAEUM HOTEL

Athenaeum Hotel. (n.d.). Retrieved from https://chq.org/athenaeum-hotel

Parisi, N. J. (2011, July/August). Chautauqua Institution's Athenaeum Hotel. *Buffalo Spree*.

Winfield, M. (2008). *Haunted Places of Western New York* (Third ed.). Buffalo, NY: Western New York Wares.

BEMUS POINT VILLAGE CASINO

Popular Meals. (n.d.). Retrieved from https://www.bemuspointcasino.com/

The Village Casino. (n.d.). Retrieved from https://www.hauntedplaces.org/item/the-village-casino/

THE BENNETT HOUSE

Bare Bones & Octagon Haunting [Television series episode]. (2012, August 1). In *Haunted Collector*. Forestville, NY: SyFy.

Newbery, J. (2017, December 07). Why Buy A Real Haunted House? Retrieved from https://www.huffpost.com/entry/why-buy-a-real-haunted-ho_b_10704884?guccounter=1&guce_referrer=aHR0cHM6Ly93d3cuZ29vZ2xlLmNvbS8&guce_referrer_sig=AQAAAD6E4xlADoLGPj5WKgFxsyjIZ0YlvhaCu96VSnkwVdOm9RolMTCPBRgomlyRTpfgqRNdLBCBvwQk92ZfwYJqjOCz7UMnkpC-kd0U7BV3ECa3-iI1lQTk3hy2EvRi-ZwcLqcFGhGmzsf6_x0i0eC5Dqt5vpRAypbiHPaeM3zDCcRB

BIGFOOT

Tracking Belief in Bigfoot (Infographic). (2012, March 21). Retrieved from https://www.livescience.com/19178-tracking-belief-bigfoot-infographic.html

Wiemer, P. (n.d.). I've Seen Bigfoot®. Retrieved from https://wewanchu.com/Ihaveseenbigfoot/

Winfield, M. (1997). *Shadows of the western door: Haunted sites and ancient mysteries of upstate New York* (Fourth ed.). Buffalo, NY: Western New York Wares.

DEWITTVILLE CEMETERY

Haunted New York. (n.d.). Retrieved from http://www.ghostquest.net/haunted-new-york.html

DUNKIRK LIGHTHOUSE

Dunkirk Lighthouse. (n.d.). Retrieved from https://www.dunkirklighthouse.com/

HOLLENBECK CEMETERY

Hollenbeck Cemetery. (n.d.). Retrieved from https://www.hauntedplaces.org/item/hollenbeck-cemetery/

HOLY CROSS SEMINARY SITE

Passionist Historical Archives. (2013, November 14). Retrieved from http://www.cpprovince.org/archives/histsummary/dunkirk-sum.php

Shepard, D. (n.d.). Holy Cross Seminary. Retrieved March, 2011, from http://app.chautauquacounty.com/hist_struct/Dunkirk/4680WestLakeRoadDunkirkTheHolyCrossSeminary.html

HOTEL LENHART

Frontier Mixology. (2015, September 15). Destination Cocktail: The Lenhart Rocker. Retrieved from https://frontiermixology.wordpress.com/2014/07/20/destination-cocktail-the-lenhart-rocker/

Hotel Lenhart. (n.d.). Retrieved from http://www.hotellenhart.com/

Mulville, M. (2019, July 12). A Closer Look: Late 19th century Hotel Lenhart in Bemus Point. *Buffalo News*. Retrieved from https://buffalonews.com/2019/07/11/gallery12431/

HOUSE OF SEVEN SECRETS

EverHaunt. (2016, March 18). Our Area's Most Haunted Places... Jamestown, NY. Retrieved from https://www.facebook.com/notes/everhaunt/our-areas-most-haunted-places-jamestown-ny-little-theatre-the-house-of-seven-sec/1226933167336219/

IGOE HALL

Igoe Hall. (n.d.). Retrieved from https://www.fredonia.edu/student-life/residence-life/igoe

Igoe Hall, SUNY Fredonia. (2015, August 15). Retrieved from https://www.newyorkhauntedhouses.com/real-haunt/-igoe-hall-suny-fredonia.html

Winfield, M. (2008). *Haunted Places of Western New York* (Third ed.). Buffalo, NY: Western New York Wares.

INSPIRATION STUMP

Gethard, C., Moran, M., & Sceurman, M. (2010). *Weird New York: Your travel guide to New Yorks local legends and best kept secrets* (Second ed.). New York: Sterling Pub.

Inspiration Stump. (n.d.). Retrieved from https://lilydaleassembly.org/place-to-see-points-of-interest/inspiration-stump/

JACQUINS POND

Jacquins Pond. (n.d.). Retrieved from https://www.hauntedplaces.org/item/Jacquins-pond/

Jacquins Pond Wildlife Management Area. (n.d.). Retrieved from https://www.dec.ny.gov/outdoor/83075.html

JEFFERSON MIDDLE SCHOOL

195-197 Martin Rd, Jamestown, NY 14701 - 168037895. (n.d.). Retrieved from https://www.realtytrac.com/property/ny/jamestown/14701/195-197-martin-rd/168037895/

Jefferson Middle School / Homepage. (n.d.). Retrieved from https://www.jpsny.org/Jefferson

THE LADY IN GLASS

Kirst, S. (2017, October 28). Legend of 'Lady in the glass case' begins with singer who died too young. Buffalo News. Retrieved from https://buffalonews.com/2017/10/28/sean-kirst-legend-of-lady-in-the-glass-case-begins-with-singer-who-died-too-young/

Mullville, M. (2018, January 10). The true story behind Jamestown's haunting Lady in Glass. *Buffalo News*. Retrieved from https://buffalonews.com/2017/10/31/gallery9278/

Przepasniak, E. (2019 September 12). 15 Places in Western New York sure to send a shiver down your spine. *Buffalo News*. Retrieved from https://buffalonews.com/2019/09/12/gallery11434/

LUCILLE BALL LITTLE THEATRE

Lucille Ball Little Theatre. (2015, August 15). Retrieved from https://www.newyorkhauntedhouses.com/real-haunt/lucille-ball-little-theatre.html

Lucille Ball Little Theatre of Jamestown. (n.d.). Retrieved from http://www.lucilleballlittletheatre.org/

MAPLEWOOD HOTEL

Gethard, C., Moran, M., & Sceurman, M. (2010). *Weird New York: Your travel guide to New Yorks local legends and best kept secrets* (Second ed.). New York: Sterling Pub.

Lily Dale Hotels. (n.d.). Retrieved from https://lilydaleassembly.org/general-information/accommodations/lily-dale-hotels/

REG LENNA CIVIC CENTER

Reg Lenna Center For The Arts. (n.d.). Retrieved from https://reglenna.com/

Winfield, M. (2008). *Haunted Places of Western New York* (Third ed.). Buffalo, NY: Western New York Wares.

SHERMAN BEAST

Lamoureux, A. (2019, January 30). This Sloth Monster Is Said To Roam The Amazon Rainforest – Here's What The Evidence Says. Retrieved from https://allthatsinteresting.com/mapinguari

Morphy, R. (2012, November 16). Mystery Beasts of Sherman: (New York, USA). Retrieved from https://www.cryptopia.us/site/2011/04/mystery-beasts-of-sherman-new-york-usa/

STOCKTON HOTEL

Stockton Hotel/ NY/ Hotel. (n.d.). Retrieved from https://www.stocktonhotelny.com/

WHITE INN

Stafford, M. (2019, March 30). Mortgage holder buys White Inn. *Observer*. Retrieved from https://www.observertoday.com/news/page-one/2019/03/mortgage-holder-buys-white-inn/

Strickler, L. (2010, March 05). Paranormal Mysteries at the White Inn. Retrieved from https://www.phantomsandmonsters.com/2010/03/paranormal-mysteries-at-white-inn.html

Winfield, M. (2008). *Haunted Places of Western New York* (Third ed.). Buffalo, NY: Western New York Wares.

AUNT HANNAH'S GRAVE

Black Hannah Gone. (1883, June 28). *Tonawanda Herald*. Retrieved from http://www.nthistory.com/items/show/1037

Exploring a Legend--The Story of Black Hannah and the Ku Klux Klan. (2006, August 7). *Tonawanda News*. Retrieved from http://www.nthistory.com/items/show/1036

Reed, D., Jr. (n.d.). Hannah Johnson. Retrieved from http://www.nthistory.com/collections/show/8

BLACK NOSE SPRING ROAD

Winfield, M. (2008). *Haunted Places of Western New York* (Third ed.). Buffalo, NY: Western New York Wares.

CLET HALL

Clet Hall. (n.d.). Retrieved from https://www.niagara.edu/clet-hall/

Pearl, M. (2016, January 11). The Ghost Of Clet Hall. *Odyssey*. Retrieved from https://www.theodysseyonline.com/ghost-clet-hall

Winfield, M. (2008). *Haunted Places of Western New York* (Third ed.). Buffalo, NY: Western New York Wares.

COLD SPRINGS CEMETERY

Gill, S. (2018, April 24). These 8 Haunted Cemeteries Near Buffalo Are Not For the Faint of Heart. Retrieved from https://www.onlyinyourstate.com/new-york/buffalo/haunted-cemeteries-buffalo/

History. (n.d.). Retrieved from https://coldspringscem.weebly.com/history.html

Linnabery, A. (2017, November 5). Niagara Discoveries: Niagara County is home to many ghosts, part II. *Lockport Journal*. Retrieved from https://www.lockportjournal.com/news/lifestyles/niagara-discoveries-niagara-county-is-home-to-many-ghosts-part/article_7a7c5f94-d243-53ff-8383-8b0bd96f78cf.html

Rug, N. (2016, October 5). Niagara's haunted history is fun to explore. *Lockport Union-Sun & Journal*. Retrieved from https://www.lockportjournal.com/opinion/niagara-s-haunted-history-is-fun-to-explore/article_db726ccd-f50f-5a8d-a9f1-f6c80722e424.html

COLD SPRINGS ROAD

Linnabery, A. (2017, November 5). Niagara Discoveries: Niagara County is home to many ghosts, part II. *Lockport Journal*. Retrieved from https://www.lockportjournal.com/news/lifestyles/niagara-discoveries-niagara-county-is-home-to-many-ghosts-part/article_7a7c5f94-d243-53ff-8383-8b0bd96f78cf.html

Winfield, M. (2008). *Haunted Places of Western New York* (Third ed.). Buffalo, NY: Western New York Wares.

DEVIL'S HOLE STATE PARK

Gethard, C., Moran, M., & Sceurman, M. (2010). *Weird New York: Your travel guide to New Yorks local legends and best kept secrets* (Second ed.). New York: Sterling Pub.

Niagara Falls - Devils Hole & the Devils Hole Massacre. (2012, February 20). Retrieved from http://www.niagarafrontier.com/devilhole.html

Parks, Recreation and Historic Preservation. (n.d.). Retrieved from https://parks.ny.gov/parks/42/

The Ultimate Niagara Falls Ghost Guide. (n.d.). Retrieved from https://maps.roadtrippers.com/trips/14520492

Winfield, M. (2008). *Haunted Places of Western New York* (Third ed.). Buffalo, NY: Western New York Wares.

DICK BLOCK

National Register of Historic Places Listings. (2012, December 14). Retrieved from https://www.nps.gov/nr/listings/20121214.htm

ECHO CLUB

DeLuca, M. (2013, March 5). Falls' Echo Club's ghostly secrets explored on SyFy channel. *Niagara Gazette*. Retrieved from https://www.niagara-gazette.com/news/local_news/falls-echo-club-s-ghostly-secrets-explored-on-syfy-channel/article_9580b27b-4bd2-51d9-9bf9-5b0d06ee2926.html

Farm Stalker & Echo Club Spirits [Television series episode]. (2013, March 6). In *Haunted Collector*. Niagara Falls, NY: SyFy.

Fink, J. (2018, October 31). A piece of Niagara Falls' history goes on the market. *Buffalo Business First*. Retrieved from https://www.bizjournals.com/buffalo/news/2018/10/31/a-piece-of-niagara-falls-history-goes-on-the.html

Moose, Jr. (2013, April 9). The Echo: Present, Past and Haunted History in Niagara Falls. Retrieved from http://www.niagarafallsreporter.com/Stories/2013/Apr09/The Echo.html

FRONTIER HOUSE

Andrews, C. (2011, October 12). The Haunted McDonald's and the Legendary Restaurateur. Retrieved from https://www.thedailymeal.com/haunted-mcdonalds-and-legendary-restaurateur

Joe, B. (2019, February 12). Frontier House sold in the Village of Lewiston. *Niagara Gazette*. Retrieved from https://www.niagara-gazette.com/news/local_news/frontier-house-sold-in-the-village-of-lewiston/article_2ccdec5a-2f18-11e9-94bc-4b0f70a9b6bb.html

Maloni, J. (2019, February 12). SOLD! Frontier House has new owners. *Lewiston Porter Sentinel*. Retrieved from https://www.wnypapers.com/news/article/featured/2019/02/12/135922/sold-frontier-house-has-new-owners

GHOSTLIGHT THEATRE

Ghostlight Theatre. (n.d.). Retrieved from https://www.starrynighttheatre.com/

GRAESTONE MANOR

Hoffman, C. (2018, May 6). Owners hope to transform Graestone Manor into bed and breakfast. *Lockport Journal*. Retrieved from https://www.lockportjournal.com/news/local_news/owners-hope-to-transform-graestone-manor-into-bed-and-breakfast/article_f8a27d40-1823-5954-830e-a57228294a1f.html

Graestone Manor. (n.d.). Retrieved from https://www.graestonemanor.com/

HALL'S APPLE FARM

Hall's Apple Farm. (2013). Retrieved from http://www.hallsapplefarm.com/

Phillips, M. (Producer). (2012, June 30). The Bride Wore Black [Television series episode]. In *My Ghost Story*. Lockport, NY: Biography.

Wolcott, B. (2012, June 29). Lockport's Ghost Story. *Lockport Union-Sun & Journal*. Retrieved from https://www.lockportjournal.com/news/local_news/lockport-s-ghost-story/article_e73a996b-cbcb-5c49-9755-fc383b742528.html

HOLY TRINITY CHURCH

Historicht. (n.d.). Retrieved from https://www.historicht.org/

The Ultimate Niagara Falls Ghost Guide. (n.d.). Retrieved from https://maps.roadtrippers.com/trips/14520492

KENAN CENTER

Kenan Center. (n.d.). Retrieved from http://kenancenter.org/

Linnabery, A. (2017, November 5). Niagara Discoveries: Niagara County is home to many ghosts, part II. *Lockport Journal*. Retrieved from https://www.lockportjournal.com/news/lifestyles/niagara-discoveries-niagara-county-is-home-to-many-ghosts-part/article_7a7c5f94-d243-53ff-8383-8b0bd96f78cf.html

LEGENDS BAR & GRILL

Dining at Quality Hotel & Suites "At the Falls". (n.d.). Retrieved from http://qualityniagarafalls.com/dining.php

The Ultimate Niagara Falls Ghost Guide. (n.d.). Retrieved from https://maps.roadtrippers.com/trips/14520492

LEWISTON PUBLIC LIBRARY

Lopez, G. (2017, December 6). Ghosts might be anything but fiction at Lewiston Public Library. *Lewiston Porter Sentinel*. Retrieved from https://www.wnypapers.com/news/article/current/2017/12/06/130727/ghosts-might-be-anything-but-fiction-at-lewiston-public-library

Welcome to Historic Lewiston, New York. (n.d.). Retrieved from http://historiclewiston.org/

LOCKPORT CAVE

Lockport Cave & Underground Boat Ride. (n.d.). Retrieved from https://lockportcave.com/

Tunnels of Terror [Television series episode]. (2012, October 31). In *Ghost Hunters*. Lockport, NY: SyFy.

MARJIM MANOR

Bittner, M. S. (n.d.). *The Legend of Appleton Hall*. Appleton, NY: Marjim Manor.

Bottled Spirits [Television series episode]. (2008, October 15). In *Ghost Hunters*. Appleton, NY: SyFy.

Rotter, J. (Writer). (2010, October 22). Most Terrifying Places in America Part 7 [Television series episode]. In *Most Terrifying Places in America*. Appleton, NY: Travel.

Winery at Marjim Manor in Appleton, NY, Niagara Wine Trail. (n.d.). Retrieved from https://www.marjimmanor.com/

Winfield, M. (2008). *Haunted Places of Western New York* (Third ed.). Buffalo, NY: Western New York Wares.

OAKWOOD CEMETERY

DeLuca, M. (2017, October 17). Spirits with the spirits at Oakwood Cemetery. *Niagara Gazette*. Retrieved from https://www.niagara-gazette.com/news/night_and_day/spirits-with-the-spirits-at-oakwood-cemetery/article_52f390a3-dc31-5ef2-978f-824da460f482.html

Oakwood Cemetery: Niagara Falls, NY. (n.d.). Retrieved from https://oakwoodniagara.org/

OLD FORT NIAGARA

Old Fort Niagara. (n.d.). Retrieved from https://www.oldfortniagara.org/

Well of Horror [Television series episode]. (2011, October 5). In *Ghost Hunters*. Youngstown, NY: SyFy.

Winfield, M. (1997). *Shadows of the western door: Haunted sites and ancient mysteries of upstate New York* (Fourth ed.). Buffalo, NY: Western New York Wares.

Winfield, M. (2008). *Haunted Places of Western New York* (Third ed.). Buffalo, NY: Western New York Wares.

RAPIDS THEATRE

Coin, G. (2015, May 07). Rapids Theatre in Niagara Falls: One of New York's 'most haunted places'. Retrieved from https://www.newyorkupstate.com/niagara-falls/2015/05/rapids_theater_niagara_falls.html

Stage Fright [Television series episode]. (2011, October 19). In *Ghost Hunters*. Niagara Falls, NY: SyFy.

The Rapids Theatre. (n.d.). Retrieved from https://www.rapidstheatre.com/

RED COACH INN

Episode 69 [Television series episode]. (2013, January 19). In *Celebrity Ghost Stories*. Niagara Falls, NY: Biography.

Historic Bed & Breakfast Hotel in Niagara Falls, NY – USA. (n.d.). Retrieved from https://www.redcoach.com/

RIVIERA THEATRE

Bishop, C. (2014, October 29). Haunted Theatre of the Tonawandas. *USA Today*. Retrieved from https://www.usatoday.com/story/news/features/2014/10/29/haunted-wny-riviera-theatre/18102963/

Riviera Theatre. (2019, August 07). Retrieved from https://rivieratheatre.org/

THIRTY MILE POINT LIGHTHOUSE

Golden Hill State Park. (n.d.). Retrieved from https://parks.ny.gov/parks/143/details.aspx

Przepasniak, E. (2019 September 12). 15 Places in Western New York sure to send a shiver down your spine. *Buffalo News*. Retrieved from https://buffalonews.com/2019/09/12/gallery11434/

Thirty Mile Point Lighthouse. (n.d.). Retrieved from https://www.lighthousefriends.com/light.asp?ID=302

TONAWANDA ISLAND GIANTS

Dell'Amore, C. (2012, November 10). Ancient Roman Giant Found-Oldest Complete Skeleton With Gigantism. Retrieved from https://news.nationalgeographic.com/news/2012/11/121102-gigantism-ancient-skeleton-archaeology-history-science-rome/

Linnabery, A. (2016, January 30). NIAGARA DISCOVERIES: Tonawanda Island, Stephen White and his magnificent mansion. Retrieved from https://www.lockportjournal.com/news/lifestyles/niagara-discoveries-tonawanda-island-stephen-white-and-his-magnificent-mansion/article_657aa96e-c9eb-54ca-8237-dc7dcc2e0afb.html

Winfield, M. (1997). *Shadows of the western door: Haunted sites and ancient mysteries of upstate New York* (Fourth ed.). Buffalo, NY: Western New York Wares.

VAN HORN MANSION

Kunz Goldman, M. (2015, October 15). Van Horn Mansion has plenty of history--haunted or otherwise. *Gusto*. Retrieved from https://buffalonews.com/2015/10/15/van-horn-mansion-has-plenty-of-history-haunted-and-otherwise/

Newfane Historical Society: Van Horn Mansion: About the Mansion. (2017, February 01). Retrieved from https://www.newfanehistoricalsociety.com/vanhornmansion_about.html

Winfield, M. (2008). *Haunted Places of Western New York* (Third ed.). Buffalo, NY: Western New York Wares.

AURORA PLAYERS PAVILION

Aurora Players - Aurora Players. (n.d.). Retrieved from https://www.auroraplayers.org/

Roycroft Pavilion. (n.d.). Retrieved from https://www.hauntedplaces.org/item/roycroft-pavilion/

Rust, R., & Turgeon, K. (2004). *Images of America The Roycroft Campus*(Third ed.). Charleston, SC: Arcadia Publishing.

Winfield, M. (2008). *Haunted Places of Western New York* (Third ed.). Buffalo, NY: Western New York Wares.

BESSIE

Associated Press. (1990, September 30). Legend of Lake Erie Monster Rises Again : Myths: New reports of sightings of the huge, snakelike creature are causing a stir. Marine researchers remain skeptical. *Los Angeles Times*. Retrieved from https://www.latimes.com/archives/la-xpm-1990-09-30-mn-2507-story.html

Schaffner, R. (Ed.). (1991, October). South Bay Bessie. *Creature Chronicles*, (14).

Winfield, M. (1997). *Shadows of the western door: Haunted sites and ancient mysteries of upstate New York* (Fourth ed.). Buffalo, NY: Western New York Wares.

CURTIS HALL

Daemen College. (2015, August 15). Retrieved from https://www.newyorkhauntedhouses.com/real-haunt/daemen-college.html

Facilities. (n.d.). Retrieved from https://www.daemen.edu/about/facilities

Kirkham, R. (2018, March 5). A Closer Look: Curtis Hall, the former Coplon Mansion, at Daemen College. *Buffalo News*. Retrieved from https://buffalonews.com/2018/03/06/gallery9261/

Top 10 Most Haunted Places in Buffalo, NY (Updated 2019). (n.d.). Retrieved from https://www.hauntedrooms.com/10-haunted-places-buffalo-ny

Winfield, M. (2008). *Haunted Places of Western New York* (Third ed.). Buffalo, NY: Western New York Wares.

DELAWARE ROAD

Delaware Road. (n.d.). Retrieved from https://www.hauntedplaces.org/item/delaware-road/

Top 10 Most Haunted Places In WNY 8 - Buffalo Digest: Web Design: Social Media Marketing. (n.d.). Retrieved from https://www.buffalodigest.com/top-10-most-haunted-places-in-wny-8

Welshofer, K. (2018, October 31). Kate and Kevin Investigate Delaware Road in Clarence to see if it's haunted. Retrieved from https://www.wgrz.com/article/entertainment/television/programs/daybreak/kate-and-kevin-investigate-delaware-road-in-clarence-to-see-if-its-haunted/71-609875413

DOS ON THE LAKE

Claud, D., & O'Connor, C. (2009). *Haunted Buffalo: Ghosts of the Queen City*. Charleston, SC: History Press.

Dos716. (n.d.). Retrieved from https://www.dos716.com/

Winfield, M. (2008). *Haunted Places of Western New York* (Third ed.). Buffalo, NY: Western New York Wares.

ELMLAWN CEMETERY

Elmlawn Cemetery. (2015, August 15). Retrieved from https://www.newyorkhauntedhouses.com/real-haunt/-elmlawn-cemetery.html

Salmons, S. R., & Salmons, P. G. (n.d.). Elmlawn Cemetery in WNY - Buffalo, NY Cemetery Services. Retrieved from https://elmlawncemetery.com/

ERIE COUNTY HOME

Haunted New York. (n.d.). Retrieved from http://www.ghostquest.net/haunted-new-york.html

WGRZ. (2018, July 25). Former Erie County Home for Sale. Retrieved from https://www.wgrz.com/article/news/local/former-erie-county-home-for-sale/71-577422048

ETERNAL FLAME FALLS

Eternal Flame Falls at Chestnut Ridge County Park. (2013, August 12). Retrieved from https://www.atlasobscura.com/places/eternal-flame-falls-2

Harris, K. (2018, August 06). Mysterious New York Waterfall Defies the Laws of Nature. Retrieved from https://historydaily.org/mysterious-new-york-waterfall-defies-the-laws-of-nature

Indiana University. (2013, May 9). Geologists study mystery of 'eternal flames'. Retrieved from http://newsinfo.iu.edu/news-archive/24236.html

Winfield, M. (2008). *Haunted Places of Western New York* (Third ed.). Buffalo, NY: Western New York Wares.

FORMER AMHERST SYNAGOGUE

Gethard, C., Moran, M., & Sceurman, M. (2010). *Weird New York: Your travel guide to New Yorks local legends and best kept secrets* (Second ed.). New York: Sterling Pub.

Winfield, M. (2008). *Haunted Places of Western New York* (Third ed.). Buffalo, NY: Western New York Wares.

FORMER HOLIDAY INN

Cichon, S. (2016, September 7). Oct. 30, 1994: Ghostly child spooks guests at Grand Island hotel. *Buffalo News*. Retrieved from https://buffalonews.com/2014/10/30/oct-30-1994-ghostly-guest-spooking-grand-island-hotel/

Winfield, M. (2008). *Haunted Places of Western New York* (Third ed.). Buffalo, NY: Western New York Wares.

GARDENIER HOUSE

Hawkins, J. (n.d.). A Look Back: The Mystery of JP Myers. *Springville Times*. Retrieved from http://www.springvilletimes.com/2018/05/03/a-look-back-the-mystery-of-jp-myers/

Historical Presentation on J.P. Myers. (n.d.). Retrieved from http://springvillechamber.com/event/historical-presentation-on-j-p-myers/

Otto, D. M. (n.d.). A LOOK BACK: The Gardinier House Haunted or Bastion of Despair? *Springville Times*. Retrieved from http://www.springvilletimes.com/2016/10/20/a-look-back-the-gardinier-house-haunted-or-bastion-of-despair/

Winfield, M. (2008). *Haunted Places of Western New York*(Third ed.). Buffalo, NY: Western New York Wares.

THE GLOBE RESTAURANT

The Globe Restaurant. (n.d.). Retrieved from https://www.theglobeea.com/

GOODLEBURG CEMETERY

Gethard, C., Moran, M., & Sceurman, M. (2010). *Weird New York: Your travel guide to New Yorks local legends and best kept secrets* (Second ed.). New York: Sterling Pub.

Winfield, M. (2008). *Haunted Places of Western New York* (Third ed.). Buffalo, NY: Western New York Wares.

HULL FAMILY HOUSE

Home. (n.d.). Retrieved from https://www.hullfamilyhome.com/

LACKAWANNA BASILICA

Nickell, J. (2014, July/August). The ‘Miracles’ Of Father Baker. *Skeptical Inquirer*, *38*(4).

OLV Basilica & National Shrine. (n.d.). Retrieved from http://www.ourladyofvictory.org/

Winfield, M. (2008). *Haunted Places of Western New York* (Third ed.). Buffalo, NY: Western New York Wares.

LANCASTER OPERA HOUSE

Lancaster Opera House. (n.d.). Retrieved from https://www.hauntedplaces.org/item/lancaster-opera-house/

Lancaster Opera House. (n.d.). Retrieved from http://lancasteropera.org/

Winfield, M. (2008). *Haunted Places of Western New York* (Third ed.). Buffalo, NY: Western New York Wares.

LINDBERGH ELEMENTARY SCHOOL

Getzville, New York Ghost Sightings - PAGE 2. (n.d.). Retrieved from http://www.ghostsofamerica.com/1/New_York_Getzville_ghost_sightings2.html

McNeil, H. (1990, June 30). Repair of Damage Caused by Arson OK'd by Kenmore-Tonawanda School Board. *Buffalo News*. Retrieved from https://buffalonews.com/1990/06/30/repair-of-damage-caused-by-arson-okd-by-kenmore-tonawanda-school-board/

MURDER CREEK

Buffalo, Nov. 22. (1890, November 23). Caused by Jealousy—Sadie McMullen's Fearful Crime Prompted by Unrequited Affection. *The Pittsburgh Dispatch*. p 9.

Buffalo, N.Y., March 5. (1891, March 6). On Trial for Her Life.—Is Sadie M'Mullen Guilty of Child Murder?—So Young and So Pretty—Could She Have Done Such a Deed?—What Promises to be a Notable Case Now Before the Supreme Court at Buffalo—A Great Field Open to Insanity Experts—Meanwhile, Sadie's Indifference is Hard to Understand. *The World*. p. 3.

Legend of Murder Creek. (n.d.). Retrieved from http://www2.erie.gov/parks/index.php?q=legend-murder-creek

Quickly, Buck. (2016, October 27). Murder Creek: the Sorry Case of Sadie McMullen. *Artvoice*. Retrieved from https://artvoice.com/2016/10/27/murder-creek-sorry-case-sadie-mcmullen/

MYSTERY GOO

Katrandjian, O. (2011, January 20). Mystery Goo Turns Icicles Green and Yellow in Snyder, N.Y. Retrieved from https://abcnews.go.com/US/splatterings-green-goo-fall-sky-snyder-ny/story?id=12649849

Morphy, R. (2011, January 24). Mystery Goo Falls on New York. Retrieved from https://www.cryptopia.us/site/2011/01/mystery-goo-falls-on-new-york/

NEW ERA FIELD

Lowinger, A. (2012, June). The Bills Curse. *Buffalo Spree*.

Roth, L. (2015, October 30). The Buffalo Bills' ghostly gridiron. *Democrat & Chronicle*. Retrieved from https://www.democratandchronicle.com/story/sports/columnist/roth/2015/10/30/roth-buffalo-bills-ghostly-gridiron/74865990/

Winfield, M. (2008). *Haunted Places of Western New York* (Third ed.). Buffalo, NY: Western New York Wares.

OLD MAIN CEMETERY

Historical Cemeteries. (n.d.). Retrieved from http://www.westseneca.net/about-west-seneca/history/historical-cemeteries#gsc.tab=0

Kotz, K. (2010, October 28). Ghostly legend surrounds Old Main Cemetery. *West Seneca Bee*. Retrieved from https://www.westsenecabee.com/articles/ghostly-legend-surrounds-old-main-cemetery/

Winfield, M. (2008). *Haunted Places of Western New York* (Third ed.). Buffalo, NY: Western New York Wares.

PIGMAN ROAD

Newkirk, D. (2014, October 01). Pigman Road is home to a blood-thirsty axe-wielding maniac... and he wants your head. Retrieved from https://maps.roadtrippers.com/stories/pigman-road-is-home-to-a-blood-thirsty-axe-wielding-maniac-dot-dot-dot-and-he-wants-your-head

Vogel, C. (2014, January 4). 'The Angola Horror': The mass rail tragedy in Buffalo's backyard. *Buffalo News*. Retrieved from https://buffalonews.com/2014/01/04/the-tragedy-in-angola/

Winfield, M. (2008). *Haunted Places of Western New York* (Third ed.). Buffalo, NY: Western New York Wares.

ROYCROFT INN & CAMPUS

Home. (2019, March 20). Retrieved from https://roycroftinn.com/

Rust, R., & Turgeon, K. (2004). *Images of America The Roycroft Campus*(Third ed.). Charleston, SC: Arcadia Publishing.

Winfield, M. (1997). *Shadows of the western door: Haunted sites and ancient mysteries of upstate New York* (Fourth ed.). Buffalo, NY: Western New York Wares.

Winfield, M. (2008). *Haunted Places of Western New York* (Third ed.). Buffalo, NY: Western New York Wares.

SNYDER BAR & GRILL

Snyder Bar and Grill Home. (n.d.). Retrieved from https://www.sbgbuffalo.com/

VIDLER'S

Vidlers 5 and 10: Largest Variety Store In The World! (n.d.). Retrieved from https://www.vidlers5and10.com/

Winfield, M. (2008). *Haunted Places of Western New York* (Third ed.). Buffalo, NY: Western New York Wares.

WESTERN HOUSE

Western House. (2015, August 15). Retrieved from https://www.newyorkhauntedhouses.com/real-haunt/western-house.html

WHITEHAVEN CEMETERY

Whitehaven Cemetery. (n.d.). Retrieved from https://www.hauntedplaces.org/item/whitehaven-cemetery/

Whitehaven Cemetery. (2003, July 8). Retrieved from http://wnyroots.tripod.com/index-grand-white1-cem.html

Winfield, M. (2008). *Haunted Places of Western New York* (Third ed.). Buffalo, NY: Western New York Wares.

BEECHWOOD CEMETERY

Beechwood Cemetery. (n.d.). Retrieved from https://www.hauntedplaces.org/item/beechwood-cemetary/

Halsey, D. (2012, October 23). Dick's Genealogy & History Corner. Retrieved from http://rochistory.com/blog/?p=1889

Kerridge, S. A. (1998). Beechwood Cemetery. Retrieved from http://orleans.nygenweb.net/cemeteries/cembwd3.htm

COBBLESTONE INN

State of New York. (n.d.). Retrieved from https://data.ny.gov/widgets/iisn-hnyv

Drawn to Evil [Television series episode]. (2017, March 11). In *Dead Files*. Medina, NY: Travel.

COUNTY HOUSE ROAD

Gethard, C., Moran, M., & Sceurman, M. (2010). *Weird New York: Your travel guide to New Yorks local legends and best kept secrets* (Second ed.). New York: Sterling Pub.

FORD STREET BEAST

Gethard, C., Moran, M., & Sceurman, M. (2010). *Weird New York: Your travel guide to New Yorks local legends and best kept secrets* (Second ed.). New York: Sterling Pub.

History.com Editors. (2017, August 23). Werewolf Legends. Retrieved from https://www.history.com/topics/folklore/history-of-the-werewolf-legend

FULLER ROAD

Gethard, C., Moran, M., & Sceurman, M. (2010). *Weird New York: Your travel guide to New Yorks local legends and best kept secrets* (Second ed.). New York: Sterling Pub.

HART HOUSE HOTEL

Euro-Inspired Boutique Hotel: Hart House Hotel: United States. (n.d.). Retrieved from https://www.harthousehotel.com/

PILLARS ESTATE

Canales, K. (2018, October 26). This magnificent New York estate is selling for a mere $500,000, and the owner says it's haunted. Retrieved from https://www.businessinsider.com/pillars-estate-new-york-tour-2018-10

Wooten, M. (2018, October 31). Haunted mansion for sale in Orleans County. Retrieved from https://www.wgrz.com/article/news/local/orleans-county/haunted-mansion-for-sale-in-orleans-county/71-610050240

TILLMAN'S HISTORIC VILLAGE INN

Tillman's Historic Village Inn. (n.d.). Retrieved from https://www.tillmansvillageinn.com/

Tillman's Historic Village Inn & Fair Haven Inn. (n.d.). Retrieved from https://hauntedhistorytrail.com/explore/tillmans-historic-village-inn-and-fair-haven-inn

Tillman's Historic Village Inn History. (n.d.). Retrieved from https://www.tillmansvillageinn.com/history.html

GENESEE FALLS INN

Genesee Falls Inn. (n.d.). Retrieved from https://hauntedhistorytrail.com/explore/genesee-falls-inn

Genesee Falls Inn: Portageville NY: The Genesee Falls inn. (n.d.). Retrieved from https://www.thegeneseefallsinn.com/

HEAVEN SENT BED & BREAKFAST

Dillon, J. (2018, May 4). Paranormal activity: Portageville B&B gains a haunted reputation. *The Daily News*. Retrieved from https://www.thedailynewsonline.com/bdn01/paranormal-activity-portageville-bampb-gains-a-haunted-reputation-20180504

Heaven Sent Bed & Breakfast. (n.d.). Retrieved from https://www.gowyomingcountyny.com/listings/heaven-sent-bed-breakfast

ST. JOHN'S CEMETERY

Goose Hill Cemetery – Saint Johns Cemetery. (n.d.). Retrieved from https://www.hauntedplaces.org/item/goose-hill-cemetery-saint-johns-cemetery

Powers-Douglas, M. (2016, March 22). Symbols. Retrieved from http://www.thecemeteryclub.com/symbols.html

Town of Sheldon Cemeteries. (n.d.). Retrieved from http://wyoming.nygenweb.net/ceminfo.htm

SILVER LAKE SERPENT

Haunted Silver Lake Serpent: Perry, NY. (n.d.). Retrieved from https://www.trytoscare.me/legend/silver-lake-serpent-perry-ny/

Nickell, J. (1999, March/April). The Silver Lake Serpent: Inflated Monster Or Inflated Tale? *Skeptical Inquirer*, *23*(2).

Perry, NY - Silver Lake Serpent. (n.d.). Retrieved from https://www.roadsideamerica.com/tip/59893

WATER STREET

Haunted New York. (n.d.). Retrieved from http://www.ghostquest.net/haunted-new-york.html

ABOUT THE AUTHOR

Writer, former international English teacher, and the great-great-grand-niece of Leon Czolgosz, Amanda R. Woomer was born and raised in Buffalo, NY. With a degree in anthropology, she won her first award for her writing when she was only 12 years old. With publications in anthologies and magazines all over the globe, she is currently a featured writer for the award-winning *Haunted Magazine* and the owner of Spook-Eats.

NOTES

NOTES

NOTES

NOTES

NOTES

NOTES

NOTES

NOTES

Made in the USA
Middletown, DE
07 April 2022

63674475R00216